Coinage in the Latin East

The Fourth Oxford Symposium on Coinage and Monetary History

edited by

P. W. Edbury and D. M. Metcalf

BAR International Series 77
1980

B.A.R.

B.A.R., 122 Banbury Road, Oxford OX2 7BP, England

GENERAL EDITORS

A. R. Hands, B.Sc., M.A., D.Phil.
D. R. Walker, M.A.

B.A.R. International Series 77, 1980: 'Coinage in the Latin East'.

© The Individual Authors, 1980.

The author's moral rights under the 1988 UK Copyright.
Designs and Patents Act are hereby expressly asserted.

All rights reserved. No part of this work may be copied. reproduced. stored. sold. distributed. scanned. saved in any form of digital format or transmitted in any form digitally without the written permission of the Publisher.

ISBN 9780860540861 paperback
ISBN 9781407351056 e-book
DOI https://doi.org/10.30861/9780860540861
A catalogue record for this book is available from the British Library

This book is available at www.barpublishing.com

BAR publishes monographs and collections of papers on all aspects of archaeology and on related subjects such as anthropology, classical and medieval history and numismatics.

BAR publishes BAR International Series which is concerned with world archaeology and BAR British Series which covers the British Isles.

CONTENTS

	Page
Foreword	i
Abbreviations	iv
The Templars as bankers and monetary transfers between West and East in the twelfth century, by D. M. Metcalf	1
Marseilles, Acre and the Mediterranean, 1200-1291, by David Abulafia	19
The billon and copper coinage of the county of Tripoli to c. 1268, by C. J. Sabine	41
The baronial coinage of the Latin Kingdom of Jerusalem, by Peter W. Edbury	59
The supply of money and the direction of trade in thirteenth-century Syria, by R. Irwin	73
The Amalricus coins of the Kingdom of Jerusalem, by Roberto Pesant, with contributions by C. J. Sabine and D. M. Metcalf	105

Notes

A note on the repayment of loans in mid-thirteenth-century Acre, by Peter W. Edbury	123
Crusader coin finds from Caesarea Maritima, Israel: the Joint Expedition's excavations, 1971-1979, by Robert L. Hohlfelder	127
Some coin exports from twelfth-century Yorkshire to the Holy Land, by Paul R. Hyams	133
Three recent parcels of Helmet deniers of Bohemund III of Antioch concealed at about the time of Saladin's conquests, by D. M. Metcalf	137
The Symposiasts	147

FOREWORD

The Fourth Oxford Symposium on Coinage and Monetary History took place at Wolfson College during the weekend of 6-8 September, 1979. The twenty-five guests (of whom nine came from abroad) heard papers which ranged all the way from numismatics to economic history but which were centred around the monetary history of the Crusader states in the Near East— the Latin Kingdom of Jerusalem, the county of Tripoli and the principality of Antioch.

As in previous years, when the subjects discussed were Edwardian monetary affairs (1976), medieval Scottish currency (1977) and the coinage and economic development of the Low Countries (1978), the purpose of the gathering was to bring together numismatists, archaeologists and historians to discuss a theme of common interest and to explore the ways in which numismatic evidence can be interpreted for monetary history.

The monetary history of Lusignan Cyprus and Cilician Armenia is closely connected with that of the Latin territories of Syria and Palestine. Both these states drew their prosperity from their position on the shipping routes of the Eastern Mediterranean, and their coinages deserve to be studied in the context of the silver supplies and bullion movements in the region as a whole. Logically they might have been included in our discussion. Perhaps the omission can be corrected at some future symposium.

This volume contains versions of all but one of the papers delivered at the Symposium, most of them having been considerably revised as a result of discussions at the meeting and subsequently. Jacques Yvon, the doyen of Crusader numismatics, was sadly unable to be with us and to read a paper, as he had hoped and intended, giving a general survey of work on Crusader numismatics. This would undoubtedly have been of benefit to numismatists and historians of the Crusades alike. All too often the latter have not been quick to make use of developments in numismatic research, and conversely numismatists have not always succeeded in keeping abreast of the considerable advances made over the years in the history of the Crusades and of the states in the Near East founded by the crusaders.

All but the most recent numismatic publications are conveniently listed in H. E. Mayer's Bibliographie zur Geschichte der Kreuzzüge (1960) and the same author's 'Literaturbericht über die Geschichte der Kreuzzüge', in the Historische Zeitschrift (Sonderheft 3), 1969. These should be supplemented by the more specialist and critical bibliographies published on the occasion of successive International Numismatic Congresses, and, for the latest work, by the American Numismatic Society's twice-yearly Numismatic Literature.

The last attempt at a general survey and classification of the coins of the Latin East, Gustave Schlumberger's Numismatique de l'Orient latin was published a century ago, in 1878, with a supplement which followed in 1882. It was so thorough and successful that it inhibited further work for fifty years, and indeed it is still constantly referred to.

An American archaeologist, Dorothy H. Cox, gave renewed impetus to numismatic research by her publication in 1933 of a major hoard purchased a few years previously in Beirut and said to have come from Tripoli. It contained over 3,500 coins, including numerous west European issues. Miss Cox's monograph was quickly complemented by an article in the Revue Numismatique for 1935 by a military doctor from Mulhouse, Henry Longuet. In it he published a somewhat similar hoard containing just over 1,000 coins, also concealed within a few years of 1220, from Djebel el Akra, very near the mouth of the Orontes. This hoard from the approaches to Antioch is best known as the Kessab hoard. Also in 1935 Willy Schwabacher, whose main numismatic interests were in the ancient Greek field, published a short account of a hoard from the island of Samos which, although it contained only 7 crusader coins, has proved important for the chronology of the issues of the last quarter of the twelfth century. In 1937 Derek Allen, as a young scholar who had recently joined the staff of the British Museum, was given the task of publishing some coins from Sir Leonard Woolley's excavations at Tell Cheik Yusuf al Gharbi (usually referred to as the al Mina finds, and again from near Antioch). While listing the Antioch deniers among them he worked out a proper numismatic classification of the 'helmet' series which was extraordinarily perceptive, given the limited material on which it was based. The war years intervened, and imposed delays on the publication of two other archaeological projects which were otherwise completed in the 1930s. Dorothy B. Waage listed the crusader coins found in the American excavations of Antioch-on-the-Orontes; and G. Ploug and E. Oldenburg dealt similarly with those from the Danish excavations at Ḥamā. Both find-series are important sources of information about crusader copper coins, which turned up in considerable numbers as stray losses but which are normally absent from hoards.

Before the war crusader numismatics was very much an empty field, in which all the advances were made by students whose main interests lay elsewhere. Since then, the subject has attracted increasingly professional attention. Jacques Yvon led the way with a succession of brief but fundamental contributions in the Bulletin de la Société Française de Numismatique. Other experienced numismatists have applied the techniques developed in better-studied areas of medieval numismatics, and the insights gained there, to the coins of the Latin East. They include Paul Balog, George Miles, Philip Grierson, Jean Duplessy, John Seltman, Paul Bedoukian, Arnold Spaer, Michael Metcalf, John Porteous, Roberto Pesant, Chris Sabine and Jeremiah Brady. Thus crusader numismatics has been drawn more into the main stream.

From the side of economic history, Andrew Watson made a notably influential contribution with his article, 'Back to gold—and silver', published in the Economic History Review in 1967.

The Symposium was organized jointly by an historian and a numismatist, in an agreeable partnership. They take this opportunity to thank all those who helped to make the meeting and the publication of this volume possible. A special word of appreciation is due to the Keeper of the Heberden Coin Room in the Ashmolean Museum, under whose auspices the Symposium was held. Further financial support was provided most generously by Sotheby Parke Bernet and Co. of London, and by British Archaeological Reports. The domestic staff of Wolfson College looked after us unobtrusively and well, as did the staff of St Anne's College, which provided accommodation. Nor should one neglect to mention the symposiasts themselves who, by their comments and questions in the formal discussions after each paper and informally at other times during the two days the gathering lasted, added to the exchange of ideas which was the first object of the venture.

P. W. E.

D. M. M.

ABBREVIATIONS

ANSMN	American Numismatic Society Museum Notes
BMC Or.	British Museum Catalogue. Oriental Coins
BSFN	Bulletin de la société française de numismatique
HBN	Hamburger Beiträge zur Numismatik
NC	Numismatic Chronicle
NCirc.	Numismatic Circular
NNM	Numismatic Notes and Monographs (American Numismatic Society)
RBN	Revue belge de numismatique
RHC	Recueil des historiens des croisades, 1841-1906
RHC Arm.	RHC Documents arméniens, 1869-1906
RHC Lois	RHC Lois. Les Assises de Jérusalem, 1841-3
RHC Occ.	RHC Historiens occidentaux, 1844-95
RHC Or.	RHC Historiens orientaux, 1872-1906
RHDFÉ	Revue historique de droit français et étranger
RN	Revue numismatique
RRH	R. Röhricht, Regesta regni Hierosolymitani (MXCVII-MCCXCI), Innsbruck, 1893-1904
Schlumberger or Schl.	G. Schlumberger, Numismatique de l'Orient latin, 1878; Supplément, 1882

THE TEMPLARS AS BANKERS AND MONETARY TRANSFERS BETWEEN WEST AND EAST IN THE TWELFTH CENTURY

D. M. Metcalf

Egypt, in the Delta, May 1250: the king of France is to be set free, against an immediate ransom of 200,000 pounds.[1] The king's people began to count out the money on Saturday morning, and it took them the whole of Saturday, and Sunday until night. They were 30,000 pounds short, and Joinville (who was present, and tells the story[2]) advised the king to send for the Marshal of the Temple—the master being dead—and to ask for a loan. Joinville was sent to negotiate the matter, but he got no for an answer. The Commander of the Temple told him that he had given the king bad advice, since he well knew that the moneys held by the Temple were trust funds which could only be released to the depositors. They had a blazing row, and eventually the Marshal of the Temple intervened to say that the commander was quite correct, but the seneschal's advice was sensible, namely that if Joinville could not get the money by asking for it, he should take it. With the diplomacy which marks bankers in every age, he added that Joinville must decide for himself what to do, and that if he seized Templar funds in Egypt, there was no serious problem, because the Order held so much of theirs in Acre, that it would be easy to indemnify them.

Having confirmed his instructions with the king, Joinville went on board the flagship of the Templar squadron, which was in effect a floating bank—and a high financial risk, one would have thought. The Commander of the Temple declined to be a witness at the charade that followed, but the marshal accompanied Joinville into the hold. When the treasurer refused to hand over the keys of the strong-boxes, Joinville picked up an axe which happened to be lying around. The marshal took him by the fist and said, 'My Lord, as it is clear that you are using force against us, we will give you the keys'. The first chest which Joinville opened belonged to Nicholas of Choisi, one of the king's sergeants. After that, Joinville left the Marshal of France in charge in the hold of the galley, and stationed the Minister of the Trinity on deck, and himself took up position in the galley alongside, which was to convey the silver to the tellers.

When everything had been arranged and the whole sum was about to be handed over to the Saracens—and we are talking about something equivalent to 50 million deniers, 50 tonnes of billon, although it was presumably paid in a mixture of currencies—Philip of Nemours said to the king that there had been a counting error and that it was still 10,000 pounds short of the agreed amount. The saintly Louis was very upset, and unwilling to leave until his pledge was exactly fulfilled. At this point, as he himself tells us, Joinville kicked Philip of Nemours on the ankle, and told him that he was only joking.

The king said that he was not to make jokes like that, and that if any money was short, Philip was to see that it was paid. In the end they got safely away. But the king was lucky to escape, because his captors had almost decided that it would be more advantageous in the long run to kill him and do without the money.

Another little story, from ten years earlier: the re-building of the castle of Safet, in Galilee.[3] During a period of truce, the bishop of Marseilles had the opportunity to visit Damascus. While he was there, he kept his ear to the ground, and he gained the impression that the people were concerned and alarmed by the rumour that the Franks were intending to rebuild Safet. It had occupied an important strategic position, controlling a convenient route giving access from Damascus into the coastal strip. On his return the bishop put this to the Master of the Temple, who was unwell at the time, and had to receive him lying down on his couch. The Master sighed heavily, and said, 'My Lord Bishop, rebuilding Safet is not simple. You may recall that the King of Navarre, the Duke of Burgundy, and the counts and barons of the host promised me that they would come to Safet, so that we could work more quickly and with greater security, that they would stay for two months, and that they would donate 7,000 marks towards the expenses. They have forgotten their promises and gone home. Now you kindly suggest that we should build the castle without any assistance.' Bishops, like bankers, commonly run true to type. This one urged the master to reconsider the matter. Negotiations took place at the next level down, and in short the Order was persuaded to go ahead—to the joy of the people of Acre, who stood to benefit from the improved security. The Templars chose a military forward party, and opened their granges, their cellars, and their treasure-chests to meet the outlay, as we are told, 'magnificently and joyfully.'

They held an opening ceremony on 11 December 1240, and the bishop of Marseilles laid the first stone and (as he was, of course, there to do the decent thing) placed on it a silver-gilt cup full of money. Others were doubtless inspired to do what they could.

The Templars took two and a half years over the work of fortification, and it was reckoned to have cost 1,100,000 bezants over and above the local income (thus twenty times the promised contribution which had never been delivered). When it was finished, it stood at the heart of a lovely estate, with figs, grenadines, almonds, olives, wine, corn, animals, irrigated vegetable gardens, 12 water-mills apart from emergency mills inside the castle itself, woodland for fuel, and so on. But the annual running costs were put at 40,000 bezants (again, over and above the revenues of the estate).[4] One may compare this with the 500 bezants which has been estimated as the income from an average village. Some 1,700 people sat down to eat every day, and 2,200 in time of war. The garrison consisted of 50 knights and 30 mounted sergeants, 50 mounted turcopoles, 300 balistiers, 800 grooms and sergeants, and 400 slaves.

When the Templars were holding at least a dozen castles (the others not, of course, as large as Saphet), and also maintaining their 'convents' or mobile forces based at Tripoli and Antioch, not to mention various other establishments,[5] the regular income they required was frightening to contemplate. They were spending large sums of money that came to them partly from outside the Latin East, but mainly from their properties within the Crusader states, and the effects on the local economy must have been revolutionary. Their very heavy commitments date, however, largely from the period after the loss of Jerusalem. From then on, the orders bore much of the burden of holding the strategic lines of defence.

Before the time of Saladin the relative importance of the Templars was less. Their resources and involvement were growing, it is true, but they were hardly an independent political force, except in the north of the principality of Antioch, where a Templar march was formed as early as the 1130s.[6] Elsewhere, more typically, the orders helped in the defence of the lordships, for example by taking custody of particular stretches of city walls. This was the case as late as the third quarter of the twelfth century. But the northern marches of the county of Tripoli were gradually handed over to the orders until, after Nur-ed-Din's campaigns of 1167 and those of Saladin in 1180, the Templars guarded the coastal plains, as well as the more mountainous hinterland, against attack from the direction of Damascus and Aleppo.[7] By 1188 their domain there was in effect quite independent.[8] Seventy years before there had been (so William of Tyre tells us) just nine poor knights who tried to guard groups of pilgrims from the local banditry.[9] These knights were probably the cadre of a considerably larger force (as at Saphet), and one may doubt whether they were ever quite as poor as a later generation liked to imagine. Nevertheless, the growth of the Order's resources—and responsibilities— was dramatic.

In the same seventy years, the commercial and monetary affairs of the Levant had likewise enjoyed rapid growth, and in particular a stock of silver-based currency had been built up. From about A.D. 1025 the minting of dirhams had dwindled or at many mints ceased entirely, throughout Asia Minor, Syria, and Mesopotamis, until Saladin reopened the Damascus mint ca. 570 H. (A.D. 1174/5). This has been interpreted as evidence of a 'silver famine' lasting for a century and a half, and there is no reason to question the assessment, even if the cessation in minting needs also to be seen in terms of political weakness and confusion. Certainly there were no large monetary stocks of silver which the Franks could have drawn across their frontiers; and it was only the importation of silver in one form or another from the West which made it possible for them to strike their own billon coins in large quantities, well before 1174/5.

Andrew Watson has described the Latin states as 'a point of leverage around which the monetary history of both east and west turned. Through them the east obtained the silver which brought the silver famine to an end. And in these kingdoms Europeans ... drew considerable supplies of gold out of the neighbouring countries'.[10] Here again we need to distinguish sharply between the thirteenth century and the twelfth. As regards bullion flows between western Europe and the Latin East in the twelfth century, the technical problems of bimetallism were still unimportant, since the west relied almost exclusively on silver currency.[11]

If there was a net flow of silver eastwards, it is likely to have been the result of four main sorts of monetary transfer. First, from trade; if exports from the Latin East, including goods in transit (which may well have been the major component in terms of value), had exceeded imports, one would have expected balance-of-payments transfers to be reflected either in the import and circulation of European billon coins, or, if they were reminted, then in an increased level of activity at the local mints. The Genoese notarial records of Giovanni Scriba give us some idea of the commodities traded, and they have been used by Byrne and by Prawer as evidence for a net flow of silver eastwards as a result of trade. This questionable conclusion was influenced by the belief that western Europe was still in a state of economic and monetary backwardness in the twelfth century. 'Most transactions', Prawer writes, 'in the second half of the twelfth century involved a drain of precious metals from Europe to the Orient. The West had not yet reached the stage of an exporter whose goods could balance imports'.[12] The information from notarial records is of course selective and fragmentary in the extreme, and it should go without saying that we have no systematic evidence from the twelfth century, other than the numismatic evidence, from which we could begin to guess what the balance of trade was. And the balance of trade and the balance of payments are by no means necessarily the same, because of the other sorts of monetary transfer.

Secondly, in the long term the major source of inflow was almost certainly the money spent by the thousands of pilgrims who visited the Holy Places. Again, we have no statistics of the numbers of pilgrims per annum, but we have graphic accounts of how tightly they were packed on board the ships that specialized in carrying them, and there can be no doubt that they brought large amounts of cash into the local economy.[13] Nor should we forget the pilgrims of other religions. Both Muslims and Jews similarly brought money into the country.[14]

Thirdly, there was aid: for example the alms which the Templars collected from the faithful, at first as opportunity offered, and later through an elaborate network of preceptories and commanderies in Spain, France, England, and elsewhere.[15] Not all aid, of course, was in cash. The Houses in the West sent all sorts of riches to Jerusalem—gold, silver, fabrics, vestments, arms, harness, horses. The hazards and costs of carrying bulky and very valuable consignments on a journey which from London to Acre normally took at least sixteen or seventeen weeks were such as to make one marvel that it was undertaken so frequently.

As well as recurrent contributions, there were donations which might be loosely described as capital transfers—princely donations for the establishment of churches or monasteries, for example. The spectacular dowry of Queen Adelaide may be mentioned under the same heading.[16]

Fourth and lastly, the Crusades (that is, the military expeditions themselves, while they lasted) injected sudden large amounts of money into the economy of the Latin East.

There is no way in which one could distinguish the exact contributions of these four sources—trade, pilgrimage, aid, and Crusade—to the total monetary stock of silver in use in the Frankish states, and it is very difficult to guess at their relative importance. The last three, at any rate, must have been positive, whereas the trade balance could have been in either direction. We need also to take into account trade with Egypt and with Armenia. Subject to any non-monetary uses of silver (for plate, etc.), the coinage automatically reflected the sum of all of them. Numismatists ought to be able to define and quantify the growth of the stock of bullion during the twelfth century, and this should be worth attempting, if only because there is so little systematic evidence about the economic history of the twelfth century.

With the exception of some very rare early billon of Tripoli, the earliest issues of billon deniers of the Latin Kingdom, of Tripoli, and of Antioch all seem to have been struck first in about the 1140s. Over a period of approximately two decades, say 1140-60, an estimated 17 million deniers, or £70,000, was minted in the Latin Kingdom, plus 5½ million at Antioch, and 7 million at Tripoli.[17] In sum, these estimates should give us a realistic estimate of the total billon currency of the Frankish states up to ca. 1160, as there was a uniform currency of a single type in each of the three states, and we may presume little or no reminting during those two decades of any silver that was turned into one of the three varieties of coinage. The global estimate is undoubtedly too low in so far as it ignores the 'preferred currencies'—coins of Lucca and Valence associated with the Latin patriarchates of Jerusalem and Antioch[18]—which remained in use alongside the royal or princely issues.

We have as yet no figures from the period ca. 1160-87, although in principle, comparable numismatic estimates can be made. For the first four decades of Latin rule, there are very few hoards to guide us, and they are impossible to date precisely; but there is archaeological and other evidence which suggests that west European coins, particularly those of Lucca and Valence, were already in circulation.[19] Die-estimation of the total quantities in which these were struck would not be helpful, as their circulation was not confined to the Holy Land. The best one can do is to compare the numbers of stray losses of the coins of Lucca and Valence with those of Jerusalem and Antioch among archaeological site finds.[20] Provided the comparisons are between coinages of approximately the same face value, the numbers of stray losses of a particular issue will depend mainly on how long it remained in circulation; and the coins of Lucca and Valence seem to have been current for many decades. Even so, they are very plentiful in comparison with, for example, the coins of Baldwin in the Latin Kingdom. Such comparisons suggest that millions or possibly even tens of millions of European coins were in circulation, and this to some extent throws doubt on the idea, prompted by the reliance on copper coinage at Antioch and elsewhere, of a slow start and a gradual build-up of the stock of silver. But the total quantities are not large enough to create problems of interpretation. In order to build up a stock of billon worth £150—£250,000 by ca. 1160, starting more or less from scratch with the First Crusade, we could be talking about an average net inflow from all sources (other than the First and Second Crusades themselves) of the order of one million deniers a year—say £4,000, not more.

The history of the gold currency seems to follow a related course. The issue of Crusader bezants was apparently on only a small scale until a date which has been put between 1148 and 1159, when there was a reform of the gold currency involving a reduction in the bezant's intrinsic value, and the creation of a new alloy standard of 80% gold.[21] The reformed bezant was worth at least 120 deniers. It dominated the money supply in the Latin Kingdom, whereas at Antioch the book-value of the billon currency may have remained greater than that of the gold until the early thirteenth century.[22] How a stock of gold was built up in the third quarter of the twelfth century is something of a puzzle. If it originated from trade with Egypt or Syria, it is difficult to imagine what the Frankish states were exporting in that direction which could have given them a favourable trade balance. They were no doubt selling European cloths into the interior, together with a variety of other products, but one would have guessed that the value of goods traded in the other direction was greater. There may have been a reciprocal flow of gold and silver. Two certain sources of gold were tribute and the spoils of war. The Templars profited in this way, for example, in 1154. When the Fatimid Caliph was murdered by Nasr-ed-Din, his sister retaliated by informing the Templars. They surprised the fugitive at the oasis of Ain Mouweileh and relieved him of considerable wealth. They then turned him in for 60,000 dinars.[23] And in 1167 Cairo paid the Latin king the first instalment of a tribute of 100,000 dinars.[24]

The role of the Templars as bankers in the East in the thirteenth century, after they had moved their headquarters to Acre, is well attested, although in nothing like the degree of detail that we have about their banking activity in the West.[25] At an early date in relation to the development of professional lay banking, the Temple of Paris and that of London became bankers or treasurers to many wealthy individuals, including princes and kings, and most importantly to the kings of France from the time of Philippe Auguste onwards. This activity brought them great prestige, as did their financial services to the Holy See. Jointly with the Hospitallers, they were often given the task of transporting to the East the proceeds of various twentieths and similar alms and taxes. In 1208, they carried £1,000 provinois to the Patriarch. In 1216 and 1219 they were employed again. The earliest levy of this kind seems to have been the Saladin tithe of 1188.

Success exposed the Templars to political pressures. The Order was drawn into a role in the West which, one is tempted to say, had little or no organic connection with its military role in the Latin East. It is as if the officers of the Brigade of Guards, as well as carrying out normal military duties in Germany and Northern Ireland, had somehow become the chief financial advisors to the King of Saudi Arabia, as well as running a merchant bank in London.

There was, it is true, an obvious need for financial credit and for cash transfers to assist individual pilgrims and crusaders. We know a good deal about how such matters were arranged, at least in the thirteenth century. Lavoix has described a collection of manuscripts in the Bibliothèque Nationale consisting of contracts signed in the Latin East by crusaders with Italian bankers.[26] Three hundred of these documents survive, of which almost two hundred are notes ordering payment or promissory notes, and the rest are drafts, letters of guarantee, and letters of exchange. They allow us to understand the system of credit, and to follow the movement of money. Some examples may help.

When Joinville arrived in Cyprus, he had only 240 livres tournois left, and his knights threatened that if he did not provide himself with some cash, they would leave him. The king, who was then at Nicosia, took Joinville into his service, and put 800 livres tournois into his coffers: thus he had plenty of money, and more than he needed.

Others were no so fortunate as to find a royal patron, but each needed to set himself up on his arrival in the Holy Land. It was rare actually to send money, for the obvious reasons of the difficulty of transporting its sheer weight, and of course of the risks. Occasionally, nevertheless, sums were sent out, as when in 1250 the abbot of Ressons forwarded to Jean de Haumont 200 livres parisis from the revenues of his lands, which were being administered in his absence by the abbot. The cash was entrusted to a knight who was setting off for Palestine.

The transfer of funds by means of a letter of exchange was also uncommon, although one can cite an example from 1207 in which Simon Rubens, 'bancherius' says that he has received £34 of denari of Genoa, for which his brother William, 'bancherius' ought to pay in Palermo 8 marks of good silver to the bearer.

Much more common is the letter of credit, signed or rather sealed by a prince, a baron, or a bishop, in which he guarantees upon sufficient proof to reimburse anyone who has lent specified persons sums of money up to a specified limit. In 1217, for example, the dean of Arras in letters patent names four crusaders who are just setting out for Jerusalem and are to carry the letter with them: Baudouin de Henchin, up to 150 livres parisis a year; Gui de Hautecloque, up to 130 l.p.; Jean de Bouffles, up to 90 l.p.; and Pierre du Chatelet, also up to 90 l.p. These are the estimated annual revenues of the properties which the said persons have entrusted to the Dean, and he will repay to the lender of money, or to his nominee, sums which the four men have barrowed, up to the stated limit against letters from them acknowledging what they owe.

If he lacked letters of introduction of this kind, the crusader might go directly to a banker or group of bankers, as Alan, viscount of Rohen did at Acre, when he borrowed 120 marks of silver from Eudo di Polpeio, Herveo Roselli, Gulielmo di Haia, and Ansaldus Barbarus (citizen of Pisa), pledging his arms, his horses, his harness, and all his goods. If a knight was killed in battle, however, a debt of this kind was difficult or impossible to collect.

Generally, therefore, the crusader had to sign a bill, of which the lender was the beneficiary, and to which there had to be four witnesses—two on the borrower's side, who were knights from his own country or who knew him, and two on the banker's side, who like him were Italians. The loan was normally for a year, and repayment was usually fixed for Easter, the Assumption, or All Saints Day. Any payment of interest was concealed, because of the ban on usury. Those who endorsed the document were answerable for the sum, their property being liable.

Sometimes, several knights joined together to borrow. At Jaffa, in 1191, Guelteneus de Brucco, Alanus de Ponte Briencii, Juhellus de Tramigo, and Radulphus de Angulo, 'milites', together receive from Bertonus de Boscoro and his associates, citizens of Pisa, 150 marks of silver. If one of the signatories disappeared, the bankers could call on those who remained.

Even this was not sufficient security, and the banker usually required the guarantee of the knight's lord. In case of non-payment, the knight agreed to relinquish his property.

The king and the leaders of the army were involved with the Italian bankers, through their local branches, on a considerable scale. The same names are repeated so often in the documents—the Conti of Pisa, Rosso Consilii of Siena, numerous merchants of Genoa—that it is clear that the leaders tended each to have their accredited banker. At Damietta, the Genoese Bonfils de Porfan was the agent for the count of Anjou; at Acre, Gulielmo Boccanegra handled the business of the count of Poitiers.

From these examples it is clear enough how the extension of credit to individual crusaders was managed without the physical trasfer of money from West to East. The other point which the examples underline is that individual knights would use a considerable amount of cash in a year. So much spending by visitors and strangers, in what had previously been a fairly self-contained regional economy, will have created easy opportunities for those of the local population with the energy to take advantage of them.

The Templars grew in strength, then, in a society where a specialized need for banking services, in particular for the handling of credit transfers, is well attested in the first half of the thirteenth century, and is known to a much lesser extent in the last years of the twelfth century. The question is whether the absence of similar documentary information from the period before 1187 reflects merely the chances of survival of records, or whether banking activities were much less developed.

Richard has recently repeated, without any hesitation, the view that the banking activity of the Templars originated through pilgrims paying money into the commanderies in their own countries, and drawing on it by means of letters of credit when they arrived in the East.[27] This is conjecture: there is no evidence to support it, and all we can do is to look at the monetary model that is implied. As described, no money moves from either West to East or vice versa. Presumably either the pilgrims' creditors came to the West and withdrew cash from Templar funds in order to complete the circle; or the Templars themselves, if they were the creditors, could have looked on the loans as a paper transaction within the order's finances, with the net effect of moving money from East to West. Since a main objective of the Templars' activity in the West was to raise money to send to the East, the latter model seems unsatisfactory. What little early evidence we have from the twelfth century points in the opposite direction: pilgrims borrowed cash from the Templars, for example in Spain, to take with them on their travels, against the security of expected income from land. They felt they could afford to take time off; the Templars acted as a locum tenens; and the pilgrims spent their money abroad, thus making a real transfer of cash.

Delisle argued that since the earliest surviving documents already reveal the functioning of a complicated banking system that was perfectly well understood, one is entitled to assume that the origins of the system are earlier, and go back, if not to the founders of the Order, then at least to the earliest masters.[28] But how many years would be needed to acquire such expertise? And what prompted the Templars to embark on such a course? It is, again, the dearth of evidence relating to banking from the first half-century of the Order's development which makes the problem so difficult to grasp. The best hope of getting any further than Delisle and Piquet managed to do lies in understanding the context of Templar banking activity more clearly. That context was certainly not static. The growth of banking and the eventual prominence of the Templars institutionally in western Europe were largely a consequence of the growth of the money supply, and numismatists will not be surprised to observe that it happened in England and northern France in the thirteenth century, coinciding with a dramatic expansion the the currency from ca. 1180 onwards. When Henry I made gifts to Hugh of Payens, England too was in the depths of a silver famine, and the money supply remained very small for the first three quarters of the twelfth century. What happened in the East? We cannot yet define the trend of the money supply in the Crusader states at all accurately, although the estimates quoted above of the total numbers of billon coins struck are a first step. But gold bezants are likely to have been a major element in the money supply,[29] at least from the 1160s onwards. No figures (and no exact dates) are available, but one's impression is that there was a big increase in the numbers of bezants minted in the third quarter of the twelfth century (i.e. those on the 80% gold standard). The change may not have been proportionately as large as that which occurred in England from ca. 1180; we need to know more about the pre-reform bezants before we can say.[30] It was certainly earlier, and may have involved inflows of gold from Sicily or from Constantinople, more than from the neighbouring Muslim countries.

We cannot demonstrate that banking was a regular and important activity of the Templars before that big increase in the volume of the currency took place, but it seems that, at the least, its development followed swiftly on the heels of the monetary expansion. The original rule of the Templars was supplemented by detailed regulations, 'Les retrais', which were written in French before 1187, and probably before 1172.[31] They reveal, with a lack of comment which seems to imply that it was accepted as normal, an established banking activity in the East already at the date when they were composed. The Master can lend 1,000 bezants with the advice of some of the wiser heads, les prud'hommes. He can lend more, with the advice of most of the prud' hommes. And he can give presents (if it is to the advantage of the House) of a value of up to 100 bezants.

Of the various financial activities which comprised medieval banking-- the holding of valuables in trust, the transfer of credit at a distance, and so on--lending money at risk is the one which offers the most unequivocal evidence of the attitude and involvement of the principals. It is, especially from a modern point of view, of the essence of banking. For the Templars (who were under vows, and who were expected individually to have as little to do with handling money as was conveniently possible) lending was, naturally, an institutional activity, undertaken by the Master, with advice, and conducted to the long-term advantage of the Order. Gifts, which could be expected to attract good-will and possible future benefactions, are mentioned under the same heading. It is the upper limit of value of a routine gift which, as much as anything, creates the impression that the Order was already well-to-do. Why would a regulation like this have been added to the rule?—perhaps there had been occasions in the past when a master had lent more than some of his confrères thought prudent.

In the twelfth century bishops and monasteries were a frequent source of loans, and the Templars might in their early days have regarded lending to the needy as simply an activity that was expected of them. The provisions of the 'Retrais' suggest that that attitude, if it ever prevailed, had been overlaid by a more self-interested approach already by the third quarter of the twelfth century.

If the Templars could contemplate lending sums of up to 1,000 bezants or more, they must often have had a good deal of spare cash in their coffers. One would not expect loans to private persons to have left much trace in the existing documents, given that so little of the Order's records made in the East has survived. There is mention, however, of Bishop Aimery of Tripoli borrowing 3,000 bezants from the Templars in 1187; and Bohemund IV received 6,000 bezants from them in 1199.[32] (But there is, actually, nothing in the 'Retrais' which need imply that the Temple in Jerusalem maintained a counter for the daily transaction of business, as we know happened in the West. The locked strong-boxes on the Templar flagship in 1250 are the best evidence of what might be called a banking service for the general public in the East.)

The earliest specific evidence from the East seems to be from the time of the Second Crusade. Louis VII writes to Suger, of the Templars, 'They lent us, and borrowed in their own name, a considerable sum. Kindly repay them without delay 2,000 marks of silver.'[33] On the assumption that these are marks of ca. 245g of fine silver (argent-le-roi), they indicate a loan of 12-15,000 bezants. When kings seek to borrow money, it is of course not easy to refuse them, and the incident may not be good evidence of a general habit of lending. But it does suggest that, if the Order could not find 12-15,000 bezants on its own account in the middle of the century, even on so pressing an occasion, one may doubt whether the Master would have had the authorization to make routine loans of as much as 1,000 bezants. There is a hint here, in other words, of a marked increase in the Templar's resources between the time of the loan to Louis VII and the drafting of the 'Retrais'.

The Second Crusade obviously brought a lot of money into the Holy Land. In the years immediately following, the mopping-up of the surplus may have stimulated the banking activities of the Order. But the original impetus to make loans may have come even earlier, from the fact that the gifts of the faithful, and the booty taken from the Saracens (which the papal encyclical of 1139, Omne datum optimum, permitted the Templars to keep) brought spare cash into the treasury, and that it seemed sensible to put it to work, but imprudent or disadvantageous to invest it all in property. In the 1130s, resources in Jerusalem may sometimes have exceeded commitments, for the Order grew greatly in Languedoc and elsewhere in the West, but hardly at all, it has been claimed,[34] in Palestine. Even this seems uncertain, for many Burgundian knights were enrolled in the 1130s. And, through lack of any eastern cartularies, we have no accurate idea of the growth of local income.

What seems plain enough is that, once the numbers of knights and other personnel in the East grew—that is, probably already by the 1140s, the regular income trasmitted from the West was trifling in relation to the total needs. When the Order was suppressed in the early fourteenth century its annual income from lands in England has been calculated as £4,720 sterling.[35] In the early days it was a mere fraction of that, as the dates of the documents in the surviving cartularies[36] reveal, and of the total, not much more than a third is likely to have reached Jerusalem. Admittedly, the Templars may well have obtained more cash for transmission overseas from alms, tithes, gift days, and the like. From the very beginning, Hugh of Payens had a flair for publicity, and for starting at the top. When he had gained the support and active encouragement of Pope Honorius, Bernard of Clairvaux, Alfons I of Aragon, and Raymond Béranger of Barcelona, the Order was clearly a very respectable cause. Its success was sometimes viewed sourly by those who thought that they might otherwise have been the beneficiaries of charitable giving. A monk revising the Peterborough chronicle in the middle of the twelfth century, for example, writes under the year 1128, 'Hugh of the Temple came from Jerusalem to the king in Normandy, and the king received him with great honour and gave him great treasures, consisting of gold and silver; and then he sent him to England and there he was received by all good men and they all gave him treasures—and in Scotland also—and sent by him to Jerusalem great property entirely in gold and silver; and he summoned people out to Jerusalem, and then there went with him or after him so large a number of people as never had done since the first expedition in the days of Pope Urban— though it came to little ... it was nothing but lies.'[37] We recognize the same temperament today in those who would say that of the money collected locally by Oxfam, very little actually reaches the third-world poor. But it is true that, then as now, there was a dichotomy of experience and of purpose, which was to some extent glossed over, between the comfortable, charitable people at home, and the soldier-monks enjoying all the prestige and camaraderie (but also the dangers) of a very good regiment stationed in the East.[38] A modern equivalent would be a cavalry regiment in British India in the nineteenth century.

Their barracks were in the al-Aqsa mosque, which the Crusaders took to be the Temple of Solomon. It had fallen into disrepair in the early twelfth century,[39] but even so, what barracks, with their vast and splendid colonnaded refectory, and with stabling for over 2,000 horses.[40]

The Templars needed from the West, even more than they needed money, a supply of well-born recruits, and their network of houses was valuable as a means of propaganda. The life-expectancy of a brother-knight newly arrived in the East was probably not high in actuarial terms. If he survived to become one of the prud'hommes, there was no doubt still plenty of responsible work for him to do, in a country that was chronically short of experienced senior leadership.

But how and why the Templars in Jerusalem became the repository of so much cash that they were drawn into banking is still, it must be admitted, a problem on which the available evidence throws very little light. The idea that they acted, before the 1170s, as a kind of Securicor, relieving pilgrims of the risks of carrying cash from the West to the Holy Land, is quite unsupported by evidence, and it is implausible as an explanation of how they emerged as wealthy bankers. Nor is it convincing to refer to the money sent from the West in support of the Templars, except perhaps in the 1130s. The aid was no doubt very acceptable, but it is hard to imagine that it made up, after the 1130s, more than a small part of the Order's total expenditure in cash and kind, most of which will have come from revenues and donations locally. Perhaps the Templars went into banking, in Jerusalem, not precisely because they had cash to spare and wondered what to do with it, but rather because they saw the opportunity of securing a much higher return on their capital in that way, and thus of increasing their wealth. They may have been influenced by their early experience in Spain. A document which has survived from 1135 shows them making loans to pilgrims: a couple from Saragossa pledge their houses, lands, vines, and gardens to obtain 50 morabotins (i.e. gold coins, although the name may perhaps have been used as a money of account) in order to make their pilgrimage to the Holy Sepulchre.[41] The Templars will restore the property on their return, but meanwhile they enjoy the usufruct. Two reciprocal loans thus avoid the condemnation of ursury. We cannot judge what sort of a bargain it was, because we do not know the value of the estate. If it was worth substantially more than the round figure of 50 morabotins a year (or for however long the pilgrimage lasted), then the Templars were securing an exaggerated rate of return on their capital.

They were in a strong bargaining position in Spain, and equally in the East, because they were able to compete favourably with the Italian merchants in offering physical security for valuables, institutional continuity, the highest financial probity among the principals, and lay associates to handle estates. It was natural that they should wish, also, to maintain a 'treasure' of their own: every powerful family would do the same. Even so, capital accumulation does not happen willy-nilly, except to the extremely rich: it results from a determined policy to run a budget surplus—a determination, in fact, to be rich.

The details given in the 'Retrais' hint that money-lending was a regular and important activity of the Temple in Jerusalem. By the mid-thirteenth century the resources of the Order in Acre were massive, as the stories of the building of Safet and of the ransom of King Louis illustrate. Such financial strength must, one supposes, have taken many years to build. It was not remotely the outcome of donations from the West. It was accomplished in the East (where the Order had formidable outgoings) only by dint of shrewd and profitable management: London and Paris were three to four hazardous months distant, and the journey even from Languedoc or Spain took several weeks. The wealth of the Templars in the Holy Land should be viewed in terms of their social and political role in the East; in the West, in terms of their role there. The lines of communication within the order were good and the transmission of ideas about banking was probably swift and effective. The transmission of cash through the Order seems, however, to have been relatively unimportant, although the amounts are very difficult to judge. We may guess that, during the twelfth century, it averaged at the least a few hundred and at the most a couple of thousand pounds a year. In relation to the total liabilities of the Order in the East, sums of this magnitude would have been a dwindling fraction.

In relation to the monetary stock in the twelfth century, on the other hand, these, and similar or larger sums donated to the Hospitallers may well have been equivalent to the larger part of a postulated net average inflow of £4,000. And what of the money spent by pilgrims? Pluck a figure from the air for the average number of pilgrims per annum: 5,000? How much on average did each one spend or give in alms in the Holy Land: £10? The crusaders from Arras mentioned above made arrangements to spend about £100 a year; and the Yorkshire pilgrims whom Dr. Hyams has written about (infra pp. 133-5) seems to have budgeted for comparable sums. Thirty marks was roughly £100 tournois. Even if travel to the East was a major item of their outgoings, they must have spent a certain amount in the Latin Kingdom. A total of the order of £50,000 is, of course, pure guesswork, but it seems inescapable that the true figure was far greater than the net quantities of new coins minted annually. In an age when coinage and money were largely synonymous, a substantial balance of payments surplus was necessarily reflected in the growth of the monetary stock: if it was not, one may strongly suspect that there was not, after all, a large balance of payments surplus. Where did all the money go? One must allow that some of the silver coming in could have been put to non-monetary uses, and some could have been exported eastwards, although there is no sign of the latter in the minting of dirhams in Syria. Some could have gone to Egypt: Prawer has remarked on the scanty evidence of cargoes travelling south, and has hinted at the illegal export of timber.[42] The only other way in which the equation will balance is if there was a deficit on trade with the West, and this, almost certainly, is the real answer: pilgrimage became vital to the monetary sector of the economy of the Frankish states, producing an income which, together with aid given to the orders, roughly matched the trade deficits in various directions (but mostly the trade deficit with the West). Merchants would carry most of the surplus cash, which paid for the imports, back to the West; and they, too, would find it convenient to accept letters of credit payable in the West, thus clearing the pilgrims borrowings.

The very miscellaneous stray finds from Acre—including coins from as far away as Portugal, the Low Countries, and England—may in many cases be cash brought in by pilgrims.[43]

The monetary balance sheet that has been sketched raises quite acutely the question how silver accumulated in the more northerly states, where pilgrimage was by comparison a much smaller source of inflow. The Antiochene deniers of Raymond of Poitiers are scarce, but the similar 'bare-head' issues of Bohemund III amounted to an estimated $5\frac{1}{2}$ million coins, or £22,500, minted between 1149 and (probably) 1163. The issue of these and of the 'helmet' deniers which were minted thereafter, apparently in very much larger quantities up to 1187, may have been made possible partly by the transfer of bullion northwards from the Latin Kingdom by the military orders to meet their heavy commitments in the north.

But the numismatic evidence from the 1160s onwards remains to be explored, and it will be interesting to see what trends it reveals.

NOTES

Bibliography. A useful guide to the literature is available in M. Dessubré, Bibliographie de l'ordre des Templiers (imprimés et manuscrits) (Bibl. des initiations modernes, 5), 1928, H. Neu, Bibliographie des Templerordens, 1927-65, mit Ergänzungen zur Bibliographie von M. Dessubré, Bonn, 1965, and L. Dailliez, Bibliographie du Temple, 1972. The best historical introduction to the Templars is probably that by Marion Melville, La vie des Templiers, 1951, and the most thorough and up-to-date study of their financial operations is J. Piquet's Des banquiers au moyen âge. Les Templiers, 1939.

1. A million bezants was the sum originally discussed. This was reduced to 800,000, of which half was to be paid before the king was freed, and half at a later date (i.e. 400,000 was the realistic figure). This was equated with 200,000 pounds (tournois?). The sum reappears in the king's accounts later as 167,000 pounds (parisis?)—there seems to have been some confusion. At 2 bezants to the pound, these were evidently the bezants of the Latin Kingdom, and not the more valuable dinars. For a summary, see K. M. Setton, ed., The Crusades, vol. II, 503f and the references given there, in particular A. Schaube, 'Die Wechselbriefe König Ludwigs des Heiligen von seinem ersten Kreuzzuge und ihre Rolle auf dem Geldmarkte von Genua', Jahrbücher für National-ökonomie und Statistik^3 XV (1898), 603-21, 730-48, at p. 615. Louis's financial arrangements are discussed more comprehensively in A. E. Sayous, 'Les mandats de St. Louis sur son trésor et le mouvement international des capitaux pendant la septième croisade (1248-1254)', Revue Historique CLXVII (1931), 254-304.

2. Jean de Joinville, Histoire de Saint Louis, ed. and trans. into modern French by N. de Wailly, 1874. Joinville wrote many years after the event. His book was unfinished in 1305. Its central section, however, may have been written by 1272, i.e. shortly after the death of St Louis. See R. Hague, The Life of St. Louis, by John of Joinville, 1955, pp. 5-7.

3. R. B. C. Huygens, 'Un nouveau texte du traité "De constructione castri Saphet" ', Studi medievali^3 VI (1965), 355-87; cf. Stephanus Baluzius, Miscellanea, ed. J. D. Mansi, vol. I, Lucca, 1761, pp. 228-31.

4. J. Riley-Smith, The Feudal Nobility and the Kingdom of Jerusalem, 1973, p. 28 implies that these were recurrent building costs. The meaning of the text, however, seems to be that the construction of the castle was essentially completed in two and a half years, at an annual outlay averaging 440,000 bezants over and above the local receipts, after which the average annual deficit (on food, supplies, minor works, etc.) was 40,000 bezants. The wording is as follows: 'In primis duobus annis et dimidio expendit domus Templi in edificando castro Saphet, preter redditus et obventiones dicti castri, undecies centum milia bisantiorum Sarracenorum, et singulis sequentibus annis secundum magis et minus XL milia bisantiorum Sarracenorum. In cotidianis expensis dantur victualia MDCC personis..." The point that is being made is that Saphet was a heavy drain on Templar funds.

5. Melville, op. cit., pp. 136-49 and 185-94.

6. J. Riley-Smith, 'The Templars and the Teutonic Knights in Cilician Armenia', in T. S. R. Boase (ed.), The Cilician Kingdom of Armenia, Edinburgh, 1978, pp. 92-117: 'The acquisition of the castles in the Amanus [in 1131 or 1136-7] was probably the consequence of the first really important gift in the Latin East to the Order'.

7. J. Richard, Le comté de Tripoli sous la dynastie toulousaine (1102-1187), 1945, pp. 62-70. Riley-Smith, Feudal Nobility, pp. 28ff. discusses the burden of defence borne by the feudatories.

8. Richard, op. cit., p. 66.

9. The origins of the Order before it received its rule in 1128 are obscure. The main source is William of Tyre; see M. Barber, 'The origins of the Order of the Temple', Studia Monastica XII (1970), 219-40.

10. A. S. Watson, 'Back to gold—and silver', Economic History Review[2] XX (1967), 1-34, at p. 11.

11. Sicily and, to a limited extent, the Iberian states are exceptions to this rule.

12. E. H. Byrne, 'Genoese trade with Syria in the twelfth century', American Historical Review XXV (1919-20), 191-219; J. Prawer, The Latin Kingdom of Jerusalem, 1972, pp. 397ff.

13. On shipping, Prawer, op. cit., pp. 195-204. On the inflow of cash, note the comments made by crusading theorists in the late thirteenth and early fourteenth centuries, who argued that pilgrims going to Jerusalem provided the Muslims with a good deal of cash—e.g. Fidentius of Padua, cap. 7.

14. The most obvious example of Muslim pilgrimage is Ibn Jubair, who was liberally furnished with his patron's gold, but we may assume that there were many pilgrims, coming either via Damascus, or from Egypt. On Jewish pilgrimage, see Prawer, op. cit., pp. 238f.

15. Alms were a relatively important source of income at an early date in the order's history: the Council of Troyes recognized the Templars' rights to them, which were however often resisted locally. Cf. also V. Carrière, "Les débuts de l'ordre du Temple en France", Le Moyen Age XXVII (1914), 308-35.

16. Adelaide's dowry is described by Albert of Aachen, RHC OCC. vol. IV, pp. 696-7.

17. D. M. Metcalf, 'Coinage of the Latin Kingdom of Jerusalem in the name of Baudouin', NC[7] XVIII (1978), 71-84; for Tripoli see C. J. Sabine, in NC[7] XX (1980), 71-112.

18. D. M. Metcalf, 'Crusader coins associated with the Latin patriarchates of Jerusalem and Antioch', NCirc. LXXXVII (1979), 445-6.

19. Id., 'Coins of Lucca, Valence, and Antioch. Some new hoards and stray finds from the time of the Crusades', HBN XXII/XXIII (1968-9), 443-70.

20. Ibid.

21. A. A. Gordus and D. M. Metcalf, 'Neutron activation analyses of the gold coinage of the Crusader states', Metallurgy in Numismatics I (1980) (in press).

22. Die-sampling remains to be undertaken for the bezants, and these comments are based only on a preliminary assessment. The problem is complicated by the difficulty in recognizing the better modern forgeries, where die-duplication is a feature.

23. Melville, op. cit., p. 66. He was then tortured by the women of the harem for several days before being put to death.

24. Ibid., p. 73.

25. Piquet, op. cit. (Not available at the time of writing, but consulted in the form of Piquet's thesis, Les Templiers. Etude de leurs opérations financières, Paris, 1939; I understand that the text was unaltered when the work was published.)

26. 17,803 fonds latin. H. Lavoix, Monnaies à légendes arabes frappées en Syrie par les croises, 1877, pp. 5-21. As this book is not widely accessible, I have repeated the examples which Lavoix gives at some length. For another version, discussing the contents of the same manuscript, see Anon., 'Die Kreuzfahrer und ihre Banquiers', Das Heilige Land XXIX (1885). Some similar documents are printed in J. de Laborde (ed.), Layettes du trésor des chartes (Archives Nationales, Inventaires et Documents), vol. III, 1875, nos. 3800, 3810-11, 3821, 3823, 3879, 3948, and 3954.

27. J. Richard, The Latin Kingdom of Jerusalem, tr. J. Shirley, Amsterdam, 1979, p. 116.

28. L. Delisle, 'Mémoire sur les opérations financières des Templiers', Mémoires de l'Institut national de France. Académie des inscriptions et belles-lettres XXXIII (1888-90), part II, 1-246, at p. 2.

29. It has recently been demonstrated that, contrary to the general opinion, the introduction of a gold coinage in fourteenth-century England increased the effective money supply in accordance with its book value: see M. Mate, 'The role of gold coinage in the English economy', NC CXXXVIII (1978), 126-41. I am not in the least disposed to believe that the Crusader bezants were connected especially with foreign trade, although of course wealthy merchants in any country were among the main users of high-value coins.

30. The uncertainty of the evidence at this point, pending the discovery of a hoard of bezants concealed before the reform, is discussed more fully in Gordus and Metcalf, loc. cit.

31. Melville, op. cit., 84-101; H. de Curzon, La Règle du Temple (Société d'Histoire de France), 1886.

32. Richard, Le comté de Tripoli, p. 68.

33. Migne, P. L. CLXXXVI, cap. LVIII, col 1378.

34. J. Leclercq, 'Un document sur les débuts des Templiers', Revue d'histoire ecclésiastique LII (1957), 81-91. But this evidence should perhaps not be pressed too hard.

35. C. Perkins, 'The wealth of the Knights Templars in England', American Historical Review XV (1909), 252-63.

36. B. A. Lees (ed.), Records of the Templars in England in the Twelfth Century (British Academy, Records of the Social and Economic History of England and Wales, IX), 1935; A. M. Leys (ed.), The Sandford Cartulary (Oxfordshire Record Series, XIX, XXII), Oxford, 1938. The The Sandford cartulary includes charters going back to the second quarter of the twelfth century.

37. D. Whitelock et al. (ed.), The Anglo-Saxon Chronicle. A Revised Translation, 1961, s.a. 1128.

38. The style of daily life in Jerusalem emerges vividly from the detailed regulations of the 'Retrais'.

39. H. Hagenmeyer, Fulcheri Carnotensis Historia Hierosolymitana (1095-1127), Heidelberg, 1913, I, XXVI, 10: 'alterum Templum ... quod nunc satis dolendum est ... non potuimus tecti eius structuram reformare, postquam in manus Balduini regis et nostras devenit.' William of Tyre believed that the Temple was originally the palace of the Latin Kings, but he may have derived this idea from the habit of the Templars of referring to their headquarters by that name—'le palais'. Fulcher would surely have mentioned its use as the royal palace.

40. Melville, op. cit.

41. Dr. Forey has pointed out to me, however, that it is not clear that the Templars obtained any immediate profit on this occasion, where the outcome depends on one's interpretation of the clause, 'quod mittant nobis in compoto hoc quod habuerant preso nostro hereditate'.

42. Prawer, op. cit. pp. 398f.

43. L. Y. Rahmani and A. Spaer, 'Stray finds of medieval coins from Acre' Israel Numismatic Journal III (1965-6), 67-73; D. M. Metcalf, 'Some hoards and stray finds from the Latin East', ANSMN XX (1975), 139ff., at pp. 141-9.

Acknowledgements.

I am grateful to Dr. Edbury, Dr. A. J. Forey, Miss Shefali Rovik, and Mr. J. Johns for much kind criticism and advice on the basis of earlier drafts of this paper.

MARSEILLES, ACRE AND THE MEDITERRANEAN, 1200-1291

David Abulafia

For long, one non-Italian city has been placed alongside Genoa, Pisa and Venice in histories of the Levant trade in the twelfth and thirteenth centuries: Marseilles has been accorded a special rôle, as the precocious forerunner of other non-Italian towns who learned the methods and copied the successes of the commercial revolution in Italy. Nor has this been without the best credentials: Marseilles could offer an imposing series of charters in which substantial trading privileges were conferred on its merchants by the rulers of Jerusalem from the time of Baldwin I or II—privileges as generous as those offered to the Venetians or other Italians, in their promises of total tax exemption and of property in all the cities of the kingdom. Nor have these been the only 'proofs' of the prominence of Marseilles: several series of notarial acts, the earliest dating to 1200, and the most detailed dating to 1248, have been taken to bear witness to the success of the Marseilles merchants in building on their privileged status. The notarial acts testify to the massive strength of the Levant trade in the years for which documents survive. Not surprisingly, there has been a strong tendency to extrapolate backwards from 1200 and 1248, and to argue that what was by then a profitable area of trade must long have been so: the Levant trade could not, surely, be built overnight. The view that Marseilles should be bracketed with the Italian communes in the intensity of its Syrian trade was the natural product of the methods of research adopted by those excellent nineteenth-century scholars, Heyd and Schaube: they, with their interest in the commercial privileges, could see how well Marseilles was placed so early in its relations with the Levant, and could easily assume that the receipt of favours from the kings of Jerusalem would be followed by vigorous attempts to take advantage of the newly created chances. In other words, Marseilles, like Genoa and Pisa, owed much of its commercial strength in the late twelfth and thirteenth centuries to the opportunity seized at the start of the twelfth century to break into eastern Mediterranean waters.[1] Schaube's work emphasized, in addition, the interest of the Marseilles merchants in specific commodities—the export of western woollens in the thirteenth century; the import of eastern dyes such as indigo.[2] Marseilles seemed to fit the classic image of the western commercial towns, first spending silver and then exporting textiles to pay for the import of Levantine silks, spices and colours. This view rapidly settled to become the standard image of the city. In the Histoire du commerce de Marseille produced under the patronage of the Chambre de Commerce de Marseille after the Second World War, Régine Pernoud provides exactly the static image of Marseilles' Levant trade which the original documents suggested: in the first place, this is a golden age as far as the commercial health and success of Marseilles are concerned, ending in the late thirteenth or early fourteenth century as a result of Angevin interference or mismanagement; in the second place, it is an era in which the Levant trade assumed major importance among the commercial objectives of Marseilles, so that the loss of Acre in 1291 gravely weakened the city's economy.[3]

Recently, much new light has been shed on the early development of Marseilles, not by the discovery of new materials but by the destruction of one of the pillars on which interpretation of the trade of Marseilles has always rested: the commercial privileges of the kings of Jerusalem. In 1972 Hans Eberhard Mayer demonstrated, with great elegance and, in my opinion, with certain success, that the charters supposedly conferred on Marseilles before 1187 were thirteenth-century forgeries, produced in Acre probably between 1248 and 1257.[4] They were not proof that the twelfth-century status of Marseilles merchants was high or well-protected; rather were they proof that the merchants of Marseilles hoped to strengthen their position much later by allusion to a series of charters attributed to rulers whose documents were largely destroyed after Hattin. The earliest genuine privilege in favour of Marseilles dates, according to Mayer, shortly after Hattin, when Conrad of Montferrat had arrived in Tyre full of hopes of recovering lost lands and of claiming the crown of Jerusalem. But it is a privilege to many others than the merchants of Marseilles. The citizens of St. Gilles, Montpellier, Barcelona, Nîmes and Marseilles itself are rewarded for their services in the defence of Tyre with exemption from customs dues in Tyre, with a warehouse and colony in Tyre, with certain judicial rights and with a promise of rights in towns to be recovered in future.[5] It is not just a token of gratitude; it is an attempt to buy help from the Provençal and Catalan fleets, an attempt to confer on them rights analogous to those possessed by the Italian towns who had fought and been rewarded the same way in the first twenty-five years of the kingdom of Jerusalem. In retrospect it seems strange that scholars were not quicker to recognise Conrad's privilege for what it clearly is: the conferment of rights on communities that previously <u>lacked</u> special status— communities among whom Marseilles was not necessarily the most important, given the appearance in the privilege of St Gilles and Montpellier in particular.

Mayer's discovery acts as a salutary reminder that, simply because documentation exists about a commercial centre, that centre should not automatically be elevated to a higher standing than cities such as Montpellier or Nîmes, about whose trade so very little is known. It would be inaccurate, for instance, to assume that Dubrovnik was a serious rival to Genoa or Venice in late medieval trade simply because its archive is nearly as large as those of the two Italian cities. Mayer argues convincingly that it is possible to recover a 'Secret History' of Provençal trade with the Levant which, in its early stages, is very different to the image projected by Pernoud's vivid account. For Mayer, rivalry between Montpellier and Marseilles was an important determinant of the commercial development of twelfth-century Provence. Marseilles benefited handsomely from close co-operation with Pisa, and it was under the tutelage of this wealthier, more experienced, maritime town that the Levantine trade of Marseilles was really established. Merchants of Marseilles travelled in Pisan boats to the east and were counted as Pisans; privileged communities were generally trusted to define their 'citizens' in the manner that most suited themselves and their alliances.[6]

Equally, Marseilles was shunned by the Genoese—the city appears very rarely in Genoese commercial contracts of the twelfth century, even by comparison with Genoa's arch-rival Pisa.[7] Genoa turned its interest towards Montpellier and St Gilles, and tried hard to ensure that long-distance Provençal trade should be channelled through Liguria.[8] In 1156 the Genoese even secured a promise from William I of Sicily to exclude Provençal merchants from his kingdom—a measure which, if effected, would also have constricted Provençal access to the Levant. Probably the Genoese were simply trying to ensure that those Provençaux who came to Sicily, or passed through Sicily to the East, would be their own allies, sailing under their own flag, as honorary Ligurians.[9] The prospects for regular trade between Marseilles and Syria in the 1150s were not auspicious. A hundred years later the forgers of Acre would present to view a privilege of Baldwin III in which complete freedom to trade without payment of taxes would be offered the merchants of Marseilles, alongside estates and warm promises of esteem.[10] It is hardly an exaggeration to say that the forged privilege presents the reverse of the real position Marseilles merchants held in the kingdom of Jerusalem at that time.

II

Mayer's book concentrates more on the legal status of the merchants of Marseilles in the Holy Land than on their economic activities. The second pillar upon which assessments of Marseilles' Levant trade have been based, the commercial contracts, receive less attention, for Mayer's purpose is not to rewrite the whole history of Marseilles' involvement in Syria. However, the commercial acts have long received close attention from scholars, and it may not be too ambitious to attempt to see what are the implications of Mayer's revision of the history of Marseilles for the economic historian of the Mediterranean. Recently J. H. Pryor has made use of these commercial contracts to present a thesis and some articles on the <u>Commenda</u> contract in the thirteenth-century Mediterranean.[11] I have myself visited the provincial and communal archives in Marseilles, and have examined those contracts that concern trade between Marseilles and the kingdom of Sicily. In earlier work on the Genoese notaries I have tried to establish satisfactory methods for handling the mass of information about Mediterranean trade offered, often in a higgledy-piggledy way, by collections of commercial contracts.[12] My aim here is to suggest ways in which the Marseilles evidence might need special handling, and to consider the real worth of the plentiful commercial contracts that speak of Marseilles' contacts with the Levant, in the light of Mayer's revolutionary work.

In 1884-5 the archivist Louis Blancard published two volumes of thirteenth-century documents which are the foundation of knowledge about the trade of Marseilles.[13] His first achievement was simply that of identifying the groups of material which would provide substantial information about the trade of Marseilles; since his time no substantial group of commercial contracts from the thirteenth century has come to light in Marseilles. His first group of texts consisted of 151 charters dating between 1200 and 1263, concerning a single merchant family, the Manduel. At the end of that time Jean de Manduel was involved in a plot against the new lord of Marseilles, Charles of Anjou, and was executed; his property and his title deeds were confiscated, and thus many commercial documents, above all those out of which legal claims arose, found their way into the Angevin archives in Provence.[14] Blancard's second series of documents dated to a single year within the period of ascendancy of the Manduel family, though it had little to say about any of the Manduels themselves. Blancard published a notarial register of 1248, compiled by a certain Amalric or Almaric, much of whose business lay with merchants trading to Acre, Sicily and North Africa.[15] Amalric's register, in its concentration upon the grandes lignes of Mediterranean trade, is by any standards an exceptionally precious fragment. Precisely because Amalric's work survives for only a very short period, four and a half months in a single trading season, scholars such as Pernoud and Sayous have tended to treat his contracts as a minutely detailed image of a typical year.[16] For there are no standards of comparison: Amalric's acts are a random survival with no equal in depth until the fouteenth century. Though the details of Marseilles' trade might have differed from year to year, the general character of that trade has been presumed fairly consistent. How valid this interpretation in fact is we shall have to see; we shall have to try to find ways to assess how 'typical' material with no points of comparison to other material from the same city could actually be. Until a conclusion on this issue is reached, the value of any assessment of Marseilles' Levant trade based on Blancard's documents seems to me rather doubtful.

Blancard provided an orthodox, full edition of the Manduel acts concerning Marseilles trade. The acts of Amalric proved too cumbersome and he was content with a combination of summaries of fairly standard documents with editions of the text of Amalric's more interesting documents. Because notarial acts are often very repetitive, except in the names of participants, the sums of money involved, and the destination of the trading expedition, this was a reasonable decision on Blancard's part; however, he was not always accurate in copying the sums of money invested in overseas trade; and indeed Sayous calls his readings 'fantaisiste' at times.[17] The original manuscript needs also to be checked. The same method was employed by Blancard in the final section of his edition, where he presented summaries, and sometimes texts, of commercial contracts extracted from notarial registers of the late thirteenth century.[18] A thirty-year hiatus between Amalric's fragment and the earliest notary whose work next survives makes comparison between Amalric and his successors hazardous enough; in addition, the later notaries concentrate more heavily on domestic business, such as land sales and personal loans. Our good fortune in having Amalric's work available to us is simply not matched by Amalric's successors, until the fourteenth century where E. Baratier found a substantial new haul of merchant acts.[19] J. H. Pryor could only find 14 contracts for trade in Acre and one for trade in Syria in the period 1278-1300; more striking still is the lack of material concerning Marseilles' near-neighbours, the north African towns. Neither Ceuta nor Tunis appear, and Bougie is mentioned only once over the whole 23 year period.[20] Generally, scholars have treated the late thirteenth-century documents with reserve. Since little of meaning can be said about Syrian trade after 1248, I propose to concentrate here on the documents about which less reserve has been shown: the Manduel charters and the register of Amalric.

From the first piece of parchment, the Manduel documents seem to argue for a close, well co-ordinated, network of Marseilles traders spread throughout the Mediterranean (B.I). We are mid-way between Marseilles and Acre, in Messina, observing a contract between Barthélemy Mazellier and Pierre Vital on the one hand and Étienne de Manduel and Guillaume Benlivenga on the other; the former receive, on 15 February 1200, 1006 gold tari, or about 34 ounces, valued at £146.13.4 regalium coronatorum, and as guarantee of repayment they offer in pawn 141 hams, liquorice measured in the weight-standard of Acre, and other articles. The presence of a product of Syria might certainly seem to imply that we have to deal with merchants at home as much in the kingdom of Jerusalem as in that of Sicily; the readiness to deal in the gold coin of Sicily implies some familiarity with the markets of the central Mediterranean too, and the presence among the witnesses to the deed of a certain Petrus R. de Narbona suggests Provençal links with Messina were possibly well established. I simply want to suggest that there are two ways of reading this document. If two merchants have received 1006 tari against the value of certain goods, it is by no means certain that they are actually offering those goods in the ordinarily understood sense of pawning them. Analogous Genoese documents use this device to enable merchants to raise money at interest while avoiding visible resort to usury. Money is advanced in one currency, not secured by the value of so many hams, sticks of liquorice, and so on, but in order to enable merchants to buy the hams, liquorice and other items in the first place; profits are concealed from public view if the moneylenders, Manduel and Benlivenga, demand repayment in Marseilles money. It is then for the debtors to make their own profit on the sale of the hams and liquorice; and, should their receipt from the sale of these goods fall short of the stipulated sum in Marseilles silver, Manduel and Benlivenga may have recourse to law and can demand seizure of the debtors' goods.[21] Now, the implication here is that the items marked de Accon in the contract were very possibly bought in Messina, where indeed the hams were almost certainly bought (for salted pork was one of the major exports of eastern Sicily in the twelfth century).[22] And the implication of that is, that the importation of the spices and dyes of the east into Marseilles around 1200 did not depend necessarily on possession of direct access to, or of large markets in, the kingdom of Jerusalem. Sicily and Tunisia acted as entrepôts where these products could be bought from other merchants, and where the opportunity for comparison of quality and price may often have been better than in Acre itself—just as we might not choose to go to Bordeaux if we wished to buy both Burgundies and clarets but might opt for Paris where we could compare more equally the advantages of such diverse wines.

Nor do the Manduel acts testify to very heavy involvement in the Levant trade in the next few decades. Documents from 1210, 1213 and 1229 refer to trade in Acre, but the sums of money cited are small, £30 regalium coronatorum at most (B. III, VII, XXII). A certain Bernard Balbo of Marseilles co-operated with Étienne de Manduel in many of his ventures, and if we take into account the fact that not one, but two, people are investing in overseas trade, the individual level of investment seems very modest. On the other hand, Manduel wealth was clearly increasing greatly. By the early 1230s Étienne's sons were investing more substantial sums in trade—primarily in trade with Bougie and Ceuta (e.g. B. XXVII, XL, XLII). In 1233 three members of the family are seen to possess alum and cloth to the value of £1120 regalium coronatorum; a year later they also claim to own 19 sacks of cotton brought from Bougie at a price of 1980 north African bezants (millares) (B. XLIII, XLV). It is clear from a document of the same year that their alum at least came from the Levant, from Aleppo, but the principal emphasis of the early Manduel records is always on the western Mediterranean (B. XLVII). From 1234 onwards Acre becomes a regular destination for the factors appointed by the Manduel family.

An explanation of the gradual rise to prominence of the Levant trade can be hazarded. Blancard believed that the Manduel family came to Marseilles only late in the twelfth century, probably from the region of Nîmes, where a small town bore the same name, Mandolium.[23] As will be seen, they were one family among many from Languedoc, Provence and Liguria who made their fortunes rapidly in a growing city. And because the Manduel record stretches over a period of sixty years, it is possible to see patterns in the development of the family's commercial interests that coincide with changes in the headship of the family itself. The first Manduel of whom the Marseilles documents speak, Étienne, seems very much preoccupied with Sicily and north Africa, as far as it is possible to generalise from a series of only 25 charters bearing his name; it is under his elder son Bernard, from 1230, that the horizons of Manduel enterprise become enlarged to include regular dealing in the produce of the Levant and of the Maghreb. When Bernard himself died in 1237, he left his younger brother Jean de Manduel considerable capital resources and an established interest in Syrian trade.[24] In 1234 Bernard had initiated heavy direct investment in the Levant trade with a Commenda worth £360 regalium coronatorum, by which his agent Pierre Brun Audouard was instructed to carry lead, salted meats, Douai cloth and the luxurious stanfort of Arras to Acre or elsewhere in Syria, on board the ship Paradisus (B. LI). Although signs exist that this was not the first major venture into Syrian trade, it is the first Commenda contract for a large sum of money which survives naming Acre as destination. In subsequent years the Manduel family rarely reached the giddy heights of £360, settling in the ten year period 1235-1244 for sums between about £50 and £150; the overall average for all Manduel contracts for trade in the eastern Mediterranean during the period 1200-63, in regalium coronatorum, is £$87\frac{1}{2}$, according to Pryor.[25] Sayous noticed, in addition, the increased emphasis on the export of commodities rather than of money, and linked this to the growth of the Manduel business house.[26] As will be seen, there is another possible interpretation, that not merely the trade of the Manduels but that of Marseilles was becoming more complex and sophisticated.

Perhaps, indeed, the Manduels had burned their fingers in the Levant. The Commenda of £360 has additional interest since it gave rise to a legal claim against the factor of the Manduels, Pierre Brun Audouard (B. XCII). He had been sent east in 1234, as has been seen; but only in 1241, after a seven year delay, could the Manduels catch up with him and bring him to justice. Seven years without satisfaction could weigh heavily upon a thirteenth-century merchant who was accustomed to putting his capital and his profits to good use whenever opportunity offered. Above all, the legal case against

Pierre Brun illustrates the difficulties presented by an attempt to trade with a land as far distant as Syria: the lack of control over the actions either of ships' captains or of factors; the danger that goods destined for the port of Acre might be sold prematurely elsewhere—as Pierre Brun claimed, in Sicily and Sardinia, and for good reason. It is worth pausing to examine what was said in court on 6 July 1241 by Manduel's lawyer and by Pierre Brun the wayward factor. In the first place, the Manduel lawyer summarised the text of the seven-year old charter which had brought £360 into the hands of Pierre Brun, in the form of lead, cloth and salted meat. And then he added a demand for a further £100 in interest in addition to the repayment of all the original capital; considering the profitable use to which the capital might have been put during these years, £100 does not seem an extravagant demand. But Pierre Brun, in reply, first attempted to deny that the contract was made— respondit Petrus Brunus se non credere, nisi reperiatur per instrumentum publicum massiliensis notarii—and then stated that even if such a contract were found, the arrangements the Manduels had made were more complex than their lawyer admitted. He was undoubtedly right to insist that the onus was on the Manduels to produce the original charter, but he was wrong if he supposed they might be unable to find it. So he shifted his defence, and advanced two arguments. First, that there had been tempests in the west Mediterranean; the bad weather had made the ship unsafe enough, but the weight of lead in her hold was a great risk in stormy seas, and some of the lead had been unloaded even before the vessel reached Sicily, in Cagliari, on Sardinia. Nor was it Pierre Brun's wish to dump his metal there, but certain peregrini milites on board, armed pilgrims, compelled him to lighten his boat whether he wished it or not. His second argument was that the goods he had received from the Manduels were themselves security against a sum of 694 bezants of Acre, sold to the Manduels by a Pisan merchant, Jacopo Tinto, against a promise of repayment in Acre to the Pisan or his deputy; and he stated that this very Pisan merchant had accompanied him on the route east, and had decided, on the arrival of the ship in Messina, to claim repayment of the debt due to him from the Manduels. So, of his own will, he went into the markets of Messina and sold a high proportion of the lead, much of the cloth, and some of the salt pork that Pierre Brun was carrying to Acre. The Pisan kept 34 ounces $17\frac{3}{4}$ tari for himself, as repayment of the 696 bezants he was owed, or at least of $234\frac{1}{2}$ bezants. And, to be sure, the Pisan merchant could not be blamed: the Paradisus had arrived in Messina at Michaelmas and did not move out of port the whole winter; she needed to be recaulked after her bad voyage from Marseilles, and could not set out again until spring brought hope of calmer seas. Justice clearly lay partly with each side, and in the end the Marseilles judge ordered Pierre Brun to pay only a small sum, £15 regalium coronatorum, so that for the Manduels this was really a Pyrrhic victory.

This legal case is an important reminder that even trade contracts in which the destination Acre is stipulated do not necessarily indicate that a journey to Acre was finally achieved. The early Manduel contracts show greater interest in the Maghreb and Sicily precisely because the journeys there were shorter and money was committed to agents for less lengthy a period. Syria brought handsome rewards, but at the price of high risks; and the middling merchant did not regard Acre as a safe destination for more than a small proportion of his funds.[27] The Manduels can probably not be counted merely as middle-range investors, however. Documents survive listing sums owed to Étienne, Bernard and Jean de Manduel, which suggest that they did profitable business as loan bankers; Jean de Manduel was owed about £6,000 by 1263, plus large sums in other money, and accruing interest (B. CXXXIX). Within their city, the Manduels were very wealthy, very influential; compared to eminent families in Genoa and Venice, they perhaps were less than outstanding in possession of funds or status. In their business methods, they were at best the equals of the Genoese and Tuscans of the end of the twelfth century, practitioners of the traditional Commenda contract, of the sea-loan and maritime exchange; they did not imitate, though they certainly encountered, the sophisticated techniques of networks of Sienese and other Italians who operated in Marseilles, Messina and other ports they knew. The Manduels were primarily interested in profitable trade in commodities and, probably, in moneylending too; they had resort to, but did not pretend to be, dealers in foreign money or large-scale deposit bankers.

What is particularly striking in the trade with Acre conducted by the Manduels is the strong emphasis placed on the export of western goods to the east. The picture of Marseilles' Levant trade which the Manduel contracts present is to that extent in accord with evidence from Genoa: the Genoese had paid in the twelfth century for eastern commodities more often in western silver than in western exports; by the late twelfth century, as pressure grew on sources of silver in the west, and as Egyptian industries went into decline, western merchants were able to substitute the cloth of Flanders and northern Italy for the bullion they once had exported.[28] The Manduel documents include several contracts for Acre which do not mention commodities, and may indicate the export of bullion; thus in August 1229 Bertrand de Cavaillon took £30 regalium coronatorum, valued at 90 bezants of Acre, to Syria in the ship of the Templars (B. XXII). But it is clear that the Manduels moved energetically into the commodity trade with the Levant, selling western coral, canvas or hemp, textiles from Châlons, Arras, Douai and elsewhere, and bringing from Acre alum, pepper and dyes. The Manduels dealt at least in their early years of success with Egypt too, for they sent wine to Damietta in 1227 (B. XV). Judging from the Manduel contracts for trade with northwest Africa, the Manduels moved more heavily towards the export of finished goods and raw materials in the 1230s, and away from the export of bullion— which, in the case of Bougie, could take the form of ingots of gold and silver and not merely of the coin of Marseilles or of north Africa.

I have been careful not to try to quantify the evidence presented by the Manduel contracts. Those that survive exist, we must assume, because they gave rise to, or were used as evidence in, contests at law; and as such, they may not be very typical of the Commendae which the Manduels completed to their full satisfaction with trusted and regular factors. Thus simple, uncomplicated trade with the Spanish coast or the west Mediterranean islands could easily have been their chief concern, even though very few Manduel documents speak of Spanish destinations. My conclusion about the Manduel evidence should therefore bring little comfort to historians of the Levant trade in the thirteenth century. It is impossible to make any judgement about the relative level of trade in Syria as compared to Sicily or north Africa on the basis of the Manduel texts—neither the level of trade of Marseilles, nor that of the family itself, is revealed in these charters. But the charters do show sufficient similarity to evidence from Genoa and elsewhere to let us argue that Marseilles in the early thirteenth century was participating in the Italian attempt to sell western commodities in the east, and to reduce the export of bullion to Syria and elsewhere; if the Manduels were indeed typical in this respect, Marseilles lagged slightly behind its Italian rivals in the move towards the sale of western finished goods—this may, however, be an optical illusion produced by the fact that the Manduels themselves were rising higher in wealth and status during the 1220s and 1230s, and were perhaps therefore making more vigorous use of their capital rather than participating in a brand new trend. This, of course, was Sayous' reading of the evidence.[29] On the Manduels then, a broadly negative conclusion about the value of their evidence.

III

It may seem churlish to look at length at the Manduel charters when a second body of material, the register of Amalric, provides so much more evidence about the Levant trade, and can be used to produce an impressive series of statistics. There are many ways of adding together the sums of money listed in notarial acts of the Middle Ages; and in quoting Pryor's figures for the register of Amalric I am consciously choosing a list of totals lower than I myself have been able to achieve. Pryor indicates that 184 out of 462 Commendae listed by Amalric concern Acre, Syria and Cyprus—that is, 39.8%. This is a higher proportion of the total numbers of Commendae than for Sicily, the Maghreb or Spain—Sicily achieves 25.1%, north Africa a mere 15.6% and Valencia a paltry 3.5%. There are rather few documents indicating direct trade with rival commercial powers: 14 for Pisa, 13 for Genoa, five for Barcelona, three for Montpellier.[30] The total sums invested in each region present an even more vivid picture, accentuating the emphasis on the Levant trade. Just over three quarters of the Levant documents mention sums of money invested in the local Marseilles currency known as moneta miscua: Pryor gives a total figure of moneta miscua invested in the Levant trade of £12505.18.7—my own attempts at addition achieved an even higher figure, approximately £16460. On top of this there are about £300 in the money of Melgueil, over £1000 of Tours, and about £400 Genoese, as well as sums of regalium coronatorum and bezants of Acre. The average amount of moneta miscua invested in the Levant trade on the evidence of Amalric is £89½ per contract. This is in noticeable contrast to the average for the kingdom of Sicily—£54—or for the Maghreb, £37½. Indeed, the only figures to produce a higher average investment per contract are those for trade between Marseilles and northern France. A small sample only, of six documents naming sums in moneta miscua, to be sent to the Champagne fairs, produces an average of £145 moneta miscua.[31] The Manduel evidence also suggests that large sums were sent to Champagne; but, at least as far as maritime trade is concerned, Acre is the clear winner.

On the surface, certainly, the Levant emerges as the most tempting destination for merchant investments in the Spring of 1248. Pryor remarks that 'the higher average value of commendae shipped to the Levant reflected both the general profitability and attractiveness of the Levant and also the fact that more capital was required to make the longer voyage profitable'.[32] I have remarked elsewhere on a similar phenomenon in twelfth-century Genoese trade contracts, where business bound for Syria shows a heavier commitment of funds than business bound for Sicily, Sardinia or Africa; the Genoese evidence suggests that trade with the Levant demanded commitment of a merchant's funds for so long, at such a high risk, that only a small section of the merchant community would regularly invest large sums in trade with Syria—that section consisting of the city aristocracy and a few very wealthy 'new men'.[33] And we know from the story of Pierre Brun Audouard that the merchants of Marseilles were in no way able to escape the risk that cargoes might have to be dumped in Sardinia, or delays encountered in Sicily, well before leaving Latin waters for the east Mediterranean. The first question in handling Amalric's evidence must therefore be whether a merchant aristocracy emerges which dominated the Levant trade, or whether the strength of Marseilles' trade with Syria by 1248 lay precisely in the involvement in that trade of a catholic selection of all merchants. In other words, if the Levant trade meant so much to Marseilles, as Amalric's evidence might be taken to indicate, was it something on which the whole city was able to thrive? On this problem depends our assessment of the real importance of the Levant trade to Marseilles.

Amalric's evidence does indicate that the leading families of Marseilles seized eagerly the opportunity to invest in Syrian trade. During March, 1248, two members of the Gasc family sent blue and green cloth of Châlons to Acre, investing a total of £302.17.7 *moneta miscua* aboard the ship *Sanctus Spiritus* (B. 84, 88). Another well-born citizen, Bonaventura Du Temple, was sufficiently closely involved with the *Sanctus Spiritus* to entrust his goods, worth an estimated £220 *moneta miscua*, to the ship's owner, Raimond Suffren, and sent in addition a large sum in money of Melgueil (B. 89). His name, Du Temple, and that of another eminent family, Jérusalem, seem to indicate a real closeness to the Holy Land, and it can be surmised that these families were descendants of Provençal residents in the kingdom of Jerusalem.[34] At the end of March Vivaud de Jérusalem sent two bales of cloth worth £188.11.0 *moneta miscua* to Acre on the *Sanctus Spiritus*, a relatively heavy investment (B.319). Generally, indeed, it seems that the heaviest investments in Acre were made by members of illustrious families or alternatively by complete outsiders—Genoese or citizens of other southern French cities. The Gasc family takes pride of place among the native merchants, with investments of vast sums in gold wire, copper, tin and textiles; members of the family individually invested medium or large sums with a variety of agents, so that the grand total of Gasc investments is concealed by a multiplicity of single contracts.

A noticeable characteristic of contracts for trade in Acre drawn up on behalf of the Marseilles upper class is the presence of named commodities from Flanders, Genoa or elsewhere. The wealthiest merchants treated their home-city as a mid-point between trading destinations. Despite the profits they were probably able to make on the Acre run alone, they were not content to specialise. There were many other merchants in 1248 who sent Flemish textiles eastwards; but it is the Gascs, or the Du Temples, or the

Casaulx, who seem with greatest consistency to have avoided the direct export of bullion. This despite the description the documents offer of members of the Gasc family as campsores, dealers in money (B. 84, 85, 194). Not merely did they treat Marseilles as mid-point between Syria and Flanders, but they did not scorn other profitable business in the Mediterranean. On 23 March a member of the Du Temple family, Hugues son of Guillaume, agreed to travel to Sicily as factor for a certain Hugues Bouvier, with £40 moneta miscua; and a few days later he accepted Arras cloth worth £20 from Martin Magne for sale in Messina (B. 158, 192). Martin Magne was himself an investor in Acre, but he was not prepared to risk all his investments in trade with one remote destination. So, keeping his cloth for Sicily, he sent an entirely different article to Acre: £28 worth of the gold wire of Lucca, used in the ornamentation of fine robes (B, 190).

A second group easily visible in Amalric's register is merchants from outside Marseilles; however, it is often difficult to be sure whether those carrying a name such as 'Carcassonne' are visitors, or whether they are descendants of settlers of years ago, as were by now the Manduels (B. 36, 174, 349). Certainly, there were many visitors from Montpellier. Guillaume Rocadour, agent of Guillaume Desvignes of Montpellier, entrusted Raimond Benet, also of Montpellier, with textiles worth £8.7.0 in money of Melgeuil, for transport to Acre on the Sanctus Spiritus; and later that spring Benet himself sent goods worth an estimated 200 bezants of Acre eastwards on the same ship, with the popular factor Pierre Bellaygue (B. 55, 185). Moreover, one of the most interesting of Amalric's acts is a transfer of a Commenda for Acre made in Montpellier to a new representative in Acre—a rare sight of the business methods of Montpellier itself (B. 251). The presence of citizens of Montpellier should cause little surprise. The rivalry of the twelfth century between Marseilles and Montpellier gave way to co-operation in the early thirteenth—perhaps the existence of Aragonese lordship both over Montpellier and, until the rise of the house of Anjou, over the county of Provence acted as a stimulus to more productive contact. In 1229 Frederick II issued a charter in favour of merchants from Montpellier trading in the kingdom of Jerusalem, allowing them equal status with the men of Marseilles, in whose ships, we are told, they had previously travelled to the east.[35] Similarly in 1236 King Henry I of Cyprus issued a charter to the merchants of Marseilles and Montpellier jointly.[36] Thus, just as the men of Marseilles had once traded under the flag of Pisa, so for a time did the men of Montpellier under that of Marseilles. And in 1236 it appears that a member of the illustrious Conques family of Marseilles, old allies of the Manduels and possibly settlers from the south French city of Conques, had been appointed consul in Acre of the community of merchants from Montpellier.[37] But there were others trading from Marseilles whose names betray origins beyond Provence and Languedoc. Martin Gasc sent a Commenda worth 250 bezants of Acre to Syria with a Pisan merchant; someone who seems to be a member of the Zaccaria clan of Genoa sent German cloth worth £29 to Acre; and an international group met on 26 March to arrange for the passage of a large number of pilgrims travelling to Syria aboard the ship Sanctus Franciscus—a certain Andrea di Ventimiglia, Olric of Valence or Valencia, and a Venetian named Jacopo (B. 123, 126, 165). The only large group of foreign merchants identifiable in Amalric's register who shunned the Acre sailings were the Sienese, though on one occasion Dioteviva Alberto of Siena sent 171 lb of saffron, worth over £160, to Acre on the Sanctus Spiritus with the trusted agent R. Caire (B.230). Saffron, produced in large quantities near Siena, was the major dye that western Europe was able to produce for export, at a time when very many dyes were imported from the eastern Mediterranean, or Spain at least.[38] The presence of a Sienese businessman dealing in saffron through Acre should cause no surprise; but mose Sienese in Marseilles concentrated on the trade routes to Champagne, and above all in money advances and money changing, employing techniques that were more sophisticated and better co-ordinated than those of the Marseilles campsores (e.g. B. 816-9, 821-2, 825-6). Although the Sienese received a privilege for trade in the Holy Land in 1268, Amalric's register does not suggest that Provence, at least, was used as a base for their Syrian business.[39]

Another group prominent in the business affairs of Marseilles was the Jewish community, a protected, secure community with rights of citizenship and a degree of self-government. After Charles of Anjou finally asserted his lordship over Marseilles, he had to agree not to interfere with the status of its Jews.[40] When they appear in Amalric's charters they perform the same tasks as the Christians, and indeed make investments in partnership with non-Jews no less than with Jews. Trade in Acre was one of their concerns, as befitted a people who in the thirteenth century were experiencing anew the appeal of the land of Israel, under the influence of Spanish and Provençal leaders.[41] Jews seem actually to have travelled to Acre as factors for Marseilles Christians. On 6 April 1248 Benaciat received £4.10.8 worth of saffron from Guillaume Gros for transport to Acre aboard the ship Sanctus Antonius, and another Jew (or perhaps Benaciat with his name differently rendered) took £5.2.8 worth of nuts on the same ship bound for Syria (B. 388, 411). A tentative comparison of Jewish business revealed by Amalric's contracts seems to suggest that the Jews were primarily interested in trade with the north African coast and with Sicily—we encounter a certain Joseph, son of Moses of Palermo, who seems to be settled in Marseilles, and trades with Bougie (B. 598, 599). Another Jew, Mossé Daccon, citizen of Marseilles, bears a name suggesting a link with Acre itself, but we find him sending 44 Metz capes not there, but to Sicily (B. 576).

Amalric's cartulary lists several ships bound for Acre, but it is the Sanctus Spiritus of Raimond Suffren which appears most often. The ship appears as early as the second surviving act of Amalric, on 14 March 1248, and disappears from the register after 31 March; during this brief period she is mentioned in no less than 144 documents compiled by Amalric. The use in Marseilles of so many types of money makes it difficult to express the exact proportion of Levantine trade assigned to this ship, out of all the trade contracts listed by Amalric for Syrian commerce; a figure between two-thirds and three-quarters can be suggested. Moreover, the Sanctus Spiritus was apparently available each year to merchants wishing to do business in Syria. In 1249 the vessel makes appearances in the Manduel documents; on 28 September of that year Jean de Manduel sent £404 moneta miscua, in the form of textiles, to Acre in nave Raimundi Sifredi et sociorum ejus, que vocatur Sanctus-Spiritus (B. CX). The Sanctus Spiritus might easily be taken to typify the ships sent east each year from Marseilles. Since Schaube's time, indeed, scholars have studied the cargoes placed aboard this ship to gain an idea of the average value of the Syria trade to the Provençal merchants, and to learn the likely capacity of the ships sent to Acre at this period. Thus, Sayous wrote that 'la multiplicité des intérêts dans les exportations pour la Syrie par un seul bateau, et encore d'après les actes d'un seul notaire, nous donne une idée de l'activité et du rôle des principaux armateurs à cette époque.'[42] Since Amalric provides extensive evidence that other ships were also being fitted out for merchant expeditions to Acre in 1248, it is tempting to conclude that in an average year the merchants of Marseilles invested hundreds of thousands of pounds in the Levant.

Was 1248 a typical year? Was the Sanctus Spiritus a typical ship? Cerainly no other ship makes such persistent appearances. The Rosetta of St Denis, bound for Acre later the same summer, makes only nine appearances in Amalric's cartulary, between 24 April and 18 May; from then to 29 July, the date of the final document recorded by Amalric, she is not to be seen. Thus she probably sailed in late May; and there is no doubt that much business for the Rosetta was recorded not by Amalric but by other notaries whose work is now lost. Nonetheless, we find the same discrepancy between the Sanctus Spiritus and other ships mentioned by Amalric: the Sanctus Antonius, of Guillaume and Bernard Narbonne, (perhaps two ships), makes twelve appearances; the Sicardus is identified twenty times; and each seems to have left Marseilles well before the Rosetta. There is a nagging impression left, first, that Amalric must have recorded the greater part of business for the Sanctus Spiritus, because the sums invested there are so greatly out of proportion to all other sums; and, second, that the Sanctus Spiritus was indeed a very capacious ship, an outstanding vessel built to withstand the long haul to Acre. Indeed, it is striking that the Sanctus Spiritus seems not to intend to put in at any port en route to Syria, whereas a competitor, the Cygnus, will do business in Cyprus as well as Acre, as will the Sicardus.[43]

Other ships too appear ad navigandum de Massilia apud Ciprum with the novel rider, vel alibi ubicunque dominus Rex Francie et alii barones applicare voluerint ultra mare (B.777). These are not, as far as can be seen, ships utilised by the merchants for commerce in Acre, but ships hired on behalf of the king of France for his crusade. 1248 was indeed a special year for Marseilles and for Acre. In mid-April Amalric recorded a visit from the agents of Guy, comte de Forez, who were in Marseilles to arrange the hire of a ship still on the stocks, to carry a crew of 41 sailors and to provide space for 60 horses. The charge for hire was 975 marks sterling (B. 549; cf. 860). On 25 May the agent of the comte de Dreux hired another ship for £2600 tournois (B. 777). Marseilles became a major arsenal of the crusade, providing not merely the hulls the crusaders needed, but food, water and armaments. Commercial contracts for Acre continue to appear in late May and early June, but Amalric's evidence suggests that in these weeks the Levant promised not so much the profits of trade, as the profits of the dockyard. St Louis himself made use of Genoa and of his new port at Aigues-Mortes to equip part of the crusading armies, and Marseilles certainly had to share business with rivals. But those close to the French king did not eschew Marseilles; the chronicler of St Louis' life, Jean de Joinville, was among those who elected for the older port.[44] Now, the crusade undoubtedly meant that more Marsilian ships than merchant vessels only set out for the east in 1248. And Amalric seems to indicate that the crusaders hoped to hire new or at least empty ships, rather than to use vessels already commissioned by merchants. Thus the Sanctus Antonius or the Sicardus are not mentioned in the negotiations for the hire of ships. Ideally, the crusaders used purpose-built ships, as the comte de Forez intended to do. But how did the crusade affect trade? Did it perhaps lead to a diminution, since merchants might fear to be caught in cross-fire? Or did the merchants assume the rôle of camp-followers, bringing supplies of food and arms, to succour at least their Christian brethren, and maybe the Muslims also?

To answer this question it is necessary to move beyond Amalric's evidence to that provided by the Genoese notaries of the late twelfth century. Just as Amalric's evidence survives for the year of St Louis' crusade, Guglielmo Cassinese's cartulary survives from the year of Richard I's. It is clear that, in 1190, Genoese businessmen were greatly attracted by the prospect of trade in the Levant. Moreover, they were not merely interested in provisioning the crusaders, but were anxious to carry bullion and textiles to the east.[45] This, too, when Acre was still in Saladin's hands and the beleaguered port of Tyre was the only certain place of sale. The evidence from Amalric's cartulary seems to me to tend in the same direction, except that Acre was now in Christian hands, and the Provençal merchants ran less risk of losing their market or of finding themselves trapped by Muslim armies. Italian and Provençal merchants did regularly expect to do very handsome business from crusades, and from other Mediterranean expeditions such as Henry VI's invasion of Sicily or Charles of Anjou's war against the Hohenstaufen.[46] It has even been suggested that the Tunis crusade of St Louis and of Charles of Anjou, in 1270, was prompted by the desire to create a major foothold for Marseilles in Africa—a view now descredited.[47] Crusade business lay partly, but by no means entirely, in the sale of arms and provisions. In a threatened city the price of luxuries might fall so that foreign merchants could purchase silk and gems at ridiculously low cost; the price of foodstuffs would certainly rise, to make importers of grain welcome and wealthy. This seems to explain the explicit instructions that the ships Sanctus-Michel and Cygnus visit Cyprus, where St Louis' crusaders were to gather, as well as Acre (B. 446, 452). The Sanctus Spiritus is a different case; she sailed in early April well ahead of the French troops, and announced no plan to visit Cyprus. But a connection with the crusade still seems likely: the Sanctus Spiritus would attract heavier investment than usual because it would arrive in the east before the region became a theatre of war; in other words, it would escape some of the risks of travelling through the war zone. Moreover, many Marseilles merchants may have feared that intensive war in the east might interrupt Levantine trade for several years. Now was the time to invest in Acre; autumn might be too late, or too risky, if one sought to purchase oriental exports rather than to provision western armies. Thus we have to deal with two types of mercantile response to the prospect of a crusade, one 'optimistic', another, as it were, 'pessimistic'.

Amalric's cartulary seems to present major problems of interpretation, as far as commercial contracts for the Levant are concerned. There are reasonable grounds for the belief that 1248 saw more intensive trade with the Levant than may have been normal; in other words, the voyage of the <u>Sanctus Spiritus</u> may not have been typical of that ship's career. An additional problem needs to be raised, though any verdict must be inconclusive. Sailings to Syria were concentrated in a few weeks in spring and autumn each year—in the case of twelfth-century Genoa, often in the autumn alone. Amalric's evidence survives from precisely the weeks during which investment in Syria had to take place; but investment in ports nearer home could be spread more thinly over time. There were only brief periods in the depths of winter when a voyage to west Mediterranean ports was utterly impossible. Thus, if Amalric's work survived only from November 1248, Syria might only receive passing reference, with casual mentions of sums of Acre bezants perhaps; and Valencia, Majorca and Naples might receive a plethora of contracts. In addition, it is likely that many business deals for short-range trade were not brought before a notary, to avoid fees or because merchants were as happy to work alone as in partnerships. A contract for trade in the Îles d'Hyères (B. XIX) is unusual evidence of the value placed on business in areas very near at hand. Of course, similar doubts can be entered for much of the Genoese and Venetian material upon which scholars, including myself, have often relied. But the Italian cartularies do provide internal comparative evidence which is crucial to their proper handling—evidence from a sequence of years, evidence from more than one notary, evidence from other sources such as chronicles and treaties for a probable increase or decrease in the level of trade. Amalric, by contrast, offers usable evidence in more restricted spheres. He is, as Schaube and Sayous appreciated, an invaluable guide to the identity of commodities taken east; and, in a general way, he gives clues to the composition of the business community of Marseilles. I shrink, however, from any attempt at serious statistical handling of his evidence. It is significant, too, that the most useful recent study of Amalric's cartulary, by J. H. Pryor, has concentrated on the evidence there contained for the growth of certain types of business contract.[48] It is the nature of Amalric's commercial contracts, not the level of the contracts, that proves in the end truly revealing.

IV

Marseilles was poor in natural resources—set among rocky coves with few natural products apart from almonds and wine, which it exported to Syria and to Sicily in the thirteenth century. If the city was to acquire food it had to search beyond its own area of jurisdiction, in the more fertile parts of Provence, in Sicily and the western Mediterranean.[49] In many ways trade in these regions remained more vital to the fortunes of Marseilles than did trade with Acre. Indeed, if we agree to regard the evidence of Amalric as exceptional, we can argue that north Africa, Sicily and Spain, as well as intensive local trade, were what really dominated the business life of Marseilles. There is no doubt that the rôle of Marseilles in Acre was modest in the twelfth century; the struggle in the 1250s to show that the merchants of Marseilles had always been privileged indicates a strong interest in the Levant, but it does not indicate any necessary success in making Syria the prime source of profit to Marseilles. If we place together Mayer's evidence for the rise to prominence of Marseilles, and Lesage's study of Marseilles in its early decline under Angevin suzerainty, only a short period is left which can serve as a golden age of Marsilian trade—the mid-thirteenth century. Amalric's contracts show Marseilles at its height, but it is unclear whether it was at its height for more than a few decades. Under Charles of Anjou there began a slow process whereby the city was transformed into a great naval base; the orders completed for the counts of Forez and of Dreux are the ancestors of others for the brother and nephew of St Louis. Under Robert the Wise Marseilles suffered a recession: trade with Acre was suspended after 1291, and little success was achieved in the new centre of Italian business in the Levant, Famagusta in Cyprus; Robert did not, moreover, allow extensive privileges to merchants of Marseilles trading in his Neapolitan realms, for it was the Florentines and other Italians who had most to offer in cash advances and political alliances. Paradoxically, Marseilles gained less privileges as an Angevin subject than Florence as an Angevin ally.[50]

My scepticism about the real importance of Marseilles in the Levant trade must, however, be tempered by the belief that Marseilles continued to deal in one cargo, human beings, from the late twelfth to the late thirteenth century. It was a prime point of departure for pilgrims travelling from France and Provence to Acre; its reputation as a source of shipping for pilgrims surely helped attract to it those kings who fitted their crusades there—not to mention the poor hopefuls of the Children's Crusade in 1212. In the twelfth century the Genoese seemed to be prepared to allow Marseilles a rôle as a source of pilgrim transport; it was competition from merchants the Genoese really wished to suppress.[51] The Manduel charters speak of the _peregrini milites_ who forced Pierre Brun Audouard to dump his lead in Sardinia in 1234 (B. XCII). Moreover, Amalric's cartulary seems to indicate that the pilgrim traffic was a source of great profit in the mid-thirteenth century. On 25 March 1248, Andrea di Ventimiglia promised Olric de Valencia and Jacopo of Venice that he would make proper provision of food and other wants for the pilgrims setting out that spring for the Holy Land aboard the ship _Sanctus Franciscus_, at a charge of 18 _solidi_ of _moneta miscua_ per person. It is clear from the charter that several hundred pilgrims were expected to travel east— as many as four hundred, in which case the cost of provisions would be £360, apart from the additional cost of servants assigned to the pilgrims by Andrea di Ventimiglia (B. 165).[52] It would certainly be interesting to know the effects on the pilgrim traffic of the Mongol and Mamluk wars in the east; the loss of Acre did not, of course, mark the end of pilgrimage to the Holy Land, but the effects of any changes on Marseilles might be profitably considered. The lack of Marsilian interest in Cyprus after 1291 may indicate that the pilgrim traffic had fallen largely into other hands.

Marseilles in the thirteenth century seems to emerge as a city of shipping entrepreneurs above all else. We could characterise Florence in the same period as an industrial centre; Genoa we could call a centre for commercial exchange. Evidently, the interests of each of these cities overlapped, and indeed the Genoese worked hard to ensure that Marseilles should not encroach too far upon their own major interests. Perhaps, too, the Genoese really were successful; perhaps they helped channel the energies of the business community of Marseilles away from intensive capital investment in textiles, bullion and luxury goods to trade in primary products from Africa and Sicily, and the construction and maintenance of high quality ships. My suggestion is that Marseilles continued to operate within these limits even when Genoa had removed its heavy hand, for its economy had been moulded by its twelfth-century competitors. In the mid-thirteenth century Marseilles had moved some distance towards specialisation in commercial business and had developed an interest in the Levant trade. That is the Marseilles Amalric reveals to us; but it is not the whole history of Marseilles' trade at this period. Amalric also reveals that large, busy community of Sienese who, in the midst of the Marseilles merchants, had already developed commercial techniques by comparison with which Amalric's contracts were a very traditional way of doing business. For Marseilles was not in the forefront; there were indeed bright successes, in 1248 and in the years before when capital was earned for the investments of 1248. But already Marseilles was beholden to the Angevins, and nervously aware that the city's future as a free republic alongside Genoa or Venice might prove an unfulfilled dream.[53]

NOTES

1. W. Heyd, Histoire du commerce du Levant au moyen âge, transl. F. Raynaud, 2 vols., Leipzig, 1885-6, i. 186-9, 319, 328-9. But note Heyd's guarded comment about the scale of Provençal trade in the 12th century: i, 334.

2. A. Schaube, Handelsgeschichte der romanischen Völker des mittelmeergebiets bis zum Ende der Kreuzzüge, Munich-Berlin, 1906, pp. 204-8.

3. R. Pernoud, 'Le Moyen Age jusqu'en 1291', in Histoire du commerce de Marseille, ed. G. Rambert, i, 1949, pp. 138-64.

4. H. E. Mayer, Marseilles Levantehandel und ein akkonensisches Fälscheratelier des XIII. Jahrhunderts, Tübingen, 1972.

5. Mayer, op. cit., pp. 181-3, doc. no. 4; for a verdict in favour of the authenticity of this charter, see Mayer, op. cit., p. 40.

6. On this important question, compare D. Jacoby, 'L'expansion occidentale dans le Levant: les Vénitiens à Acre dans la seconde moitié du XIIIe siècle', Journal of Medieval History, III (1977), 225-64, and Mayer, op. cit., p. 65, citing a document of 1245: quod consules Pisani in Acon et in partibus Sirie et factitiis pro omnibus, qui Pisanorum nomine censentur, sive sint Florentini, sive Pistorienses, sive Senenses, sive de Sancto Geminiano sive de Tuscia, et quod predicti homines subsunt dictis consulibus (R. Davidsohn, Forschungen zur Geschichte von Florenz, ii. Aus den Stadtbüchern und Urkunden von San Gimignano, Berlin, 1900, 298).

7. D. S. H. Abulafia, The Two Italies: economic relations between the Norman Kingdom of Sicily and the northern communes, Cambridge, 1977, p. 113 (Pisa only in 1160), pp. 174 and 177 (Pisa and Marseilles in 1190), p. 182 (Pisa only in 1191).

8. Heyd, op. cit., i. 187, for evidence that even the merchants of Montpellier must limit their expeditions to the area between Spain and Genoa, under the terms of treaties imposed by Genoa in 1143 and 1155. But the transport of pilgrims to Syria was permitted: Mayer, op. cit., p. 60; cf. infra for a suggestion that Marseilles too involved itself in the pilgrim traffic at this period.

9. Abulafia, op. cit., pp. 95-6.

10. Mayer, op. cit., pp. 177-9, doc. no. 3.

11. J. H. Pryor, 'The Commenda in Mediterranean maritime commerce during the 13th century: a study based on Marseilles' (Ph. D. dissertation, University of Toronto, 1974; also available in Marseilles, archives communales); J. H. Pryor, 'The working method of a 13th-century French notary: the example of Giraud Amalric and the Commenda contract', Mediaeval Studies, XXXVII (1975), 433-44—the use of the adjective 'French' seems odd in reference to 13th-century Provence; J. H. Pryor, 'The origins of the Commenda contract', Speculum, LII (1977), 5-37; of general interest is J. H. Pryor, 'Stephanus demonasterio and the notariate at Aubenas in the early 15th century', Mediaeval Studies, XXXVI (1974), 28-55.

12. Abulafia, op. cit., pp. 8-24.

13. L. Blancard (ed.), Documents inédits sur le commerce de Marseille au moyen âge, 2 vols., Marseilles, 1884-5.

14. Blancard, op. cit., i. 3-258. Hereafter, references to Manduel documents are given in brackets in the main text, in the form B. followed by a Roman numeral, which is the document number—thus (B. I), (B. XXII), the first and the twenty-second document.

15. Blancard, op. cit., i. 261-ii.367. Hereafter, references to Amalric's register are given in brackets in the main text, in the form B. followed by an Arabic numeral, which is the document number—thus (B. 777).

16. Pernoud, op. cit., pp. 150-64; A. E. Sayous, 'Le commerce de Marseille avec la Syrie au milieu du XIIe siècle', Revue des etudes historiques, XCV (1929), 391-408.

17. Sayous, op. cit., p. 391n; cf. Pryor, 'Working method', p. 433n and Pryor, 'Commenda contract', p. 8n.

18. Marseilles, archives communales, série II, Notaires, 1; Pryor, 'Working method', pp. 433-44. My own visit to the archive, in 1977, was for the purpose of checking Amalric's Sicilian, not Levantine, trade figures against Blancard's edition; I have had in this essay to rely more often on Blancard's readings and figures than is really advisable. In addition, I have chosen to retain Blancard's French versions of names, on the ground that this is the form commonly used by modern writers. Of course, the citizens of Marseilles spoke Provençal, and not French, in the thirteenth century; they neither considered themselves French nor owed any services to the king of France—it is anachronistic to call Amalric a French notary, as does Pryor, 'Working method'. However,

the Provençal form of the merchants' names cannot easily be recovered
and the Latin form was neither very consistent in rendering nor used in
daily speech.

19. E. Baratier, 'De 1291 a 1423', in Histoire du commerce de Marseille,
ed. G. Rambert, ii, 1951, pp. 7, 206-53 and passim; Blancard, op. cit.,
ii, pp. 387-512, for a selection of acts from the late 13th century; Pryor,
diss., for tables, and editions of individual acts of interest for the development of the commenda.

20. Pryor, diss., p. 256, table I: 'Commendae exported from Marseilles
by destination'.

21. Abulafia, op. cit., p. 25n, for Genoese cambia maritima; cf. R. de
Roover, 'The Cambium Maritimum contract according to the Genoese
notarial records of the 12th and 13th centuries', in Economy, Society
and Government in medieval Italy, ed. D. Herlihy, R. Lopez, V. Slessarev,
(Kent, Ohio, 1969), pp. 15-33.

22. Abulafia, op. cit., p. 92, referring to the treaty of 1156 between Genoa
and the Norman kings of Sicily. A later Manduel document shows salt
pork being taken from Marseilles to the Levant, and some of it being
unloaded in Messina (B. II—discussed infra). Of course, there are many
examples of medieval traders carrying coals to Newcastle. Varieties
in quality, the desire for the produce of exotic lands—these and other
factors conspire to make (say) Italian shoes as attractive to modern
British buyers as British shoes to modern Italian buyers. And indeed
Britain even imports salt pork in the form of Danish bacon, Parma ham,
and so on.

23. Blancard, op. cit., i. p. xvi.

24. A. E. Sayous, 'Les opérations du capitaliste et commerçant marseillais
Étienne de Manduel entre 1200 et 1230', Revue des questions historiques,
CXII (ser. 3, XVI) (1930), 5-29; A. E. Sayous, 'L'activité de deux
capitalistes-commerçants marseillais vers le milieu du XIIIe siècle:
Bernard de Manduel (1227-1232) et Jean de Manduel (1233-1263)', Revue
d'histoire économique et sociale, XVII (1929), 137-55.

25. Pryor, diss., p. 269, table 4: 'Values of Commendae by area of destination'.

26. Sayous, 'Deux capitalistes-commerçants', pp. 138-9, 153.

27, Compare the situation in 12th-century Genoa: Abulafia, op. cit., p. 100.

28. Abulafia, op. cit., pp. 255-73 for parallel developments in Sicily; R. S.
Lopez, 'Il problema della bilancia dei pagamenti nel commercio di
Levante', Venezia e il Levante fino al secolo XV, i. Storia, Diritto,
Economia, ed. A. Pertusi, 2 vols., Florence, 1973, pp. 431-52.

29. Sayous, 'Deux capitalistes-commerçants', pp. 138-9, where Sayous does,
to be fair, ascribe some importance to changes in the trading position of
Marseilles in the early 13th century.

30. Pryor, diss., p. 256, table 1. There is more statistical material in
R. K. Berlow, 'The Sailing of the "Saint Esprit" ', Journal of Economic
History, XXXIX (1979), 345-62.

31. Pryor, diss., p. 269, table 4.

32. Pryor, diss., pp. 267-70.

33. Abulafia, op. cit., p. 100, also pp. 182-3.

34. G. Lesage, Marseille angevine, 1950, p. 167, argues that these families fought in defence of the Holy Land and made their fortune there.

35. E. Winkelmann (ed.), Acta imperii inedita seculi XIII, 2 vols., Innsbruck, 1880-5, i, pp. 272-3; RRH, no. 1014; J. La Monte, Feudal monarchy in the kingdom of Jerusalem, Cambridge, Mass., 1932, p. 272; cf. Mayer, op. cit., pp. 84-8, for invaluable comment. Marseilles was under imperial ban at this moment, and ships of Marseilles were prevented from entering ports in Syria which were under the control of Frederick II's agents or allies.

36. Mayer, op. cit., pp. 193-5, doc. no. 10.

37. Lesage, op. cit., pp. 115-17.

38. I disagree with the view of J. Richard, Le royaume latin de Jérusalem, 1953, p. 277, that saffron was mainly prized as a seasoning for food. For evidence of saffron production in Tuscany, see Davidsohn, Forschungen, vol. ii, 299-303; useful comments by Pernoud, op. cit., p. 155. See also Berlow, op. cit., pp. 353, 355-6, 361.

39. G. Müller (ed.), Documenti sulle relazioni delle città toscane coll'Oriente cristiano e coi Turchi fino all'anno 1531, Florence, 1879, no. 70, pp. 100-1; RRH, no. 1360; La Monte, op. cit., p. 275. The real importance of this privilege lies on Conradin's attempt to win Sienese support against the Angevin invaders of southern Italy; it is a privilege for trade in Sicily and Italy as well as Jerusalem. Since Conradin was king of Jerusalem by right of succession, it was natural that he should include the Holy Land in his privilege; but Sienese bankers at this period seem to have been much more interested in south Italian than in Syrian business. The privilege would certainly have been valuable to those Sienese who did trade in Acre, since it reduced tolls on exports and imports through that port to a mere 1%. Davidsohn, Forschungen, vol. ii, pp. 298, cited in n6, supra, reveals the presence in Acre of Sienese trading under a Pisan flag, and, at times when both Tuscan cities were favouring the Hohenstaufen cause, co-operation may have been very close.

40. Lesage, op. cit., pp. 92-3.

41. J. Prawer, Histoire du royaume latin de Jérusalem, 2 vols., 1969-70, vol. ii, pp. 397-418, noting the especial importance of the Provençal rabbi Moshe ben Nahman, or Nahmanides. Berlow, op. cit., p. 356.

42. Sayous, 'Commerce de Marseille avec la Syrie', p. 407; cf. Schaube, op. cit., pp. 204-8.

43. Blancard, op. cit., ii. 519-23: index of ships mentioned in commercial contracts.

44. Jean de Joinville, Mémoires de Jean sire de Joinville ou histoire et chronique du très-chrétien roi Saint Louis, ed. F. Michel, 1867, pp. 37, 40-1, offering a graphic description of the voyage from Marseilles to Cyprus, and of the mood on board ship.

45. M. W. Hall, H. C. Krueger, R. L. Reynolds (eds.), Guglielmo Cassinese, 2 vols. (Notai Liguri del secolo XII, ii, Genoa, 1938); Abulafia, op. cit., p. 178, and p. 177, table 12.

46. Abulafia, Two Italies, pp. 183-213; D. S. H. Abulafia, 'Southern Italy and the Florentine economy, 1260-1370', Economic History Review (forthcoming), for relations between merchants and Angevins.

47. R. Sternfeld, Ludwigs des Heiligen Kreuzzug nach Tunis und die Politik Karls I. von Sizilien, Berlin, 1896.

48. See especially Pryor, 'Commenda contract', pp. 5-37.

49. Lesage, op. cit., pp. 43-59.

50. See generally, Lesage, op. cit., pp. 100-2, 151-5; also G. Yver, Le commerce et les marchands dans l'Italie meridionale au XIIIe et au XIVe siecle, 1903, 217-19. Both Yver and Lesage emphasize the good things that Marseilles did receive from Charles of Anjou, but a long term view, and (above all) a comparison with Florentine successes, suggest that Marseilles was not outstandingly favoured.

51. For Marseilles, Schaube, op. cit., pp. 203-4; but it is necessary to build on a presumed analogy with Montpellier: Heyd, op. cit., i. 187; Mayer, op. cit., pp. 60.

52. Richard (op. cit., p. 16) slightly misinterprets this text by apparently confusing the fare paid by pilgrims with the cost per head agreed among three businessmen, themselves no doubt anxious for a profit. Andrea di Ventimiglia was probably free to charge more than 38s. raimondins from his actual passengers.

53. I should like to thank my former teacher and present colleague, Arthur Hibbert of King's College, Cambridge, for the extended loan of a copy of Blancard's volumes, H. E. Mayer for the handsome present of Marseilles Levantehandel, J. H. Pryor for the provision of trade figures and other indispensable material (copyright J. H. Pryor, 1974), Anna B. Sapir for reading my text, and the staff of the Archives communales and of the Archives des Bouches-du-Rhône in Marseilles for their willing help during my visit in 1977.

THE BILLON AND COPPER COINAGE
OF THE COUNTY OF TRIPOLI TO c.1268

C. J. Sabine

The coinage of Crusader Tripoli has long been the subject of speculation and some controversy, mainly due to the very limited nature of the available evidence. With the lack of documentary records large groups of coins are needed to supply reasonably reliable statistical information on which to base any hypotheses regarding the monetary history of the county. So far as Tripoli is concerned such large groups of coins are not forthcoming, and only two hoards have so far been published which contained significant numbers of Tripoli coins; both these hoards are from the first half of the thirteenth century, and neither was recorded in great detail.[1] There is no hoard evidence so far published from the twelfth century.

In recent years Tripolitan coins have been appearing on the British market in increasing numbers, and since no published system of classification can record the types in sufficient detail, the present survey was undertaken in the hope that future finds may be recorded more precisely.[2] During the course of the research certain interesting possibilities arose which gave some clues to both the relative and absolute chronology of the Tripoli series; this has resulted in certain reattributions being proposed from those given in Gustave Schlumberger's classic work on the coinage of the Latin Orient.[3] It must however be stressed that such reattributions as are proposed are tentative—the final proof must await future well-documented finds.

The survey took account of 342 coins, and whilst this may sound like a fairly large number it should be remembered that the petty coinage of Tripoli is spread over a period of more than 150 years, and comprises some 20 major types. The numbers of each type are thus at best only small, and any statistical evidence derived from the survey must be treated with caution. This assumes further significance when it is considered that many coins of Tripoli are very indifferently produced and it is not always possible to identify individual dies with certainty.

The coinage of Crusader Tripoli, when viewed as a whole, is rather different from that of the Latin Kingdom of Jerusalem, although there is of course a certain similarity between all the Crusader issues of western European type. The coins of Jerusalem most frequently met with are the billon deniers, and the same is true for the principality of Antioch. The coinage of Tripoli, however, consisted largely of copper pieces of denier size, the billon coins generally being rather scarcer than the copper today, with the exception of the last billon issue.

The mint of Antioch also struck similar copper pieces but apparently not on the same scale as at Tripoli, to judge by surviving examples. Small coppers struck for the Latin Kingdom do not make their appearance until the period immediately preceding the loss of Jerusalem to Saladin,[4] and afterwards were struck in several cities by the local barons.[5]

Both gold and silver coins were struck at Tripoli, as well as billon and copper. These series, however, form separate studies in their own right and are not considered here.[6] The billon coins are clearly deniers, but the denomination of the coppers is not certain, although they are often loosely referred to nowadays as copper deniers. The style of the lettering shows that sometimes the billon and copper were parallel issues, and therefore the copper must represent a lower denomination. Copper coins of similar size and weight to those struck in Tripoli were also struck in Acre for Henry of Champagne (1192-7), and are marked with their value PVGES (pougeois);[7] these coins were probably used as half-deniers or oboles, and the Tripoli coins may be of the same value.[8]

This interpretation gains some support from the fact that whereas the Kingdom of Jerusalem issued billon oboles of the same types as the royal deniers but of reduced module at least up to the reign of Amaury (1163-74),[9] from the reign of Guy of Lusignan (1186-92) onwards regular issues of copper began, although apparently on a fairly restricted scale.[10] We may see in this the direct influence of Tripoli, since Raymond III of Tripoli (1152-87) seems to have struck copper coinage at Beirut during his custody of that city from 1184-6 while regent of the Latin Kingdom.[11] After the loss of the city of Jerusalem to Saladin in 1187 the coinage of the Latin Kingdom becomes much more 'northern' in character with the continued striking of copper coins at Acre, Beirut, Tyre, and Sidon. As far as monetary matters are concerned the northern ports of the Latin Kingdom may well have been to some extent under the influence of Tripoli since coins of the county are reported as being found as far south as Acre, but apparently no further.[12] It thus seems that the billon obole of Jerusalem may have been replaced by the copper pougeois, corresponding with a common denomination in Tripoli; nor is this surprising when one considers the large influence wielded in the Latin Kingdom by Raymond III, and subsequently by the members of the 'baronial party'.

The foregoing might suggest that the coinage of Tripoli should not be studied out of context with other Crusader issues, and as far as the commencement of autonomous issues from Tripoli is concerned this context is of the utmost importance, since it gives us our best available evidence for the first issue of western European style coinage struck in the Latin East.

The coinage of the county of Edessa consisted of heavy bronze pieces, somewhat akin to the Byzantine follis, and being further from western influence than the other three Crusader states the coinage shows little in the way of western features.[13] The principality of Antioch was at least nominally a part of the Byzantine empire, and links with Constantinople must have been many. The early autonomous coinage of the principality again consists of heavy bronze coins very similar in inspiration to those of Byzantium. There is no known early autonomous coinage from the Latin Kingdom, but it has recently been shown that both Antioch and Jerusalem had their own so-called 'preferred' western currencies which are known to have circulated in considerable quantity.[14] These preferred coinages were the denari of Lucca for Jerusalem and the deniers of Valence for Antioch.[15] It seems likely that these coins were imported to Antioch and Jerusalem in large quantities, beginning at a very early date. Autonomous billon deniers seem to have commenced at Antioch with those of Raymond of Poitiers (1136-49),[16] and in the Latin Kingdom with the BALDVINVS series which seems to belong essentially to Baldwin III (1143-63).[17]

The county of Tripoli had no strong links with the Byzantine empire at its founding c. 1102, although Raymond IV of Toulouse, subsequently Raymond I of Tripoli, had been on good terms with the emperor Alexius I. The county was a small territory sandwiched between two large Crusader states, and, lacking a major seaport or commercial centre, can have had little economic significance in the Levant until the capture of Tripoli itself in 1109. From its founding until the capture of the city the county's currency needs would no doubt have been considerably less than those of Antioch and Jerusalem; however, these two states had large quantities of the preferred coinages which may not have been readily available in the emergent county, with most commercial traffic passing it by to the north or south. In its earliest days the county may therefore have been somewhat starved of currency, for although commercial activity may not have been great there were doubtless many economic demands that Raymond had to meet, including pay for his army and the expenses of building his castle of Mount Pilgrim. Lack of readily available currency may thus have necessitated the early striking of autonomous issues at Tripoli. Count Bertrand (1109-12) is known to have struck billon deniers in the county, and this at a much earlier date than any other Crusader ruler. The billon issues of Antioch and Jerusalem may have commenced in the late 1140s as a recoinage of the preferred western issues; but no such theory can be advanced for the autonomous issues of Tripoli, which clearly started much earlier.

The coinage of Bertrand cannot however be seen as satisfying the county's need for currency in its earliest days, but might become more understandable had there already been an issue in the county before his time. Such a coinage would have been struck by Raymond I, or possibly his successor William-Jordan (1105-9), and being issued for economic reasons might have been struck on a fairly large scale. Lack of silver in the county might have necessitated the issue being struck in copper, and it would therefore have been the prototype for the later small copper coins—there seems no good reason for Antioch to have issued small coppers instead of billon oboles unless it was due to some previous precedent, since the very large volume of billon deniers produced in the principality shows there was no lack of silver there. And there is indeed a very unusual issue of Tripoli which gives every indication of being early, and which for several reasons appears to fulfil the previously stated requirements for an autonomous coinage in the county of Tripoli's earliest days.

The Moneta type copper coin (see Fig. 1) was recognised by Schlumberger as being early. He also noted the most unusual legends MONETA TRIPOLIS / RAIMVNDI COMITIS, but considered that the issue probably belonged to Raymond II (1137-52).[18] Further consideration of the legends in conjunction

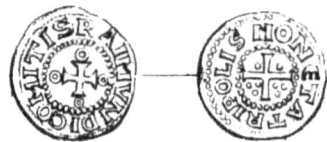

Fig. 1. Moneta copper, type 1

with the monetary situation in the surrounding Crusader states raises the possibility that these coins in fact constitute the first issue of petty coinage in the county of Tripoli. The obverse legend MONETA TRIPOLIS is quite unlike any other known issue of Tripoli, all of which mention the city itself in some such form as CIVITAS TRIPOLIS, or a variation of this. Thus the MONETA TRIPOLIS legend, by deliberately omitting to mention the city, might be thought to imply that the city itself was not at that time in Crusader hands. This was the situation only during the rules of Raymond I and William-Jordan. It therefore seems likely that the Moneta coppers in fact belong to Raymond I, although their issue might have been continued by his immediate successor. A similar instance of a Crusader ruler without a city may be found in the deniers struck for the king of Jerusalem, probably by the Hospitallers during the period of the Third Crusade, whose legends similarly proclaim MONETA REGIS / REX IERL'M.[19] The Moneta coppers of Tripoli also have an unusual reverse legend, where RAIMVNDI COMITIS replaces the more usual RAIMVNDVS or RAMVNDVS COMS. Thus the legends of the Moneta coppers seem to say 'Money of Tripoli of Count Raymond', rather than the later form of 'Count Raymond / the city of Tripoli'.

With regard to the scale of issue, a statistical analysis of the dies gives an estimate of approximately $2\frac{1}{2}$ million coins,[20] which is what one might expect under the circumstances described. The pattern of dies used tells us little, except that of the four varieties of this coin, the one presumed to be first (since the legends are not abbreviated) appears to be struck from fewer dies than the other three types, suggesting that there may have been a fairly small-scale introduction followed by a gathering of impetus.

Fig. 2. a. Bertrand denier; b. Bertrand/Pons denier

Mention has already been made of the billon deniers struck in Tripoli by Bertrand (see Fig. 2a), but these are so scarce today that no statistical information can be gained. Only five specimens can at present be located, and all are from different dies. This suggests that the size of the issue may not have been as small as the coins' present scarcity might suggest. The workmanship of the dies is not generally of a good standard, and the designs on the coins reproduce those of Bertrand's deniers previously struck by him in Toulouse.[21] Four of the known examples bear Bertrand's name, while the fifth is ostensibly anonymous although clearly of a related type. This latter coin has the obverse legend TRIPOLIS divided so as to isolate the letters PO (see Fig. 2b). Schlumberger suggested that this could be a reference to Bertrand's successor Count Pons (1112-37) and that this coin might therefore belong to him rather than Bertrand.[22] No further evidence can be brought forward either for or against this, except that by Pons' time sufficient of the preferred coinages would probably have already been in circulation throughout the Latin East, and so the need for Pons to strike a coinage is not obvious. However it should also be borne in mind that the early counts of Tripoli were the only Crusader rulers of their day who enjoyed the right of coinage in western Europe. Pons never became count of Toulouse and this may provide sufficient reason for his not openly issuing a coinage in his own name. The reason for Bertrand's doing so can only be guessed at; presumably when the city of Tripoli was taken by the Crusaders in 1109 some stocks of silver also fell into Crusader hands and Bertrand may have had this coined in his name as a proclamation of his new status. It does not seem reasonable to account for the present scarcity of Bertrand's coins solely by reason of their being a small issue, although this may be partly responsible. On the whole it seems more likely that any such specimens still in circulation were recoined when the first major billon series of Tripoli was issued, perhaps in the late 1140's.

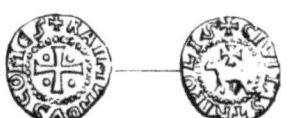

Fig. 3. Horse and Cross copper, type 1

It appears that the next type to be struck after Bertrand's coinage was the scarce copper issue with a reverse type that has usually been described as the Agnus Dei (see Fig. 3). The obverse legend RAIMVNDVS COMS evidently predates the more common RAMVNDVS, and the reverse type is apparently copied from the coins of Alfonse-Jordan, count of Toulouse (1112-48).[23] The coins both of Tripoli and of Saint-Gilles seem to show a horse looking ahead with a cross-on-staff behind the creature, rather than the more normal lamb looking over its shoulder and holding a banner with its foreleg. It therefore seems that the device is not the Agnus Dei, and it will be referred to as the Horse and Cross type. Its attribution is not certain, but the spelling of the count's name and the similarity of type with the coins of Toulouse leads one to suspect that these coins were struck by Raymond II (1137-52), and almost certainly belong to a period before the later star and crescent device came into use on the Tripolitan coinage. The dies of the Horse and Cross coinage show some blundering of the legends, and the pieces are often poorly centred. A statistical estimate of the volume of their issue, based on a study of the dies used, gives approximately one million coins. There are two basic varieties showing slight but consistent differences.

The first major coinage of Tripoli is the Star and Crescent series. Coins showing this device were struck in both billon and copper. The symbol of an eight-pointed star surmounting a crescent is of considerable antiquity, but in the context of Crusader coinage raises a number of interesting problems. As far as the Crusaders were concerned the symbol was Islamic, and it is therefore not easy to see why such a device should have been used on Christian coins. A similar symbol also appears on the deniers of Raymond V of Toulouse (1148-1194), struck at Pont-de-Sorgues, although here the star is six-pointed.[24] It has traditionally been assumed that the Tripolitan coins were copied from those of Toulouse. However one copper type of the Tripoli shows the count's name spelt RAIMVNDVS which might suggest that these coins are earlier than has hitherto been believed; just how early cannot be stated with any degree of certainty, although perhaps the mid 1140s would not be too far from the truth. The similar coins of Toulouse are mentioned in documents from 1151 onwards, and they cannot be earlier than 1148 since they bear the count's initial R. Whichever way round the borrowing was, the fact still remains that the symbol itself is not one which might be expected on a Christian coin, and since the counts of Tripoli were perhaps more 'orientalised' than the counts of Toulouse one might suspect that the Tripoli coinage was the first to use the device, although why Toulouse should have done so remains a mystery. If we were to look for a suitable reason for the exchange to have occurred, the timing would be just about right for the introduction of the Star and Crescent device in France after the return of visiting crusaders from the Second Crusade (1147-9).

There are also copper coins of Antioch which bear the star and crescent device,[25] again with a six-pointed star rather than the eight of Tripoli. Their lettering style suggests they are contemporary with the earliest 'Helmet' type issues of Bohemund III, introduced perhaps in the early 1160s. The Helmet type coins of Antioch also include a tiny star and crescent in their design, although here the device is split with the crescent to the left and the star to the right of the bust. Bohemund III and Raymond III are known to have been on good terms,[26] and this seems to have been reflected in the coinages of their two territories in the early 1160s.

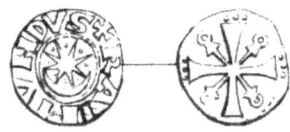

Fig. 4. Star and Crescent copper, type 1

The Star and Crescent coinage of Tripoli consists of four varieties of copper coin, and three varieties of denier. The type 1 coppers, those with the legend RAIMVNDVS (see Fig. 4), appear to be the first issue, and since the other three copper issues are all anonymous, it seems logical to attribute types 2-4 to the period of Raymond III's captivity following the Battle of Artah in August 1164.[27] In fact from this time onwards all the coppers of Tripoli are anonymous, and it could be that Raymond's captivity set the precedent for this anonymity. The deniers are however named, and the count's name is here spelled RAMVNDVS (see Fig. 5); it is thus most likely that the deniers followed from the type 1 coppers. This would make their date of introduction perhaps the late 1140s, although the issue no doubt belongs essentially to Raymond III. It is tempting to see some connection between the commencement of the major billon issues of Antioch, Jerusalem, and Tripoli, perhaps as a general recoinage of the western European issues then circulating in considerable quantity. However one should not lose sight of the fact that the datings are speculative.

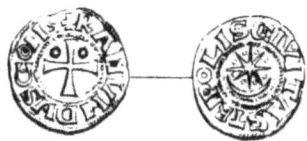

Fig. 5. Star and Crescent denier, type 2

The three types of denier are quite easily distinguished from each other by the positions of the bezants in the quarters of the obverse cross, and there are other minor differences in the reverses which help to establish the sequence of issue by means of mules or hybrids between the various types. Several coins of the last issue are of inferior workmanship, which suggests that there may have been some degeneration before the issue ceased. All the die-duplication occurs in types 1 and 3; it might therefore be that type 1 was a small issue which was succeeded by the main issue of type 2. Type 3 may have been cut short by Raymond's capture in 1164. One specimen of Star and Crescent denier has been analysed chemically, and one may suspect that the original mint standard was about one quarter fine silver.

a   b

Fig. 6. Star and Crescent coppers: a. Type 2; b. Type 4

The copper issues of the star and crescent series are again easily distinguished from each other. Type 2 bears the legend +TRIPOLIS and might be an emergency issue struck immediately subsequent to Raymond's capture (see Fig. 6a). The coins are crudely struck, and the dies of inferior workmanship. These coins are very scarce today and the issue may have been small. The two major issues of Star and Crescent copper are in completely different styles, and also the legends are quite different. Type 3 bears CVATIRIPOLIS in broad flat letters, while type 4 has CIVITASTRIPOLIS or CIVTASTRIIPOILS in small lettering (see Fig. 6b). Type 4 may be the last issue since it is found overstruck by one of the succeeding types.

Thus far it appears that the coinage of Tripoli was either billon or copper, but not both together. There are no Bertrand coppers, nor are there any deniers with the legend RAIMVNDVS. There are no anonymous deniers that can be attributed to Raymond's captivity, and so it seems that the coinage struck in the county throughout this period consisted almost entirely of coppers of types 3 and 4.

In attempting to estimate the sizes of the various Star and Crescent issues, certain problems arise. The billon is fairly straightforward with an estimate of about 7 million coins; but types 1 and 2 of the copper are so scarce that statistical evidence is worthless. Type 3 of the copper is also fairly straightforward with an estimate of about half a million coins. There is very little die-duplication in type 4 and again statistical estimates cannot be made. However it seems safe to say that type 4 was probably the major copper issue of the Star and Crescent series, especially since there are no known variations of type 3 while there are at least two varieties of type 4.

a   b

Fig. 7. a. Star denier, type 1b; b. Castle copper, type 1b

The date of introduction of the next billon coinage is again not certain, but the style of these coins is far removed from the Star and Crescent deniers and the type may possibly have been first struck after Raymond III's release from captivity. The coins themselves, the Star deniers, type 1 (see Fig. 7a), are well executed pieces, usually struck on well-rounded flans from very well prepared dies; the crescent has now been omitted in favour of a large eight-pointed star. The count's name is spelled RAMVNDVS, and it is important to note that the first letter is unquestionably an R. There has been some confusion in the past concerning the attribution of these pieces, it being supposed that they might belong to a certain Raymond IV of Tripoli who was believed to have succeeded Raymond III on his death in 1187.[28] Although Raymond III intended that Raymond, Bohemund III of Antioch's eldest son, should succeed to Tripoli, there is no evidence that his wishes were carried out, and the county passed to Bohemund III's second son, also named Bohemund, who was later Bohemund IV of Antioch.[29] Since the Star deniers of type 1 show the count's name beginning with an R, they must belong to Raymond III. Other types of Star denier exist which help to establish this attribution with more certainty, since on them the count's name begins with the letter B. These must belong to Bohemund.

At present the statistical evidence with regard to the type 1 Star deniers is conflicting, and no worthwhile estimate can be made concerning the size of the coinage. Three examples of this type have been analysed and again one may suspect that the alloy was originally about a quarter fine. It seems likely that the Star deniers type 1 were a recoinage of the previous Star and Crescent series, since there were none of the earlier coins amongst 99 Star deniers in the Kessab hoard, —although this hoard was deposited much later and apparently contained mainly the Star deniers issued by Bohemund.

The style of lettering used on the type 1 Star deniers is echoed on the copper coins of Tripoli of Castle type 1 (see Fig. 7b), and one of these coins is found overstruck on a Star and Crescent copper type 4. It is therefore likely that the Castle coppers were issued alongside the Star deniers, unlike the previous either billon/or copper situation. The Castle coppers type 1 are also fairly well produced, and we may suspect that there had been some tightening up of the mint procedures after Raymond III's release from captivity. There are some minor varieties of both the Star deniers type 1 and the Castle coppers type 1 but the position with regard to these is not clear at present. One of the varieties of Castle copper type 1 has a small doorway which seems to have been copied on the next issue of Castle copper, type 2, to be discussed later.

Mention has already been made of Star deniers on which the Count's name begins with a letter B. There has been some controversy whether these coins actually exist, or whether the B is in reality a badly formed letter R.[30] There can now be little doubt that this issue does exist, and since the type is very similar to that of Raymond III's coins, the BAMVNDVS issue must belong to Bohemund, who presumably continued the previous issue with the substitution of the letter B for R. Bohemund's coins, the Star deniers type 2, show considerable degeneration from Raymond's excellent pieces, and also exhibit a feature which shows them to have remained in production for some length of time.

During the second and third decades of the thirteenth century, many Crusader issues used wire borders to the legends rather than the more usual beaded form. This feature can be seen on the deniers of John of Brienne struck at Damietta between 1219 and 1221;[31] the anonymous deniers of Sidon of the Mosque type introduced probably c. 1230;[32] the deniers of Henry I of Cyprus (1218-53);[33] some of the deniers of Hugh I of Cyprus (1205-18);[34] some of the coppers of Antioch of the Fleur-de-lis type, which by lettering style are associated with the billon coinage of Antioch struck c. 1215-20;[35] most of the billon deniers of Beirut in the name of John I (c. 1200-36);[36] as well as some of the billon and copper issues of Tripoli. It thus seems that the use of wire borders might be a good criterion for judging the approximate period of issue of some of the Tripoli coins.

Some of the Star deniers signed BAMVNDVS show the beaded borders and some the wire borders, and some a mixture of the two, and all have a rather 'overcrowded' appearance. One would like to date the pieces with wire borders subsequent to the period c. 1215-20. The Kessab hoard, concealed c. 1225, contained 99 specimens of the Star deniers, but they were only superficially described. Longuet's original publication notes the use of the letter B in the count's name, and it has more recently been suggested that some of the coins in the hoard were those of Raymond.[37] With a date of deposit of the mid-1220s, both statements are quite possible—it would not be unusual for a hoard such as this to contain coins forty years old, but the use of the letter B shows that Bohemund's coins were also present in quantity—as one might expect. The only coin illustrated from the hoard has the count's initial obscure, but the obverse has wire borders, thus probably putting the coin after c. 1215-20—again just as might be expected with a hoard of this date. The inclusion of coins of Raymond II suggests that there had been no recoinage since the commencement of the Star denier series. The Star deniers type 2 are difficult to classify by nature of their degeneration, but this poor production standard immediately separates them from the very regular aspect of Raymond III's issues.

Fig. 8. Castle coppers: a. Type 2; b. Type 3

The issues of Castle copper subsequent to type 1 all show some form of degeneration. They have been placed in sequence according to stylistic criteria, and the validity of this must await future discoveries. Type 2 (see fig. 8a) shows dies of neat workmanship with a square castle with what appear to be dots-for-hinges on the doors, which are now smaller than before. Perhaps this was carried over from the Castle copper type 1 variety previously mentioned. All specimens of type 2 examined were defective in one way or another, and may have been produced during a period of economic hardship such as followed Saladin's campaigns of 1187-8. Their defects could also be the result of great economic activity but this somehow seems less likely. The most likely time for the introduction of this issue seems to be soon after Bohemund took control of Tripoli, perhaps c. 1187-90.

The coins of type 3 (see fig. 8b) show much inferior workmanship of the dies, but the coins retain the small divided doorway of type 2 but without the dots-for-hinges. The borders are coarsely beaded. The lettering also is coarser than on type 2, and usually has exaggerated serifs. We really have no clear guide as to the period of issue of this type, but it may take us as far as c. 1210 when viewed in context with the succeeding types.

The type 4 Castle coppers show a radical departure from type 3 in that the castle, which is even coarser in workmanship, has a large undivided doorway instead of the previously small divided one. The legends are narrow with small lettering, and some evidently early pieces of this type show the previous small divided doorway of type 3. It is in type 4 that the wire borders first make their appearance on the copper coinage, although the majority of type 4 coins have the beaded form. It thus seems possible that production of this type ended in the period c. 1215-20.

Castle type 5 is very similar to type 4, but is generally of slightly better workmanship, with larger lettering and more use of wire borders. Some type 5 coins show lettering in a style similar to that of Antioch, and also the use of stops between the letters, which is a feature of the coinage of Raymond-Roupen at Antioch, 1216-19. It therefore seems probable that type 5 is essentially of the period c. 1220 onwards, although the distinction between types 4 and 5 tends to be rather blurred. Although one specimen of type 5 examined has retrograde legends, its standard of workmanship is much better than previously. Perhaps there had been some attempt to improve the coinage which by now was of a very poor standard in both billon and copper.

That a subsequent attempt to improve the coinage was in fact made can be seen in both the billon and copper series of Tripoli, but at what time can only be approximately estimated. Hoard evidence shows that the last billon issue of Antioch, the Helmet type 6 coinage, was introduced probably about 1230, perhaps on the accession of Bohemund V in 1233.[38] These coins are of similar general type to the previous issues, but are of simplified design and very neat workmanship; also they are struck on a reduced weight standard. All these features can be seen in the billon and copper coinage of Tripoli, and it therefore seems likely that the New-Style coins are contemporary with Helmet type 6 of Antioch.

Fig. 9. New-Style Star deniers: a. Type 3; b. Type 4

The New-Style billon coinage seems to have commenced with a Star denier of good workmanship, but having only six rays to the star instead of the previous eight, and bearing the abbreviated legend :BAMUND' COMS/ :CIVITAS TRIPOL' (see fig. 9a). The initial crosses have been replaced by a pair of pellets, and this in conjunction with the use of shorter legends and a star with fewer rays may have been an attempt to improve the previously-mentioned overcrowded appearance of the type 2 Star deniers. These first New-Style Star deniers, classified as type 3, show features which link them both with the preceding coinage and with the following types. The letter R has a curled foot as on the type 1 and 2 coins, while the letter A has a crescent on top which is a feature found on some later pieces. The borders are still of the wire type.

A further new type of Star denier, type 4, is in many respects very similar to type 3, but has the novel feature of French legends. The star is again six-pointed, and the legends are :+: B O C O M S / :+: CITE TRIPOL' (see fig. 9b). The initial crosses have reappeared, and one of the three specimens examined shows a mixture of beaded and wire borders. The Djebail hoard, deposited c. 1230-5, is reported to have contained 33 specimens of the coins with French legends, but the wording of the report leaves uncertainty as to the precise nature of the Tripoli coins—there may have been some of a later type present as well. The date of deposit of the Djebail hoard tallies well with the evidence provided by the type 6 Antioch deniers, and the fact that the Kessab hoard, concealed about ten years earlier, contained none of the New-Style deniers gives a very good indication of the date of their introduction which must be the late 1220s or early 1230s. Yet further evidence is forthcoming since it was during the second or third decades of the thirteenth century, and certainly before 1228, that the chancery in Antioch and Tripoli began issuing formal documents in French instead of Latin.[39] This could well provide the reason for the use of French legends on the type 4 Star deniers, and also helps to support the suggested dating.

Both the type 3 and type 4 Star deniers are very scarce today, and this combined with the mixture of features on them and on the early coins of the following issue, suggests that they were 'experimental' pieces, and were probably both issued within a very short time of each other. The possibility also exists that type 4 is an issue outside the main development of the New-Style series, and that the true order of types should run 3 - 5 rather than 3 - 4 - 5. The muling of type 4 reverses with early type 5 obverses however shows the relative position of type 4 in the series.

a   b

Fig. 10. New Style coinage: a. Star denier, type 5; b. Castle copper, type 6

The previously-mentioned type 5 Star deniers are the last major issue of billon from Tripoli, and are easily distinguished by the use of three small dots in the second quarter of the obverse cross, and the fact that the reverse star is again eight-pointed. Some early coins of this type omit the group of three dots, and show a mixture of previous features such as crescent-topped A's, R's with a curled foot, and beaded and wire borders. The true type 5 coins have beaded borders, A's with a straight bar on top, R's with a straight foot, and the legends +BAMVND' COMS / +CIVITAS TRIPOL' (see fig. 10a). Most specimens are extremely ill-struck, suggesting that they may have been produced at a high rate. They are the commonest billon coins of Tripoli today.

The date at which the type came to an end is not readily apparent, but there is in existence an inscription dedicating a new 'Tower of the Mint' at Tripoli, the date being between 1266 and 1268.[40] The timing would be about right for the introduction of the gros and demi-gros of Bohemund VI (1251-75),[41], and it seems inconsistent that such poor quality billon coins would continue to be issued alongside the excellent large silver pieces. (But such a situation could and sometimes did exist, as is shown by other coinages.[42]) If the billon issue was large, as it seems to have been, and also produced fairly rapidly, then the continued need for striking a petty coinage after c. 1268 for so small a territory as Tripoli is not obvious.

The copper coins of Tripoli appear to have undergone a similar process to the billon, but the early stages of the New-Style copper coinage are not so clearly defined, perhaps through the accident of non-discovery. On the Castle copper type 6 (see fig. 10b) coins the obverse and reverse types have been interchanged from the earlier issues, and the castle, now on the reverse, is of the simplified 'Genoese gateway' form. The style of lettering is precisely as on the Star deniers type 5, although with the earlier anonymous legends; the wire borders have been retained on the copper series. Some early coins have a variant style of castle with four crenellations, which seems to be a hybrid between types 1 - 5 which have five crenellations, and type 6 which has three. These intermediate coins have several unusual features linking them with the experimental stages of the New-Style Star deniers; one coin shows a crescent-topped letter A, and another has the double pellet initial mark of the type 3 Star deniers and the castle is on the obverse, as on the earlier coinages. There can be little doubt that such coins stand at the head of the type 6 Castle coppers, but too few examples are known to establish whether they deserve to rank as substantive varieties or not. Both the billon and copper issues give evidence of an extensive reorganisation of the Tripoli mint c. 1230, which resulted in several experimental types being issued before the coinage was finalised as the type 5 Star deniers and the type 6 Castle coppers. Again there is no clear end to the Castle copper series, but it could be that since both New-Style coinages seem to have started together, they may also have ended together.

Both the type 5 Star deniers and type 6 Castle coppers are very difficult to classify other than in their basic types. Certain features do however occur which may give some clue to the chronology of the issues. Some type 5 Star deniers show a simple cross pattée on the obverse, with spreading limbs as on the type 3 and 4 Star deniers; it is therefore likely that type 5 coins with such features stand earlier in the issues than those which have a cross with more parallel-sided limbs and others which occasionally have the serifs added in a rather careless manner. Again with the copper coins of type 6, differences may be noted in the width of the castle; the experimental early coins have a rather broad castle, and it may be that the standard type 6 coppers with a similarly broad castle are earlier than those with a narrow castle.

Fig. 11. a. Late copper of uncertain attribution;
b. Billon/copper coins of Tripoli type - perhaps counterfeit

Certain other unattributable copper coins appear to belong to the Tripoli mint (see fig. 11a), since they are apparently found in association with Tripoli coins. They are light in weight and have unintelligible legends which on most seem to be +IIOIIOII —perhaps this is also echoed in the principal design, which is otherwise enigmatic. The best assessment that can at present be made is that this issue may have been struck by the Tripoli mint some time after the demise of the Castle coppers type 6, perhaps in response to some sudden shortage in the dwindling supply of early copper. The coins are scarce today, and the issue may have been small.

Other copper coins exist which by type seem to be linked to the billon issues of Tripoli (see fig. 11b). Most of them are so far out of character that they could be the work of contemporary counterfeiters—the legends are usually blundered or meaningless, and the workmanship is often very poor.

Throughout the period of its activity the Tripoli mint seems to have controlled the weights of the billon deniers fairly well; earlier coins average about 0.9 g, and the New-Style coinage about 0.7 g. Those billon coins analysed suggest that the alloy was originally about one quarter fine silver.

Weights of the copper coins vary wildly, especially prior to the New-Style series. Most lie between about 0.5 g and 1.75 g, and it seems that the mint's standard for these coins was rather slack. The New-Style copper coins seem to be more closely controlled and vary between about 0.5 g and 0.8 g with only one heavy piece being recorded at 1.29g.

Two copper pieces were noted which had been overstruck on previous issues. One is a Castle type 1a struck over a Star and Crescent type 4, as previously mentioned, and the other is a Star and Crescent type 4a struck over an unidentifiable coin which was perhaps a Horse and Cross type. Such overstriking has been noted in the copper coinage of Beirut,[43] and it was very common with the early large bronzes of Antioch and Edessa.[44] It seems likely that this practice was very limited in later years, and no reason for its use at Tripoli can be proposed at present.

A study of the dies used suggests that the petty coinage of Crusader Tripoli was not generally issued on a very large scale, although some issues may have been larger than previously thought. The process of recoining the billon issues seems at present to be peculiar to Tripoli—the Kessab hoard contained no Star and Crescent deniers thus suggesting a recoinage in the early 1170s, and the Djebail hoard contained no Star deniers of types 1 or 2, hinting at a similar recoinage c. 1230 for the New-Style Star deniers. In contrast, early coins are commonly found in late hoards of Antioch deniers; whilst the position with regard to the issues of the Latin Kingdom is not clear at present, there is as yet no sign of recoinage during the BALDVINVS series. The recoinage of the Tripoli billon no doubt accounts at least in part for the type 5 Star deniers being the most frequently encountered billon pieces of Tripoli today.

No reliable estimate can at present be made of the ratio of obverse to reverse dies used at Tripoli, but it seems to have probably been about two obverse to one reverse. The fact that the obverse dies are generally more numerous than the reverse suggests that the obverse was usually the upper die, and the more complicated reverse design was on the lower die.

The petty coinage of Tripoli appears to be the most complete and continuous western European coinage struck by the Crusaders. It retained its own distinctive character throughout the more than 150 years of its production. The mint of Tripoli continued to produce large silver coins bearing either the eight-pointed Tripoli star or the Castle device at least until the rule of Bohemund VII (1275-87). This makes Tripoli the longest-lived Crusader mint.

NOTES

1. H. Longuet, 'La trouvaille de Kessab en Orient Latin', $\underline{RN}^4$ XXXVII 1935, 163-83; G. Schlumberger in $\underline{RN}^4$ XI 1907, 282.

2. For full details of the survey see C. J. Sabine, 'The billon and copper coinage of the crusader county of Tripoli, c. 1102-1268', $\underline{NC}^7$ XX 1980 (in press).

3. G. Schlumberger, Numismatique de l'Orient Latin, 1878-82.

4. C. J. Sabine, 'The Turris Davit coinage and the regency of Raymond III of Tripoli, (1184-6)', $\underline{NC}^7$ XVIII (1978), 85-92.

5. Small copper coins are known from the following Crusader mints: Antioch, Tripoli, Acre, Tyre, Sidon, and Beirut. There are also the similar pieces struck for Guy of Lusignan as king of Jerusalem (Schl. III, 25) and in Cyprus (Schl. VI, 2), as well as several anonymous coppers which bear no mint name.

6. The gold has not as yet been positively identified, and the large silver (Sch. IV, 19-22) does not seem to offer such grave numismatic problems as the billon and copper.

7. Schl. III, 28.

8. Schlumberger considered the coins of Henry of Champagne (1192-7) struck at Acre to be 'pougeoises' (f.), or farthings. However Raymond d'Aguilers implies that the coins of Le Puy (pogesi) were used as half-deniers, and the term 'pougeoise' (f.) only appears in France in the thirteenth century. On the whole it therefore seems likely that Henry's coins were 'pougeois' (m.), and were used as 'oboles', or half-deniers. J. A. Blanchet, 'La pite ou pougeoise', in Études de numismatique, I, 1892, pp. 309-26.

9. Schl. III, 20 and 24.

10. Schl. III, 25.

11. Sabine, loc. cit., $\underline{NC}^7$ XVIII (1978).

12. D. M. Metcalf, 'Some hoards and stray finds from the Latin East', ANSMN XX (1975), 139-52; L. Y. Rahmani and A. Spaer, 'Stray finds of mediaeval coins from Acre', Israel Numismatic Journal III (1965/66), 67-73.

13. J. Porteous, 'The early coinage of the counts of Edessa', $\underline{NC}^7$ XV (1975) 169-82.

14. D. M. Metcalf, 'Crusader coinages associated with the Latin patriarchates of Jerusalem and Antioch', NCirc. LXXXVII (1979), 445-6.

15. For detailed information concerning these coinages see D. M. Metcalf, 'Coins of Lucca, Valence and Antioch', HBN XXII-XXIII (1968/69), 443-70.

16. Schl. II, 17.

17. Schl. III, 21-24. For the latest research see D. M. Metcalf, 'Coinage of the Latin kingdom of Jerusalem in the name of Baudouin', $\underline{NC}^7$ XVII (1978), 72-84.

18. Schlumberger, op. cit., pp. 101f.

19. Schl. III, 27.

20. The statistical method used is detailed in C. S. S. Lyon, 'Analysis of the material', in H. R. Mossop, The Lincoln mint, c. 890-1279, Newcastle-upon-Tyne, 1970, pp. 11-19.

21. F. Poey d'Avant, Monnaies féodales de France, 1858, no. 3682.

22. Schlumberger, op. cit., p. 101.

23. Poey d'Avant 3714-15 (billon deniers and oboles of Alfonse-Jordan) and 3718-19 (billon deniers and oboles of Raymond, either Raymond IV, 1088-1105, or, much more probably, Raymond V, 1148-94).

24. H. Rolland, Monnaies des comtes de Provence, XII-XV siècles, 1956, p. 105.

25. Schl. III, 3.

26. M. W. Baldwin, Raymond III of Tripolis and the fall of Jerusalem (1140-1187), Princeton 1936, pp. 140f.

27. Although it was not necessarily always the case, some crusader issues seem to have been anonymous during periods of regency. C. J. Sabine, loc. cit., $\underline{NC}^7$ XVIII (1978); also G. Schlumberger, op. cit. p. 103.

28. Longuet, loc. cit., pp. 175-7; Schlumberger, op. cit., p. 104.

29. J. Yvon, 'La succession de Raimond III (1152-1187) et la numismatique du comté de Tripoli', BSFN (1967), 114f.; and also particularly M. W. Baldwin, op. cit., p. 138 and note 14.

30. Longuet, loc. cit., pp. 175-7; Yvon, loc. cit.

31. Schl. III, 31 and XX, 4.

32. Schl. V, 8.

33. Schl. VI, 12.

34. Schl. VI, 4 and 5.

35. Schl. III, 1 and 2. Also see particularly the specimen illustrated in D. M. Metcalf, loc. cit., ANSMN XX (1975), pl. XVII, 3.

36. Schl. V, 10. See also the specimens illustrated in D. H. Cox, The Tripolis hoard of French seignorial and Crusader's coins, (NNM LIX), New York 1933, pl. VIII, 1 and 2.

37. Yvon, loc. cit. at p. 115.

38. D. M. Metcalf, 'The Maǧaracik hoard of "helmet" coins of Bohémond III of Antioch', ANSMN XVI (1970), 95-109, at p. 97.

39. RRH, no. 979.

40. Unfortunately the lower right corner of the inscription containing the last letters of the date is missing. For an illustration see J. Prawer, The World of the Crusaders, 1972, opposite p. 72.

41. Schl. IV, 19 and 20. These coins are evidently based on the gros tournois of France, introduced by Louis IX in 1266.

42. For example most English groats of the fourteenth and fifteenth centuries are of much better fabric than the pence of the same period.

43. Sabine, loc. cit., NC[7] XVIII (1978).

44. Porteous, loc. cit.; Schlumberger, op. cit., pp. 43-50.

THE BARONIAL COINAGE OF THE LATIN KINGDOM OF JERUSALEM

Peter W. Edbury

The subject of the baronage of the Latin Kingdom of Jerusalem and its relationship with the crown has received considerable attention during the past half century. In 1932 the American scholar, John La Monte, published his Feudal Monarchy in the Latin Kingdom of Jerusalem which was essentially a restatement of the older view that from the outset in the early twelfth century the kings were weak constitutionally: the king was primus inter pares with his vassals; he was obliged to rule with their consent, and his rule was hedged about by an array of feudal conventions which allowed little scope for the exercise of royal authority. Since the Second World War a number of specialists in the history of the crusades, most notably Jean Richard, Claude Cahen, Joshua Prawer, Hans Eberhard Mayer and Jonathan Riley-Smith have presented us with a fresh view, or rather, a fresh series of views.[1] La Monte is shown to have mistaken thirteenth-century legal theory for twelfth-century historical reality, and, though areas of disagreement remain, a consensus has emerged which would see the twelfth-century kings of Jerusalem as powerful men who kept the upper hand in their dealings with their nobles. As time wore on the prerogatives of the dynasty were undermined: the accession in 1174 of a king who was a leper; the accession in 1185 of a king who was a young child; the disastrous defeat for the Christians at Hattin in 1187; the consequent loss of territory and prestige and the resultant recrimination; the succession to the throne of no less than four heiresses in turn so that for the period 1186-1228 the kingdom was ruled by their consorts—all had a debilitating effect on royal authority even although some of the rulers concerned were able and vigorous. From 1228-1268 the titular kings of Jerusalem were absentees—members of the German imperial house of Hohenstaufen—and for much of the remaining period until the extinction of the Latin Kingdom in 1291 the throne was disputed by the Cypriot Lusignans and the Sicilian Angevins. No wonder that legal theorists writing in the second half of the thirteenth century could present a view of the constitution which left the impression that monarchical power was severely circumscribed and that baronial rights were extensive.

This paper sets out to consider the coinage issued by the barons of the Latin Kingdom, delving into the problems of who were involved, when were the mints in operation and under what circumstances were coins produced. But first, as frequent reference is made to Schlumberger's Numismatique, still after a century of use an invaluable work of reference, a possible source of confusion needs to be dispelled. Schlumberger shared the belief that the droit de coins possessed by many of the lords in the East comprised the right to strike money. In fact, as Chandon de Briailles showed nearly forty years ago, this privilege had nothing to do with coinage and concerned the right to use a lead seal to authenticate formal documents.[2] Schlumberger's erroneous belief led him to assume that many more lords could have issued coins than in fact did so. It is now clear that the lords of only three lordships, Sidon, Beirut and Tyre, definitely issued their own coins—western-style billon or copper deniers and oboles.[3] In addition, there is an extremely rare anonymous denier of Jaffa (Fig. 1) which is at present undated and so which may or may not have been minted during one of the periods at which Jaffa was held as a fief of the crown.[4] Attention is drawn elsewhere in this volume (pp. 94-6).

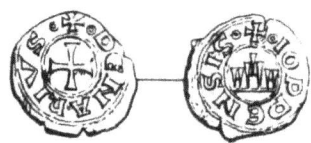

FIG. 1. Anonymous denier of Jaffa. Obv. Cross pattée. +·DENARIVS· Rev. Stylized gateway. +·IOPPENSIS·

to supposed references in Muslim sources to Jaffan and Beiruti dirhems—evidently imitative Arabic coins—but it is far from clear precisely what coins were intended by these ascriptions, and there is no way at present of knowing whether they were in reality minted by the lords of Beirut and counts of Jaffa.

To turn first to the coins issued by the lords of Sidon. We are at once confronted by a problem. In the supplement to his Numismatique de l'Orient latin, Schlumberger described a copper coin which purports to have been issued by Gerard lord of Sidon who flourished in the years 1147-65 and who died c. 1170 (Fig. 2).[5] Gerard is chiefly famous as the nobleman whose disseisin of one of his own vassals provoked the then king, Amaury, to intervene on that vassal's behalf and to promulgate the celebrated law, the Assise sur la ligece. In addition there survive self-evidently garbled reports of what appears to have been an earlier brush with the crown which may have led to Gerard being expelled from the kingdom by Amaury's predecessor, Baldwin III.[6] The difficulties surrounding the coin includes the fact that the unique example known to Schlumberger is now unlocated[7] and, although style is difficult to judge from a nineteenth-century line-drawing, Schlumberger's engraving makes the coin look more like a product of the thirteenth century than anything produced in the third quarter of the twelfth. Were it acceptable as a coin minted by Gerard, it would be of key interest as the earliest identified

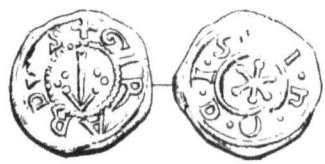

FIG. 2. Copper coin supposedly of Gerard lord of Sidon. Obv. Arrow. GIRARDVS. Rev. Chrismon. S·I·D·O·N·I·A (retrograde).

baronial issue. But unless other examples are brought to light, it must be treated with all possible reserve.[8]

With Gerard's son and successor, Raynald of Sidon (1170-c. 1204), we are on safer ground. Several deniers are known bearing his name[9] and the problem here lies in trying to establish the period at which these coins were minted (Fig. 3). Raynald first appears as lord of Sidon in a document of 1171;

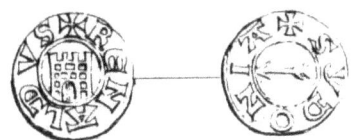

FIG. 3. Billon denier of Raynald of Sidon. Obv. Fortified tower. RENALDVS. Rev. Arrow. SYDONIA.

in 1187 Sidon, along with most of the Latin Kingdom, was captured by Saladin, and although Raynald retrieved part of his lordship by the truce agreed in 1192, it was not until 1229, long after his death, that the town of Sidon was once again fully in Christian control. Until the late 1220s it would appear that the revenues from Sidon were shared by the Muslims and the Christian lords in a condominium and that Sidon itself was in Muslim hands.[10] In the light of these developments it is more natural to assume that the minting of these coins dates from the period when Raynald had sole rule in Sidon—before 1187—and this early date may find some support in the absence of coins of Sidon from two large hoards concealed in the mid-1220s, the Tripoli and Kessab hoards, perhaps an indication that by then they had ceased to circulate.

If Raynald's coinage belongs to the period before the battle of Hattin, it needs to be considered in conjunction with the copper coins bearing the legend T·V·R·R·I·S· +·D·A·V·I·T· . It has recently been proposed that the Turris Davit coinage was issued by Raymond of Tripoli at Beirut during his custody of that lordship in the years 1184-6 while regent for Baldwin IV and Baldwin V.[11] His acquisition of the regency had meant the victory for the political faction in the Latin East which he himself led and of which Raynald was a member, and Beirut was assigned to him temporarily in order to compensate him for personal expenses incurred during his period of office. Beirut was the most northerly of the cities of the Kingdom of Jerusalem; beyond it lay Raymond's own county of Tripoli; immediately to the south stood the lordship of Sidon. Raymond and Raynald were thus political allies and near neighbours. Both employed appropriate devices on their coins: Raymond's Turris Davit coinage bore on the reverse the eight-pointed star characteristic of Tripolitan deniers; Raynald's coinage shows on the reverse the arrow, the punning device derived from the fact that the contemporary vernacular form of the name for "Sidon" had the medieval French word for "arrow" as its homonym (saiette from the Latin sagitta). Indeed, it is possible that Raynald issued his coins in the mid-1180s, influenced perhaps by the example of his political patron some twenty-odd miles up the coast.

Raynald's coinage appears to have been followed by a series of degenerate imitative forms with totally blundered legends (Fig. 4).[12] These are only identifiable as originating from Sidon by the arrow device common to them all. The arrow, however, seems to have been misunderstood: it is placed vertically instead of horizontally and has the appearance of a stylized plant with dots

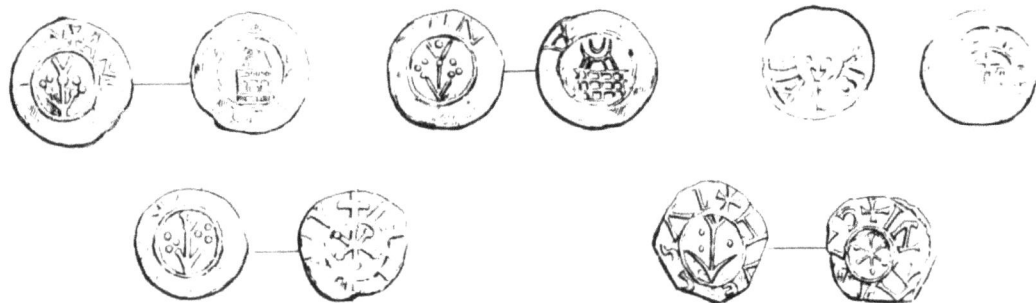

FIG. 4. Degenerate forms in billon or copper of the Sidon coinage. In no case can an intelligible reading of the legend be offered.

added to the design perhaps intended as flowers or leaves. The best specimens have the Holy Sepulchre on the other side—the design being copied from the AMALRICVS deniers (still current in the 1220s) while others have the simpler six-limbed chrismon. It is likely that they all date from the period of the condominium (1192-1229), and they could be of Arab workmanship. It may further be proposed that the GIRARDVS coin already discussed (Fig. 2) is an associated type, presumably of the same period: the form of the arrow, which shows the vertically aligned plant-like features, and the six-rayed chrismon are closely paralleled.

In striking contrast to these degenerate issues is the well-executed anonymous billon coin illustrated in Fig. 5.[13] This coin, with its French legend

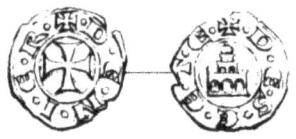

FIG. 5. Anonymous billon denier of Sidon. Obv. Cross pattée +D·E·N·I·E·R· Rev. Building with arcading and cupola. +D·E·S·E·E·T·E·

and the absence of the arrow motif, clearly signifies a new departure, and the fact that the earliest datable contexts in which it has been found are hoards apparently concealed in the 1230s[14] strongly suggests that the issue began shortly after Sidon returned to undisputed Christian control in 1229. If so, the coinage would have been first minted on the authority of Raynald's son, Balian of Sidon. Balian was a distinguished lawyer who for much of the time from 1228 until his death in 1240 acted as regent in Acre, steering a difficult course in the conflict between the Emperor Frederick II, the father of the rightful but absentee heir to the throne, and the Latin Syrian barons led by Balian's own maternal uncle, John of Ibelin lord of Beirut, who were opposed to him.[15] Writing of the events of 1251, Joinville has a story of King Louis IX of France and his knights giving deniers issued by Balian's widow, Margaret of Risnel, as an offering at the funeral of Count Walter of Brienne.[16] Unless of course the coins in question were of some unknown type specifically minted for this occasion, it is probable that Joinville was referring to coins of the type here discussed—the implication being that they were still available at that time. Whether they were still in production in 1251 is another question. The style of the surviving specimens is so uniform that the idea that their issue spanned a period of over twenty years is open to doubt.

Mention of John of Ibelin lord of Beirut leads us to the coins that he himself issued in his lordship. Beirut, lost by the Christians in 1187, was regained in 1197 and was given to John, a half-brother of Queen Isabella, at an unknown date between 1200 and 1205.[17] John thereafter held Beirut until his death in 1236; from 1205 until 1210 he was regent of Jerusalem, but he is best remembered as the leader of the Cypriot and Latin Syrian nobility who resisted the attempts by the Emperor Frederick to bring the Christian-held territories in the East under his direct control. John was a wealthy lord and Beirut seems to have enjoyed considerable commercial prosperity during his time. The famous description of his palace at Beirut by Wilbrand of Oldenburg who was a visitor in 1212 speaks of his conspicuous consumption,[18] and from the 1220s there is evidence for John developing Beirut's commercial potential by issuing privileges to encourage western merchants to come there to trade.[19] It may be surmised that it was as a direct result of this commercial activity that sufficient silver accumulated for John to mint his own deniers.

The surviving coins from Beirut are of two denominations: billon deniers bearing John's name (Fig. 6) and copper coins, some of which are anonymous while others are again in the name of John (Fig. 7). Most of the principal varieties of the deniers occurred in two hoards, the Tripoli and Kessab hoards, both of which were concealed in the mid-1220s, and this enables us to date them to the period c. 1200-c. 1225.[20]

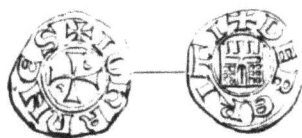

FIG. 6. Billon denier of John of Ibelin, lord of Beirut. Obv. Cross pattée; crescents in 2nd and 3rd quarters. +IOhANNES. Rev. Fortified tower. +DE BERITI.

Schlumberger suggested that the copper coinage dated from the time of John's grandson and namesake, John II, who was lord of Beirut 1247-68, but the existence of at least three examples overstruck on the Turris Davit coinage of the mid-1180s suggests that they too were minted by John I. It is true that the copper coins do not appear in either of the hoards just mentioned, but this absence would be explained simply in terms of their low value making their concealment not worth while. Probably the copper coins were issued more or less simultaneously with the billon deniers as a fractional denomination of lower intrinsic value.[21] There are three varieties of the coppers, and the sequence in which they were issued is problematic. The quality of the dies is variable, and declines in the course of the issue inscribed DE BERITO IOhE. This might be taken as a reason for placing the variety last. It is by far the most plentiful. The other two varieties are anonymous. The fortified gateway on that inscribed DE BERITENSIS is distinct, being eccentric with an entrance to one side, curved arches at the top of the central tower and single turrets on the side-works. It is scarce and could be an experimental issue standing at the head of the series. The coin with DE BARVTh resembles the more common variety in the details of its gateway and the fact that in this case the legend is in French might be an indication that this variety is late in the sequence.

FIG. 7. Copper coins of John of Ibelin, lord of Beirut. <u>Obv.</u> Fortified gateway. The legends are a) DE BERITENSIS, b) DE BARVTh or c) DE BERITO IOhE. <u>Rev.</u> Geometric, fretted design.

Schlumberger drew attention to "la ressemblance frappante" between the coins bearing John's name and the issues of Tripoli and Sidon and of the <u>Turris Davit</u> type.[22] Now that it has been proposed that the <u>Turris Davit</u> coinage originated from Beirut, the link between it and John's coinage is all the more significant. John of Ibelin would presumably have known Raymond of Tripoli's mint, and, as the existence of the overstrikes proves, the <u>Turris Davit</u> issue was still in circulation there at the time John's moneyers were at work. There were also close personal links between John of Ibelin, Raynald of Sidon and Raymond of Tripoli: John's father, Balian of Ibelin, was another of Raymond's partisans in the years before 1187 and Balian and Raynald both supported Conrad of Montferrat in the struggle to oust Guy of Lusignan from power at the time of the Third Crusade. Besides this, Raynald married John's sister, Helvis of Ibelin, a woman at least twenty years his junior.[23] The date of Raynald of Sidon's death is unknown—it occurred at some point between 1200 and 1210[24]—but it seems highly probable that he survived long enough to suggest to his brother-in-law that he might follow his own example and mint his own coins in his lordship.

The third lordship from which coins are known is Tyre. They were issued by Philip of Montfort, lord of Tyre 1246-70, and his son, John lord of Tyre and Toron 1270-83.[25] Philip of Montfort was the son of Raynald of Sidon's widow, Helvis of Ibelin, and her second husband, Guy of Montfort; he was thus the nephew of John of Ibelin, lord of Beirut. Philip is normally referred to as "Lord of Tyre", but his title to Tyre was somewhat dubious. In 1246 the regent of the Latin Kingdom of Jerusalem, King Henry I of Cyprus, entrusted Philip with custody of Tyre. Tyre was a part of the royal domain and Henry, as regent, in theory could not make permanent alienations from it. Legally Philip had only temporary control and his right to administer Tyre could last only until the regent either dismissed him or died. But despite the insecurity of his title, Philip held on to Tyre, treating it as if it were his own feudal barony. On the accession of King Hugh III of Cyprus as king of Jerusalem in 1269, the legal situation was regularized by an agreement which confirmed Philip in possession. At the same time provision was made for the marriage of Philip's son, John, to Hugh's sister. In reality, even if he had wanted to, King Hugh was too weak to take Tyre back from Philip who by then had been entrenched there for over twenty years.[26] Throughout the 1260s Philip had been at loggerheads with the Latin Syrian barons based in Acre since he supported the Genoese and they the Venetians in the wars that the two mercantile republics were fighting in the East. At one point, in 1263, he made an alliance with the Muslims against the authorities in Acre, and in 1267 he had his own truce with Baybars, the Mamlūk sultan.[27] Hugh III of Cyprus' marriage alliance with the Montforts paid off: when in 1277 his control of Acre and the other vestiges of the royal domain on the coast of Syria was allowed to slip out of his hands and pass to the officers of his rival, Charles of Anjou, John of Montfort remained loyal and allowed Hugh to use Tyre as a bridge-head for his attempt at recovery.[28]

FIG. 8. Copper coins of Philip and John of Montfort. a) Obv. Cross pattée. +PhELIP· Rev. Classical portico and pediment. DE SVR. b) Obv. Cross pattée. +IOhSTRO (recte +IOhSIRE—see Seltman op. cit. (n. 25)). Rev. Similar to a). DE SVR.

Philip and John's coins (Fig. 8) are of a similar design and it may be that they form a continuous series and were minted during a relatively short space of time around the year 1270, the date of Philip's death. The coins appear to be of copper, with little or no silver content, and so cannot have had much commercial appeal or have been of much value to the lords who issued them.

It is one thing to describe and try to date a series of coin issues, quite another to interpret their significance. The various issues span the best part of a century, and it is likely that the circumstances which prompted their appearance were far from uniform. But an adequate investigation of the coins themselves remains to be undertaken. With the exception of the Turris Davit coinage, which in any case stands apart since it appears to have been issued by the regent and not by a vassal in his lordship, no corpus of the surviving coins of any of the issues has been compiled. No analysis of provenance has been attempted, and it is not possible to assess how widely the coinage circulated. Nor have the dies and die-duplicates been counted, and until this is done the total coins minted in any one variety cannot be estimated. The metal-content of the issues similarly awaits analysis, and so no conclusions as to the intrinsic value of the coins relative to other coinages in circulation is available. (Quite likely the deniers will prove to be in the same range of fineness as the royal coins, i.e. roughly a quarter silver to three-quarters copper.) In very general terms it can be said that the baronial coins were never an important part of the economy at large. For example, in the Tripoli and Kessab hoards which were concealed in the 1220s, they accounted for less than 1% of the total in each case, and other evidence seems to point in the same direction. Nevertheless, much work is still to be done.

The historian when faced with these baronial coins is also confronted by a completely different problem. A twelfth-century law threatened vassals of the crown who minted their own coins or who fabricated imitations with the confiscation of their fiefs. Issuing coins in one's own name and the forgery of coins were just two offences in a list of twelve for which this penalty was prescribed. Others included such things as rebellion, deserting one's lord in battle and apostacy.[29] It looks as if the purpose of the law, or établissement, was to assert a royal monopoly over the minting of coins. But herein lies the difficulty. For whereas the établissement purports to have been promulagated by King Baldwin II (1118-31), recent numismatic opinion inclines to the view that the earliest royal coinage belongs to a later period, to the reign of King Baldwin III (1143-63).[30] There are three possible ways around the dilemma thus posed: first, the law was dealing with what at the time was a purely hypothetical situation; secondly, pace recent opinion, coins were being issued as early as the time of Baldwin II, and, thirdly, the law should be redated to a later period. None of these solutions is altogether satisfactory. Medieval kings did not as a rule legislate for hypothetical contingencies, and there is no definite indication from the wording of this law that this is what was happening here. But Professor Joshua Prawer has rightly drawn attention to the influence of Roman Law present in the établissement, and it may be that the two clauses concerning coinage indicate no more than an awareness of the Roman principle that the falsification of money was a crimen laese maiestatis and do not reflect contemporary circumstances.[31] Were royal mints functioning before the 1140s? After the fall of Tyre in 1124 the Christians are said to have used captured dies to strike Fatimid dinars,[32] but when royal mints properly-speaking began is another question. Precise dating of Jerusalemite coins is difficult, and although various possibilities for pre-Baldwin III issues have been mooted, none has yet been proved.[33] The simplest solution to the problem of the établissement is to redate it and ascribe it to the reign of Baldwin III. This redating has been proposed by Professor Prawer for completely different reasons. There is no need here to re-examine his arguments except to note that though he clearly prefers to date the établissement to the reign of Baldwin III, he admits to entertaining a certain measure of doubt.[34] Of course, if Baldwin III was responsible for issuing the établissement, the difficulty is neatly resolved since there is no question that a royal mint or mints were in action during his reign, and conversely, as M. Yvon has observed, the numismatic evidence supports Prawer's hypothesis.[35] Prawer may well be correct, but final and satisfactory answers to the question of the date of the établissement and the question of the date of the earliest regular coinage struck by the crown are still awaited.

If Baldwin II or Baldwin III thought it necessary to forbid vassals to mint their own coins, it is worth considering whether any had in fact been doing just that. At first sight, unless against our better judgement we accept that Baldwin III's contemporary, Gerard of Sidon, was responsible for the coin which bears his name, vassals only began to mint their coins some twenty years after Baldwin III's death. But two further possibilities remain open.

It could be that at some period during the reign of one of the two Baldwins, vassals had issued their own Saracen Bezants. Such issues might have been far more significant economically than the scarce copper and billon coins we know were issued later and so would have posed more of a threat to the royal currency and the royal control of commerce: hence the severe penalty of confiscation. It may well be that the imitative Arab coinage struck by the kings of Jerusalem was designed in the first instance as a trade-currency for use in commercial dealings with the neighbouring Muslim powers. In this connection it could be significant that the établissement links the prohibition on the minting of one's own coins with a prohibition on the development of the trading potential of one's lordship by building up port facilities and improving roads into the Muslim lands.[36] That minting coins and developing commerce with Muslims are associated here could indicate that the king regarded the minting of coins as one aspect of a threat to his control of commerce, in which case the likelihood that it was imitative Arabic coins that had been issued by the nobles is enhanced. But speculation along these lines is almost certainly doomed to remain unresolved even if a gold hoard of early date were to turn up: if barons did issue imitations of Muslim coins, it would be exceedingly difficult to identify them as such.

A second possibility concerns the county of Tripoli. At the time the town of Tripoli was captured from the Muslims in 1109, Count Bertrand did homage to King Baldwin I. In 1122, however, his son and successor, Pons; refused Baldwin II homage and declined to perform services. Baldwin II led a military demonstration to the county and mediators arranged what William of Tyre called "a suitable peace". But William gives no direct indication that Pons did homage on that occasion and he makes no further reference to counts of Tripoli doing homage to kings of Jerusalem. In 1132 Pons again came into conflict with a king of Jerusalem, this time Baldwin II's successor, Fulk of Anjou.[37] It is noticeable that after the 1120s there are far fewer instances recorded by William of Tyre of counts of Tripoli assisting the kings on their campaigns, while on the other hand there are a number of places in William's narrative from the 1130s onwards which make it plain that Tripoli was regarded as being independent of Jerusalem.[38] It is clear that in the 1120s and '30s Count Pons was making a successful bid to throw off the royal suzerainty which stretched back to 1109, and that Baldwin II and Fulk were fighting a losing battle to prevent him. There exists a unique anonymous coin from Tripoli which is tentatively attributed to Pons.[39] Assuming that this attribution is correct, it might be possible to construct the hypothesis that Baldwin II (if it was Baldwin II) included the clause forbidding vassals to issue coins in the établissement as part of an attempt on his side to counter Pons' assertions of independence. Further clauses in the établissement could relate to other aspects of Pons' resistance to Baldwin's authority, in which case it would seem reasonable to connect the promulgation of this document with the events of 1122.

After this inconclusive and speculative discussion of the circumstances and purpose of the établissement, we come now to consider its bearing on the baronial coin issues described above. A number of distinguished scholars have drawn the conclusion that Raynald of Sidon and the other lords who minted coins were usurping the royal prerogative and flouting the law as laid down by Baldwin II or Baldwin III.[40] Certainly there is other evidence that Raynald, John of Ibelin lord of Beirut and Philip and John of Montfort were all self-assertive men who took steps to safeguard their interests, and the fact that they issued their own coins is seen as a part of a wider pattern of independently-minded behaviour. The very existence of baronial coins is therefore viewed as a pointer to the rise of aristocratic autonomy and the decay of royal power. Such an interpretation has much to recommend it, but is not without difficulties.

Simply to say that baronial power was growing and royal power declining is not in itself an adequate explanation of why barons should have chosen to issue small denomination coins of billon or copper. Prawer would see the striking of these coins as a political rather than as an economic act: it was, to use his own words, "a declaration of independence by the baron and his lordship".[41] But if the coins were primarily issued as a form of propaganda, proclaiming the power of the baron concerned, it may be wondered why some of these issues were anonymous, giving only the provenance of the mint and not the name of the man on whose authority they were minted and put into circulation. On the other hand, Prawer is probably correct in saying that the coins can have brought the lords comparatively little financial reward, since they have a low face-value and their scarcity suggests that relatively few can have been minted. But if it is admitted that the coins themselves do not always have the appearance of being propagandist issues and that they may have been of little economic value to their lord, the question of why the lords should have bothered to strike them at all arises.

In the middle ages any owner of a mint would expect to make a profit out of striking coins, and the Jerusalemite barons would have been no exception, even if it is assumed that the actual return would have been modest. But it could well be that over and above the profitability of minting coins there was a further economic incentive—that the lords struck coins to make good a shortage of small change in their lordships. As in present-day Italy, there may have been simply not enough loose change in the market-traders' tills. The Tripoli and Kessab hoards both contained large numbers of small coins from western Europe and the incidence of stray finds seems to confirm the impression that in the thirteenth century western coins circulated, supplementing the royal issues.[42] Whatever the official view may have been of barons minting coins, in the early thirteenth century the royal authorities certainly allowed non-royal coins to pass from hand to hand. The conclusion here must be that the royal mints were unequal to the demand, and so it is proposed that some of the baronial issues signify efforts to alleviate the shortage, thereby protecting the normal exchange of goods and services within the respective lordships. Of course, this explanation will not serve for every instance: for example, John of Beirut's overstrikes must obviously have been issued for reasons other than increasing the volume of coin in circulation.

The accepted interpretation, that baronial coins signify a usurpation of the royal monopoly, and the hypothesis that baronial coins were minted as a means of making a profit for the lords concerned with the possible added incentive of alleviating a shortage of small change are not in themselves mutually exclusive. But the baronial issues may not have been a usurpation at all. The barons, or some of them, may have acted with the express permission of the king. Prawer is of the opinion that, as there is no evidence for the king abolishing his monopoly, the barons must have usurped it, but lack of evidence is not conclusive on its own, especially as formal privileges from the Latin East granting rights of any sort to lay vassals are extremely rare. A more radical approach, and one which seems to tilt the balance of probability more firmly against the usurpation theory is that by the early thirteenth century the établissement of King Baldwin and with it the assertion of the royal monopoly of mints may have been only dimly remembered by king and barons alike. Its text survives in the legal treatise known as the "Livre au roi" of c. 1200, but various features of it accord ill with other aspects of the treatise and Riley-Smith has tentatively suggested that its inclusion there represents a piece of legal antiquarianism brought in to answer the circumstances of a particular political crisis. As he puts it, "it was an archaic, half-forgotten piece of legislation...".[43]

What then does all this have to tell us about the nobility and its changing relations with the crown? After 1174 baronial power waxed and monarchical power waned. This much is incontrovertable. But there has been a tendency to assume that baronial power was advanced by conflict and confrontation. To take the case in point: the assumption has been that the barons "usurped" the royal monopoly, flaunting their coinage in the face of an enfeebled monarchy in an assertion of newly won power. Maybe. But there is something unreal about this picture. We are all too easily trapped into a habit of mind which imagines that there was a sort of baronial instinct which demanded that the barons "do down" the king. But why "do down" one's lord, one's military commander, the fount of patronage, the guarantor of noble privilege? After all, more often than not baronial and royal interests coincided. One view could be that normally the barons were not out to curtail royal power so much as to fill the vacuum when for other reasons royal power failed. Clearly this is a much larger subject than a paper on baronial coin issues can encompass, but the hypothesis that baronial coins represented little more than an attempt to alleviate a shortage of small change which the royal mints were incapable of remedying might be one step in the argument towards such an interpretation.[44]

NOTES

1. For bibliography, see J. Prawer, Histoire du royaume latin de Jérusalem, 1969/70, i, 51ff; J. S. C. Riley-Smith, The Feudal Nobility and the Kingdom of Jerusalem, 1174-1277, 1973, p. 232 n. 4.

2. F. Chandon de Briailles, 'Le droit de "coins" dans le royaume de Jérusalem', Syria XXIII (1942/3), 244-57. See now H. E. Mayer, Das Siegelwesen in den Kreuzfahrerstaaten (Bayerische Akad. der Wissenschaften: Philosophisch- Historische Klasse Abhandlungen. Neue Folge 83 (1978)).

3. J. Yvon, 'Les monnaies "féodales" du royaume latin de Jérusalem', BSFN XXV (1970), 550-2.

4. Schl., p. 110 and plate IV, 29.

5. Schl. supplement, p. 7 and plate XX, 6. For Gerard's career see J. L. La Monte, 'The lords of Sidon in the twelfth and thirteenth centuries', Byzantion XVII (1944/5), 183-211, at pp. 190-3, 199.

6. La Monte, 'Lords of Sidon', pp. 192-3; J. Richard, 'Pairie d'Orient latin: les quatre baronnies des royaumes de Jérusalem et de Chypre', RHDFE^4 XXVIII (1950), 67-88 at p. 76.

7. Yvon, 'Les monnaies "féodales"', p. 551.

8. In the discussion at the symposium following this paper, Mr. Porteous drew attention to a somewhat similar coin, albeit with a French legend instead of a Latin one, in the Bibliothèque Nationale in Paris. At first sight this coin would also appear to show Gerard's name, but, as Mr. Sabine then suggested, this might be a faulty rendering of SIRE DE (Seete).

9. Schl., p. 114 and plate V, 3; supplement p. 7.

10. La Monte, 'Lords of Sidon', pp. 193-200; Prawer, Histoire du royaume latin, ii, 179-80, 199.

11. C. Sabine, 'The Turris Davit coinage and the regency of Raymond III of Tripoli (1184-6)', NC^7 XVIII (1978), 85-92.

12. Schl., pp. 114-15 and plate V, 4-7; supplement p. 7 and plate XX, 5; A. J. Seltman, 'Some Crusader Coins', NCirc LXXIV (1966), 61-3 at p. 62.

13. Schl., p. 115 and plate V, 8.

14. D. M. Metcalf, 'Some hoards and stray finds from the Latin East', ANSMN XX (1975), 139-52 at p. 143 n. 16.

15. For his career, see La Monte, 'Lords of Sidon', pp. 200-5; Riley-Smith, Feudal Nobility, pp. 123, 137-40, 160, 166-86 passim, 199-207 passim.

16. Jean de Joinville, Histoire de Saint Louis, ed. and trans. into modern French by N. de Wailly, 1874, p. 466.

17. J. L. La Monte, 'Jean d'Ibelin: the Old Lord of Beirut, 1177-1236', Byzantion XII (1937), 417-48 at p. 424.

18. The passage is quoted in an English translation by J. Prawer, The Latin Kingdom of Jerusalem: European Colonialism in the Middle Ages, 1972, pp. 451-2.

19. Riley-Smith, Feudal Nobility, pp. 66, 76-8.

20. D. H. Cox, The Tripolis Hoard of French Seigneurial and Crusader's Coins, NNM LIX (1933), 1-61 at pp. 53-4; H. Longuet, 'La trouvaille de Kessab en Orient latin', RN^4 XXXVIII (1935), 163-83 at p. 175; J. Yvon, 'Monnaies et sceaux de l'Orient latin', RN^6 VIII (1966), 89-107 at pp. 97-9.

21. Schl. pp. 118-19 and plate V, 11, 12; supplement, p. 8 and plate XX, 8, 9, 11; Sabine, loc. cit., pp. 89-90, 92. The coin illustrated by Schlumberger and thought by him to be from Toron (pp. 124-5 and plate V, 13) has now been re-attributed to Beirut. Seltman, op. cit., p. 63.

22. Schl. p. 118.

23. Whereas Raynald was apparently of full age by 1171 (La Monte, 'Lords of Sidon', p. 194), his wife's parents did not marry until about 1176 (La Monte, 'John d'Ibelin', p. 419).

24. La Monte, 'Lords of Sidon', pp. 199, 200. It is usually said that Raynald had died before 1204 when his widow married Guy of Montfort. The chronicler mentions the marriage in the course of his description of the events of that year, but it is not altogether clear whether it took place then or later. Guy was again in the East in 1210-11 and it was in 1210 that Raynald's son Balian first appears as lord of Sidon. RRH no. 853; 'L'estoire de Eracles empereur et la conqueste de la Terre d'Outremer', RHC Occ., ii, 263, 311.

25. Schl., pp. 128-9 and plate V, 14-15. Seltman, loc. cit., pp. 61-2. John of Montfort inherited a claim to the lordship of Toron, lost to the Muslims in 1266, through his mother. Seltman (loc. cit. and above n. 21) has corrected Schlumberger's belief that coins were issued at Toron.

26. Riley-Smith, Feudal Nobility, pp. 215, 224-5; H. E. Mayer, 'Ibelin versus Ibelin: the struggle for the regency of Jerusalem 1253-1258', Proceedings of the American Philosophical Society CXXII (1978), 25-57 at p. 29; J. Richard, The Latin Kingdom of Jerusalem, trans. J. Shirley (Amsterdam, 1979), p. 408.

27. Riley-Smith, Feudal Nobility, pp. 27-8; Richard, Latin Kingdom, pp. 366-70, 395.

28. Riley-Smith, Feudal Nobility, p. 227; Richard, Latin Kingdom, p. 417.

29. 'Le Livre au Roi', RHC Lois, i, 616-17. Note however that the reference to the forgery of the 'coins' of the kings or barons of the realm in the 'Livre des assises de la cour des bourgeois' (RHC Lois, ii, 220) relates to seals and not coinage.

30. The belief that the regular royal silver coinage began in the middle years of the twelfth century depends on the attribution of the Baldvinvs coinage, now generally thought to have begun with Baldwin III. See J. Duplessy and D. M. Metcalf, 'Le trésor de Samos et la circulation monétaire en Orient Latin au XIIe et XIIIe siècles', RBN CVIII (1962), 173-207, esp. pp. 178-9; Yvon, 'Monnaies et sceaux', pp. 92-7; D. M. Metcalf, 'Coinage of the Latin Kingdom of Jerusalem in the name of Baudouin', NC[7] XVIII (1978), 71-84.

31. J. Prawer, 'Etude sur le droit des Assises de Jérusalem: droit de confiscation et droit d'exhérédation', RHDFÉ[4] XXXIX (1961), 520-51 continued in XL (1962), 29-42 at p. 527.

32. P. Balog and J. Yvon, 'Monnaies à légendes arabes de l'Orient latin', RN[6] I (1958), 133-68 at pp. 141-2.

33. Three possibilities are known to the present author and there are doubtless others. (i) Dr. Metcalf kindly informs me that he has isolated a group of gold bezants some of which could belong to the period before Baldwin III's accession. (ii) The Baldvinvs coinage could go back to one of the first Baldwins. This possibility is not ruled out by Yvon ('Monnaies et sceaux', pp. 96-7). (iii) It is possible that the rare anonymous denier discussed by A. Spaer ('Two rare crusader coins of the Latin Kingdom of Jerusalem', NC[7] XVII (1977), 184-6 at pp. 184-5) is early.

34. Prawer, 'Étude' (1962), pp. 38-42; idem, Latin Kingdom of Jerusalem, p. 137. Cf. his Histoire du royaume latin, i, 470 and n. 7 where he is more confident in his ascription to Baldwin III.

35. Yvon, 'Les monnaies "féodales"', p. 551 n. 1.

36. 'Livre au roi', p. 617.

37. William of Tyre, 'Historia rerum in partibus transmarinis gestarum', RHC Occ., i, 466, 469, 536, 611-13. Cf. Fulcher of Chartres, 'Historia Hierosolymitana', RHC Occ., iii, 420, 447. See J. Richard, Le comté de Tripoli sous la dynastie toulousaine (1102-1187), 1945, pp. 30-2.

38. For counts of Tripoli assisting the kings before 1130, see William of Tyre, pp. 474, 481, 485, 519, 523, 565, 579, 596. For assistance after 1130, see pp. 672, 784, 845, 1013, 1115. For Tripoli as an independant entity, see pp. 626, 754-5, 1006, 1065-6, 1077-8, 1122. See further Richard, Comté, pp. 32-8.

39. See above p. 45.

40. Prawer, Latin Kingdom of Jerusalem, pp. 137, 384, 391; Riley-Smith, Feudal Nobility, p. 27; Richard, Latin Kingdom, pp. 89, 332.

41. Prawer, Latin Kingdom of Jerusalem, p. 137; see also p. 384.

42. Cox, op. cit.; Longuet, op. cit.; Metcalf, 'Some hoards and stray finds', pp. 141-9.

43. Riley-Smith, Feudal Nobility, p. 156.

44. I should like to thank all those who attended the symposium and were kind enough to comment on this paper; the final form owes much to their suggestions. A special word of thanks to Michael Metcalf whose vigilance has prevented countless howlers.

THE SUPPLY OF MONEY AND THE DIRECTION OF TRADE IN THIRTEENTH-CENTURY SYRIA

R. Irwin

During the twelfth century and the early decades of the thirteenth the ports held by the crusaders on the Syrian and Palestinian coastline flourished commercially.[1] To a considerable extent their prosperity was based on their role as outlets for merchandise coming from the great cities of the Syrian hinterland (Damascus, Aleppo, Hama and Homs). Caravans from Damascus and Aleppo brought not only Syrian produce to the crusader littoral but also merchandise, much of it luxury goods, from Iraq, Anatolia, Iran and the Indies. Muslim merchants brought their goods to such ports as Acre, Tyre, Tripoli, Lattakia, Beirut and Jaffa. Italian and other western merchants purchased these goods and took them across the Mediterranean to sell in Europe.

In the period c. 1240-90, however, the degree to which these Frankish coastal cities depended for their prosperity on their role as ports of transit for merchandise coming from or via the Muslim cities of the hinterland was relatively slight. Nevertheless the ports remained prosperous and the interest in them of the merchant communities of Venice, Genoa and Pisa and of their southern French and Spanish competitors does not seem to have diminished until the very end.

The change in the relationship between coast and hinterland and the possible reasons for the continuing economic vitality of the coastal ports must now be examined.

Almost certainly the most important factor behind the shifting of Near Eastern trade routes and therefore in the commercial activities of the Latins in the Levant was the westward advance of the Mongol armies. The indirect effects of Mongol movements were felt in Syria long before the actual arrival of the Mongol armies before the walls of Aleppo in 1259. In the 1230s and 40s Mongol campaigns in central Asia and Anatolia led to the displacement of tribes and bands of Khwarizmian Turks, Turkomans and Kurds. Large contingents of these peoples, fleeing westwards and southwards before the Mongols, started to arrive in Syria, and as early as 1240 a Khwarizmian army threatened Aleppo.[2] In Syria such bands found employment in the cavalry of the Ayyubid princes or made a living from nomadic pastoralism or brigandage. In many cases all three activities were doubtless combined.

The disruption that the arrival of these nomadic warbands brought to settled life and commerce is well attested in the sources. Though the power of the Khwarizmians was broken at the battle of Gaza (1244), the massive influx of Turkomans into northern Syria in the late 1240s was to have more important long-term implications.[3] Latin sources record the damage done by Turkoman devastations of the northern principalities in 1247, 1250, 1252 and 1255.[4] The Turkomans moved into Palestine too, for Frankish raiding parties encountered them and large herds of cattle in the area of Beysan in 1249 and in the area of Tiberias in 1260.[5] Looking back on the reign of al-Nāṣir Yūsuf (the Ayyubid ruler of Damascus, Aleppo, Ba'labakk and much of Palestine until the Mongol invasion of 1259), Abu' l-Fidā observed that in his reign 'the roads became unsafe because of brigandage and it was impossible to travel from Damascus to Hama or elsewhere without a military escort and the mischief of the Arabs and Turkomans increased.'[6] Shahrazuri Kurds also moved into Palestine in the 1250s and eventually settled with their herds in the Gaza region.[7] The influx of Kurdish and Turkoman nomads into Palestine seems to heve encouraged a resurgence of Arab nomadism in the same area. Al-Nāṣir Yūsuf seems to have been utterly incapable of imposing the rule of law on the Bedouin. There were recurrent tensions between the Bedouin and the subsequent Mamlūk regime—tensions which exploded in a Bedouin revolt in 680/1281 and the sacking of Gaza and Nablus.[8] The Franks for their part were forced to abandon the agricultural colonies they had established on the plains of Galilee in the 1250s, and their subsequent raids into the Muslim hinterland were little more than cattle-stealing expeditions. Generally it seems likely that in the late thirteenth-century hinterland of Palestine and Syria there was a shift away from settled agriculture in favour of pastoralism (though this process is difficult to trace due to the urban bias of the sources of the period).

Most of the Syrian towns were occupied and sacked during the Mongol invasions of 1259-61. Thereafter Damascus seems to have made a full recovery—its prosperity being based to a considerable extent on the profits to be made from being the political capital and military centre of the Mamlūks in Syria and from its central role in the internal trade of Muslim Syria.[9] Other towns, however, did not recover. In Palestine, for example, a Jewish letter of 1267 described the town of Jerusalem as being grossly underpopulated as a result of the Mongol invasions.[10]

More importantly, in northern Syria Aleppo, which had experienced its heyday as a centre for international commerce in the early thirteenth century, was not able to imitate the resilience of Damascus. In the early thirteenth century the Venetians had negotiated a series of treaties with Aleppo's Ayyubid rulers which allowed the Venetians commercial concessions and a funduq in Aleppo. The last such agreement was negotiated with al-Nāṣir Yūsuf in 1254.[11] Thereafter there are no signs of any Western commercial presence in the city at all until the fourteenth century. Unlike Damascus, Aleppo was occupied by the Mongols twice in the period 1259-61 and again in 1280. Unlike Damascus, its walls and fortifications were not restored until the 1290s and, as Lapidus has put it, 'Aleppo remained without the stimulus of investment, construction or trade and production which eased the hardships of the age for Damascus'.[12] Ibn Shaddād's topography provides a wealth of evidence on depopulation, abandoned towns and pastoralist settlement in northern Syria in the 1260s and 70s.[13]

Of course the damage from the Mongol occupations could have been repaired. The real damage done by the Mongol appearance in the Near East stemmed from the nomadic influx referred to above and from two further factors; firstly the displacement of populations of towns under threat from the Mongols and secondly the closing of the frontiers between Syria and Iraq to peaceful commerce. The economic importance of refugees in this period should not be underestimated. People fled from the towns of Syria to Egypt or the Crusader principalities, and from the countryside to the towns. In many cases the displacements of population thus effected were permanent.[14]

In the first half of the thirteenth century much of the merchandise which Aleppo sent on to the West had presumably come overland to Aleppo from Mosul. Mosul was sacked by the Mongols in 660/1261. Even before then it must have experienced some disruption of its long-distance commerce.[15] Though it recovered subsequently (as Marco Polo's narrative indicates)[16] its recovery may have been hampered by the emigration of large numbers of Mosulīs into Syria and Egypt. Mosulī artificers were indeed to make a major contribution to Mamlūk arts and industry.[17]

Here we may parenthetially observe that the merchant 'Musauci Mosulini' referred to in a Latin commercial document of 1268 as resident in Acre may have resided there, not as the representative of some Mosulī based trading enterprise, but as a refugee who had restarted his business in the kingdom of Jerusalem. A similar observation applies to the Confraternity of Mosserins known to have existed in Acre in the late thirteenth century. Jean Richard believed that the membership of this confraternity would have been drawn from representatives of Mosulī commerce at their Acre branch. A subsequent study by Jonathan Riley-Smith has convincingly argued that the confraternities, including the Confraternity of Mosserins, should be seen as (evidently Christian) lay crusading brotherhoods affiliated to the great Military Orders. Now a fighting brotherhood recruited from Nestorian merchants from Mosul temporarily resident in Acre is an improbable beast. It is surely more likely that the brotherhood was formed by Christians permanently in exile from their homeland in Iraq. We have no evidence as to whether these 'Mosserins' engaged in trade or were artisans.[18]

Certainly other Arab Christians took refuge in the Crusader principalities, at least temporarily, during the Mongol invasion of Syria. Al-Makīn ibn al-'Amīd, a Christian employed in al-Nāṣir Yūsuf's chancery until 658/1260, then fled to Tyre. He stayed there five months and reported that many Christians from Damascus had done the same.[19] (As we shall see subsequently this phenomenon may have some bearing on the monetary crisis in Damascus later in the same year.) In the same year the Mongols levied a tax of a dinar per head on those inside Antioch. The tax is reported to have produced a hundred thousand dinars. As an estimate of the normal population of Antioch the figure of a hundred thousand would be preposterous, but as an estimate for a city temporarily swollen by refugees there is nothing implausible about it.[20]

A general effect of the flight of people from the countryside to the cities was to force food prices up in the short run and, in the long run, to make it likely that the harvest in the following year would be a very poor one.

There is no need here to linger over the other result of the Mongol invasion—the closing of the frontier to commerce between Syria and Iraq from the 1260s onwards. In 681/1282-3 the Mongol Ilkhan Aḥmad made proposals and indeed claimed to have taken a one-sided initiative in opening the frontier to trade, but his proposals were regarded with suspicion by the Mamlūk Sultan Qalāwūn. Aḥmad was murdered in 1284 and nothing came of this initiative. It is not until the very end of the thirteenth century that we have convincing evidence for a direct overland route for trade from the Ilkhanate into the Mamlūk Empire in the careers of merchants like al-Sawāmilī and in the diplomacy of the Ilkhan Ghazan.[21]

In the north west the Christian kingdom of Cilician Armenia entered into an alliance with the Mongols while much of Anatolia came under Mongol protection or occupation. Now the so-called 'alum of Aleppo' was actually mined Anatolia and in the early thirteenth century marketed through Aleppo.[22] In the late thirteenth century the 'alum of Aleppo' is in fact more likely to have reached Europe through the ports of Cilician Armenia.

The Mongol invasions had the effect of isolating Syria from its northern and eastern neighbours—at least as far as an overland trade was concerned.

Some commerce must have come into Syria overland from Egypt though there is disturbingly little evidence for it. As Ayalon has noted, the Mamlūk barīd (postal) route was not suitable for merchants[23] and though khans were built in Palestine in this period they were expressly intended for the use of Muslim pilgrims proceeding to Jerusalem or Hebron.[24] Though we hear of Franks plundering livestock we do not hear of them plundering caravans. A caravan proceeding from Egypt to Damascus would be obliged either to follow a coastal route through southern Palestine, through an area either dominated by or actually occupied by the Franks, or to travel east of the Dead Sea through the Transjordan. Certainly, as far as goods destined for Western markets were concerned, it would have been much cheaper to send these to Alexandria or Damietta on the Nile Delta. Egypt and Syria did not form one commercial market: their divergent monetary histories alone would suggest that.

It is difficult even to guess whether the bulk of Italian commerce in the thirteenth-century Levant was with Syria or with Egypt. Certainly Genoa's commercial interest in Egypt in the early thirteenth century and up to c. 1260 seems to have been relatively slight.[25] But undue reliance on the large number of Genoese notarial acts from the early 1250s that have survived and been published may produce a misleading impression here. The Genoese were heavily involved in Louis IX's crusade to Egypt from its earliest stages. After the Egyptian débâcle, Louis IX and his followers spent the years 1250-4 in Palestine. For Genoese merchants to have resumed trading with Egypt then would have been not only tactless but also bad business. There were profits to be made from providing supplies and financial services to the French king and his army in Palestine; Louis IX was to spend over a million pounds there.[26] Moreover the political situation in Egypt at that time was exceptionally disturbed and in 650/1253 the port of Alexandria was handed over as an iqṭāʿ (that is, very loosely speaking, a fief) to the disorderly mamlūk emir, Fāris al-Dīn Aqṭāy al-Jamdār.[27]

Some years later Genoa must have resumed trading with the Mamlūks. There were Genoese embassies to the Mamlūk Sultans in 1263, 1275 and 1285.[28] Egypt features frequently as the destination of merchants in the Genoese notarial acts witnessed in Ayas in the 1270s.[29] In 1289 the Sultan Qalāwūn seized Genoese merchants and property in Alexandria. In 1290 a new commercial agreement was drawn up to regulate affairs between Mamlūk Egypt and Genoa.[30] Venice and Pisa both traded with Egypt in the early thirteenth century. There were commercial agreements between Venice and Egypt in 1238 and 1254 and between Pisa and Egypt in 1208 and 1215-16.[31]

The Italians were not restricted to the ports of the Nile Delta, but, as emerges from the clauses of some of these agreements, could travel freely down to Cairo.[32] Though, as has already been mentioned, there was a Venetian commercial colony in Aleppo in the first half of the thirteenth century, there is little other evidence that western merchants journeyed into the hinterland of Muslim Syria. In 638/1240-1 Sāliḥ Ismā'īl allowed Franks to come to Damascus to purchase arms,[33] and in 1288 Qalāwūn guaranteed the security of Venetian merchants in Syria.[34] Although there was obviously a great deal of commerce between the Christian coastline and the Muslim hinterland in Syria, its nature is difficult to determine from Italian commercial treaties and notarial documents. Western archives are rich in documentation on trade with the Levant, but it is often difficult to be sure of the ultimate destination of goods listed in contracts as due to be despatched to the Levant— whether 'Oltramare' will refer only to the Crusader ports on the Syrian coast or to ports in Cyprus, Cilician Armenia and Egypt as well, and whether, when Acre is marked as the ship's ultimate destination, the goods to be sold there were for the consumption of the settlers on the coast or for further export to the interior. Even when Acre or Tripoli or Beirut is given as the ship's destination, it is unlikely that it was the ship's only important port of call and this makes it very difficult for us to follow the potentially complex exchange of goods that may have taken place between Genoa, Acre and Alexandria. The Pisan and Venetian merchants (whom we know of from a petition to al-'Ādil in 1207) and who, sailing from Beirut, stopped off at Cyprus before proceeding to Alexandria with a cargo mostly of fish, were not in my opinion exceptional.[35]

In what follows, therefore, I have decided to rely mainly on information from local sources, much of it in Arabic. It is likely that much of the commerce of the Levant in the thirteenth century, as in earlier and later periods, was not in luxury goods, but in such basic staples as grain. It is unfortunate therefore that one tends to find evidence about the grain trade and its direction only in years of famine and crisis. In 1244, 1279 and 1282 the Hospitallers wrote to the West appealing for grain to supplement their supplies in a time of famine.[36] In 1244 and 1282 the famines must have been caused or exacerbated by the devastations of the Khwarizmians and the Mongols respectively. Joseph de Cauncy's letter of 1282 implies that until the War of the Sicilian Vespers, the Franks in Syria had been importing grain from Angevin Sicily.[37]

Clearly it is possible that not all the grain purchased in Sicily was consumed by the Franks of the coastal principalities and that some of it was sold in the Syrian interior. Evidence from the late 1250s and early 60s certainly shows the interior as dependent upon grain grown in Egypt and imported into Syria through the Palestinian ports and upon grain grown by the Franks themselves in Palestine. Thus in 659/1261 Baybars and his emirs were bringing grain by boat from Damietta to Jaffa. Another consignment of grain was unloaded at Gaza and then presumably brought overland up the coastal plain. While Baybars was in Palestine that year he negotiated a series of treaties with Jaffa, Acre and Beirut. According to the chronicler Ibn al-Furāt the reason the sultan allowed the Franks a breathing space 'was that prices were high and the bulk of their [i.e. the Muslims'] imports were coming from the Frankish lands'. As a result of these treaties, 'The roads then became safe and there was an increase in imports (jalāb).'

Some of the best crop-growing land lay on the coastal plain between Ascalon and Caesarea. It was for this reason that in 662/1264 the Mamlūk governor of Palestine sought and got permission from the sultan to suspend hostilities with the Franks so that they could harvest their crops, thus averting the danger of famine in the hinterland.[38] It must be emphasised however that we only have references to large-scale imports of grain and such a heavy dependence of the interior upon the coast in years of crisis, and obviously, in the long run, the role of the Palestinian ports as importers of grain did not protect them from the destructive ambitions of the Mamlūk sultans.

Even in normal years the Crusader principalities derived some of their prosperity from their position as middlemen in the sea-borne commerce between Egypt and Muslim Syria, handling such commodities as soap, cotton, fruit, sesame oil and salt fish.[39]

The fullest and clearest documentation on the nature of the trade conducted across the Christian-Muslim frontiers and on the economic activities of the Crusader principalities in the late thirteenth century is to be found in a series of truces negotiated between the Mamlūk sultans and Frankish princelings. We have the whole or part of the Arabic texts of truces concluded between Baybars and Hospitallers of Crac des Chevaliers and Margat in 665/1267[40] and between Baybars and the lady of Beirut in 667/1269,[41] between Baybars and the Hospitallers of Margat in 669/1271,[42] between Qalāwūn and Bohemond VI of Tripoli in 680/1281,[43] between Qalāwūn and Acre in 682/1283[44] and between Qalāwūn and the lady of Tyre in 683/1285.[45] In addition where the truce documents themselves are missing we often have quite detailed accounts of the negotiations preserved in the Arabic chronicles of those years, for instance for truce negotiations with Tyre in 665/1267 and with Tortosa and Tripoli in 669/1271.[46] Though the main preoccupations of the truce documents were political and military, most of the agreements include economic and commercial clauses.

In the 665/1267 agreement with the Hospitallers of Crac and Margat it emerges that the Hospitallers had been collecting a range of revenues and exercising a variety of rights over those Muslim towns, technically part of the principality of Homs, which lay west of the River Orontes—among them Barīn, Masyāf, Abū Qubays, and 'Aynab. Some of these rights and revenues were now to be split half-and-half with the Sultan Baybars. From the number and detailed nature of the clauses dealing with the subject, it would appear that the main sources of revenue being thus partitioned were taxes and tolls on herds and flocks owned by Arabs, Kurds and Turks which were either permanently pastured on the west bank or else came into the partitioned area from across the Orontes. Less space is devoted to the peasantry, the concerns here being the respective jurisdictions of Christian and Muslim law, the exemption of the peasantry from forced labour and the apprehension of criminal or tax-defaulting peasants. Merchants and travellers are covered in one perfunctory clause. They are to be safe in the sultan's territory and in the Hospitallers' and in the partitioned area and they are to be free to take whatever road they choose. Other sources of Hospitaller revenue mentioned in the agreement came from rights over fishing, hunting, and the gathering of nenuphar (water lilies) on the banks of the Orontes. These revenues were now to be partitioned with the Sultan. Until 1267 the Hospitallers had also collected a levy on straw. According to the new agreement they renounced this tax in return for 50 Ṣūrī dinars annual compensation. Since blood prices for murder were covered in the agreement, the profits of justice may be considered a further source of Hospitaller revenue. Finally and most importantly the Hospitallers had been levying tributes in money and in kind on Hama (400 dinars), Abū Qubays (800 dinars), and the Ismāʿīlī territories of Masyāf and Ruṣafa (1,200 Tripolitan dinars and 50,000 mudd of wheat and barley). These tributes the Hospitallers now relinquished.

In 666/1268 Crac des Chevaliers surrendered to the army of the sultan. The next agreement negotiated by the Hospitallers of Margat with Baybars in 669/1271 was much less favourable to the Hospitallers. In this agreement the Hospitallers were obliged to share on a half-and-half basis all harbour and shipping taxes coming from places situated on the coast from al-Qanṭāra the north to Balda in the south. In addition there was to be an equal division of taxes on imports, exports and merchandise in general. These taxes were to be entered in two separate sets of accounts and there was to be no change in the taxes. A further clause stated that goods going to the castle of Margat and its suburb are to be taxed, except for corn, provisions, clothes and horses destined for the personal use of the Hospitallers and their servants. Other clauses specify that the taxes are to be collected jointly by the deputies of the sultan and the Hospitallers, that the Hospitallers are not to supply the Ismāʿīlī castles, that merchants coming through the territory of Margat were to be provided with military protection free of charge by the party concerned, and that when merchants from the Sultan's lands travelled into the region, of Margat and its dependant ports escorts and the patrol of the roads were to be the responsibility of both parties. There was also a naufragium clause in the agreement covering the security of lives and property in cases of shipwreck.

In Baybars' agreement with Beirut concluded in 665/1267 we find none of the interest in pastoralists and pasturage we found in the first of the Hospitaller treaties. Among the clauses that are of economic interest are: the stipulation that Baybars' subjects and their property should be safe from harm by the lady's subjects and her servants and ships; reciprocally, her subjects and servants should be safe from harm in the sultan's lands (Lattakia and Jabala are singled out for special mention here) from the sultan's subjects and his ships; there is to be no alterantion in the customary taxes by either.

side; if a Frankish merchant enters the sultan's territory from Beirut he is protected by the treaty, but if he then goes on elsewhere (presumably this refers to re-entering Christian territory at Acre, Tyre or other Crusader cities) he is no longer protected by the treaty.

Only a part of the text of the truce concluded between Qalāwūn and Bohemond VI of Tripoli seems to have been preserved in Ibn al-Furāt's chronicle. Nevertheless that part of the agreement which covers the partition of revenues is of the greatest interest. One of the stipulations here was that the port of Lattakia and its harbour should be taxed and that the revenues should be partitioned. How the partition was to work is not altogether clear for the agreement refers back to a clause in an earlier agreement between Baybars and the count of Tripoli which has not been preserved. However the document then goes on to state that an inspection post was to be set up on the Artūsia bridge (over the river Barīd, a few miles to the north of Tripoli) and that this port was to be staffed by the sultan's men. These would comprise a mushidd (senior inspector), a shāhid (junior inspector), a kātib (scribe), three slaves and a picket of ten soldiers. The main job of the inspector was to prevent forbidden articles (the possible nature of which will be considered later) from entering the territory of Tripoli. It is expressly laid down that the mushidd was not to hinder the import of cereals from Arqa (to the north of the Artūsia bridge and still held by the Franks) but only to impose taxes on what did come in.

Another clause in the treaty provides for the security of the sultan's and the count's ships from attacks by one another. Doubtless there were other clauses in the treaty providing for the safety of merchants, etc., but these have not been preserved by Ibn al-Furāt.

The truce document drawn up between Qalāwūn and the city of Acre in 682/1283 is perhaps the longest and certainly the most interesting of all the treaties. Among its many provisions we wish here to single out only those relating to commerce: it is forbidden to import certain articles into the Frankish territories including horses and weapons; those who try to break this embargo will have their goods confiscated; the property of merchants shipwrecked on the territory of either side must be returned as must the property of a merchant who dies in the territory of either of the contracting parties; debt defaulters who fly across the frontiers to escape prosecution must be returned; when the treaty expires or is terminated there is to be a forty-day period of grace to allow stranded travellers to reach their home territory safely.

The clause on contraband articles is particularly interesting as we have another official document preserved in Ibn al-Furāt's chronicle which shows how this embargo was enforced. The document in question is a tadhkīrat— that is a diploma of appointment to office—issued in Muharram 685/Feb-Mar 1286 to the Emir Shams al-Dīn Ibrāhīm b. Khalīl al-Tūrī. The Emir Shams al-Dīn was to replace another emir in the administration of an area close to the Frankish occupied coast of Palestine. The post was described as the Wilāya of al-Rūhā and the Roads to the Franks of Château Pèlerin, Haifa and Acre. The area he was to govern ran from a little way south of Haifa to a little way north of the port of Jaffa. Some of the area was partitioned with the Franks, some was not and his area of authority lay to the west of places like Qaqun and Nablus which were more firmly in the hands of the Muslims. Shams al-Din's job is described in the tadhkirat as being first to enforce law and order in the area and secondly to enforce the truce with Acre. 'What had been forbidden should remain so, that is to say, the import of horses, mules and weapons and anything that had been previously banned in the reign of al-Ẓāhir Baybars'.[47]

Finally we have the text of a truce between Qalāwūn and Margaret lady of Tyre negotiated in 684/1285. In this treaty too there is protection for ships at sea, for the property and lives of those shipwrecked on the coast and for the property of foreign merchants dying in each other's lands. The forbidden articles may not be imported into Tyre (it is taken for granted that it is known what these are). Finally merchants are given a forty-day period of grace at the expiry or cancellation of the truce to regain their home territory in safety.

The preoccupations of the Hospitaller treaty of 1267 indicates the economic importance of livestock breeding, at least in northern Syria. Clauses in the treaties with Beirut, Acre and Tyre suggest that there was nothing unusual in western merchants trading in the Muslim interior—though we have no other evidence for it in this period. However it must be emphasised that, with the exception of the treaty with Beirut in 1269, clauses covering the security of merchants and the levying of trade tolls constitute only small sections of agreements which appear to have been more concerned with agricultural revenues and the maintenance of law and order in the areas covered. Moreover the clauses on the security of merchants and on naufragium, etc. are drafted in vague and standardized terms. Though the Mamlūk regime presumably took the protection of merchants seriously and hoped to profit from commercial tolls, it would seem that its main aim was to restrict and control commerce across the frontiers, not to encourage it—or, to put it another way, it was concerned with contraband not commerce.

This is hardly surprising for a great deal of the Franks' commerce was not open and above board, nor was it conducted with the law-abiding, city-dwelling merchant communities of Damascus and Hama. Rather it was trade with what we may loosely call the dissidents and disaffected in Muslim Syria. As we have seen already, until the late 1260s the Hospitallers had been supplying the Ismāʿīlīs.[48] In Palestine there was a surreptitious two-way trade in arms. Sometimes the Franks bought from the Muslims. In 687/1288-9 the Egyptian wazir Sanjar al-Shujāʿī was accused by a rival of selling arms from the royal stores to the Franks. Sanjar at first successfully defended himself to the Sultan Qalāwūn by claiming that he had only been selling inferior quality weapons to the Franks and at a profit to the Mamlūk state, but subsequently Qalāwūn came to the conclusion that even selling inferior quality weapons to the Franks redounded badly on Mamlūk prestige, and so Sanjar was deposed from the wazirate and fined 65,000 dinars.[49]

On other occasions it was the Franks who were selling arms and other supplies to the disorderly Arabs of Palestine,[50] and we know from references in Arabic chronicles that the Arabs for their part sold Muslims as slaves to the Franks. As Riley-Smith has pointed out, Acre possessed an important slave market and it is possible that the sale of slaves, taken in warfare or purchased from the Arabs of the interior, constituted one of Acre's main exports to the West.

Moreover, looking at Christian commerce in Syria in broader terms, it is remarkable how little attention hitherto has been paid to the question of whom the Italian merchants and settlers in the Christian principalities traded with in Muslim Syria. As suggested above, much of their trade would have been with pastoralist tribesmen. But the civilian merchant community of the Syrian cities would have had other competitors too. Mamlūk emirs had capital to invest and surplus produce from their lands to dispose of. They had no prejudice against engaging in trade and it is clear that they were important as investors and salesmen. No class in Muslim society was better placed to take financial advantage of a harvest failure in Egypt or Syria than the Mamlūk military elite who had iqtās in Syria and Egypt and often large stockpiles of grain to dispose of.[51]

Everywhere the interest of the state and of individual Mamlūk emirs in commercial activity is apparent. Baybars personally invested money in the purchase of slaves.[52] His atābak was an immensely wealthy emir; in 665/1267 the authorities in Beirut agreed to compensate him for his ship which had been captured at sea by pirates and further to free the merchants who had been taken from the ship.[53] As we have seen above, Qalāwūn's wazir supervised the sale of arms to the Franks. Some Mamlūk emirs in Egypt collected their iqtā revenues from the customs tolls levied in the ports of the Nile Delta.[54] There is not space here to do more than indicate the variety of Mamlūk economic interests, but insofar as Mamlūk policies towards the Crusader principalities were swayed by commercial considerations, entrepreneurs from the military class were best placed to sway them. Arab merchants do not seem to have enjoyed any influence at court until the reign of al-Ashrāf Khalīl (689/1290—693/1293).[55]

Another general observation seems worth making. It is of course true that in the eastern Mediterranean shipping from western ports such as Genoa, Venice, Pisa, Marseilles and Barcelona shared a near-monopoly of sea-borne trade. But it was not total, and there was a Muslim merchant marine operating in eastern waters, although its existence can only be traced from indirect references in the sources. Not all the Muslim ships referred to necessarily belonged to Egyptians or Syrians, and it is possible that some of the shipping was north African in origin. A ship attacked by Marseillais pirates in 670/1271 belonged to a subject of the Khan of the Golden Horde.[56] But some ships were clearly Egyptian—for instance the atābak's ship, already mentioned, which was attacked by Beiruti corsairs in the 1260s. Another Egyptian ship was attacked by the Genoese at Candelore in 1287.[57] The Sultan Baybars negotiated with the Byzantine Emperor Michael VIII to secure the right to send one ship a year through the Bosphorus to purchase slaves in the Black Sea area, though according to Greek contemporaries he actually sent two.

The concern of the Egyptian sultans to stamp out or at least restrict the damage done to Muslims by piracy is apparent in their diplomacy—not only in their negotiations with the Crusader principalities discussed above, but also in Mu'izz Aybak's treaty with the Venetians in 1254, Qalāwūn's negotiations with Michael VIII in 1285,[58] his agreement with Cilician Armenia in the same year,[59] his agreement with Aragon in 1286[60] and, above all, his treaty with Genoa in 1290. Of course not all Muslim money and merchandise was invested in Muslim ships. Partnerships and investments could be shared between Muslim and Italian. There is no way of knowing, for instance, whether the ship, captured by the Genoese Lucchetto Grimaldi in the Armenian harbour of Gorighos with the property of subjects of the ilkhān of Persia, the king of Cilician Armenia and Muslim residents in the Crusader principalities on board, was Muslim or not.[61]

It is highly unlikely that any Muslim ships from Egypt visited western ports. But they would have traded with the Crusader ports and certainly with the Syrian ports of Jabala and Lattakia. In the first half of the thirteenth century Jabala and Lattakia (the best port on the Syrian coastline) were under Muslim government,[62] but they were reoccupied by Bohemond VI during the Mongol invasion of 1259-60. An important part of the population remained Muslim, however, and the threat to evacuate the population of Lattakia was one of the levers which Baybars used to secure a partition of authority and revenue in these two places.[63]

This takes us to another important observation. Lattakia and Jabala were singled out for special mention in Baybars' treaty with Beirut. In Baybars' second treaty with the Hospitallers there is a clause specifically dealing with the string of tiny harbours from al-Qantara to Balda. Grain was imported through Gaza and Jaffa. From the perspective of investors and notaries in Italy it was the trade across the Mediterranean with the great ports of Acre, Tyre, Tripoli and Beirut that was important. But the Christians and Muslims in Syria are unlikely to have shared that perspective. Then, as in later periods, much Levantine commerce must have hugged the coast. There was a lot of cabotage and tramping, a lot of carrying and selling of foodstuffs and other staple commodities to quite small ports up and down the Syrian coast and short-haul journeys between Syria and Egypt.

Moreover, because ships hugged the coast even when engaged in commerce over longer distances with more valuable commodities, the ports on the Syrian coast were able to operate, effectively, as toll gates and also to profit from supplying provisions and services to ships that took refuge in their harbours. It is likely that a large portion of the harbour dues that were partitioned with Mamlūks along the coast were from activities of this kind.[64]

The importance of this sort of role for the Syrian and Palestinian ports becomes obvious, when we consider that, as far as the Mamlūk sultans in Egypt and the Genoese in the Levant were concerned, an important long-distance route—perhaps the most important route—ran between the ports of Alexandria and Damietta in Egypt and the ports on the coast of Cilician Armenia, most notably Ayas. As Riley-Smith has pointed out, on the basis of the registers of Genoese notaries active in Ayas, Lattakia and Beirut, there were eleven separate sailings from Ayas to Egypt between February and June 1274 and thirteen between February and December 1279.[65] (Earlier in the century it seems that the Venetians trafficked between Constantinople and Alexandria.[66]) On the Muslim side it is evident from Qalāwūn's agreement with the Armenians in 684/1285 that large numbers of Muslims, some of them Qalāwūn's subjects, some of them not, were trading in Cilician Armenia, and that a particularly important part of this commerce as far as the sultans were concerned was in slaves. Since Caffa and Tana in the Crimea only became important as slave-trade ports in the fourteenth century, it is open to speculation that Ayas in the late thirteenth century was the main supplier of white slaves to Egypt. Also of course Cilician Armenia must have been the main outlet on the Mediterranean for trade coming through Mongol lands on a northern route, from Mosul, from Tabriz and from places further east.[67]

Thus the Crusader ports were well placed to profit from their position as intermediaries in a long-distance, sea-borne trade, but their economically strategic position lay on a north-south axis from Ayas to Alexandria, not on an east-west one from Damascus to Italy.

These suggestions about the nature of Levantine commerce in the thirteenth century have relied heavily upon source material in Arabic. To an extent the arguments are the victim of the biases and silences of those sources. Therefore they are only suggestions and it is probable that a clearer picture will emerge only after more work has been done in Italian archives.

* * * * *

Turning now to the question of money, it must be said at the outset that it is impossible to get any clear overall picture of how moneys circulated in thirteenth-century Syria. Not all the Ayyubid and Mamlūk mints in Syria have been identified. We are uncertain as to the extent to which moneys minted by the Latins circulated in the hinterland of Syria, and we are similarly uncertain as to the extent to which Egyptian-minted coins circulated there. Some coin hoards must have been buried by refugees, and, in view of what has already been remarked above about the movement of refugees in this period, the evidence of coin hoards, though crucial, may be misleading. Even the extent to which transactions depended upon money is difficult to discover; tributes were often levied in kind, the endowments of the pious might be fixed in kind, iqtā revenues might be collected in the form of crops and the army paid with the dīnār jayshī, a notional currency covering payments which were mostly made in kind. When and where money did circulate and whether that money circulated at a fixed face value or by weight are matters of controversy.

Many of our uncertainties arise from our ignorance about the extent to which the Ayyubid and Mamlūk regimes directly controlled the minting of coinage and the extent to which they were able to enforce the acceptability of particular coins in the market-place and our ignorance too of the sort of considerations which may have influenced their monetary policies. Much depends also on the ability of the ordinary trader in the market-place to distinguish a 'good' coin from a 'bad' one, or an imitation from its genuine prototype. In view of contemporary numismatic difficulties in this area, it must remain doubtful whether he could.

The mint was an important source of revenue for the ruler. In the late 1230s the Cairo mint seems to have been producing a profit of about 36,000 dinars annually as revenue.[68] In the 1250s the mint in Aleppo produced 100,000 dirhams annually for its Ayyubid prince.[69] In Mamlūk Egypt the profits of the mint were sold as a farm, as a reference in Ibn 'Abd al-Ẓāhir's chronicle to a petition of the farmers of the mint to the Sultan in 662/1264 indicates.[70] However we do not know what sort of person purchased the right to the profits of the mint (the petitioners of 662/1264 may well have been Mamlūk emirs or Italians), nor should we assume that the purchasers of the farm had any control over the operations of the mint. In Mamlūk Damascus at least, the operations of the mint continued to be supervised in the 1260s by a state-appointed official, the Nāzir Dār al-Darb (supervisor of the mint).[71]

When money was struck it was not always struck to meet economic needs. The propaganda value of coins was obvious. When Baybars' son al-Sa'īd was invested with the nominal co-rule of Egypt and Syria in 662/1264 the proclamation drawn up by Baybars' head of chancery included the statement 'There should be no sort of dirham or dinar which will not shine with our (i.e. Baybars' and Sa'īd's) names.'[72] This was an aspiration which could not be realized Probably the bulk of the coinage in circulation in the late thirteenth century continued to be Ayyubid. But the statement was propaganda and reveals the value of coins as such. Again, when Baybars briefly occupied Kayseri in Anatolia in 675/1277 one of his first acts was to have the khutba said in his name in the mosque and Ẓāhirī dirhams struck.[73] The issue of such a coin seems closer to the striking of a victory medallion than it does to the issue of money.

On the other hand the decision whether or not to suppress an older issue of coinage was not necessarily taken on a purely economic basis either. Some time before 569/1174 Nūr al-Dīn received a petition in the Dar al-'Adl (House of Justice) at Damascus from certain merchants requesting that he suppress a certain coin known as the qirtās and that he should replace it with dinars struck in his own name. Nūr al-Dīn refused to do this, fearing, he said, to ruin those of his subjects who might have ten or twenty thousand of those coins in their possession. Abū Shāma concludes this little anecdote with the exclamation 'Consider how often and how much he showed concern for the welfare of his subjects.'[74]

Similarly the petition presented in the Cairo Dar al-'Adl by the farmers of the mint to Baybars, of which mention has already been made above, was to the effect that the minting of dirhams had now ceased and that the old Nāṣirī dirhams should be suppressed (implicitly to make way for a new issue of dirhams of superior fineness). Baybars refused this petition. He instead reduced either the amount they paid for the farming of the mint or their obligation to mint (it is not clear which) from 250,000 dirhams to 200,000 dirhams and remarked that 'the people should not suffer any loss of wealth from this'. The point here is that in both cases the decision not to suppress bad coinage is presented as the act of a virtuous ruler—there is even perhaps an element of public charade in such performances in the Dar al-'Adl.

Though Egypt and the Syrian towns had all been ruled by various Ayyubid princes in the early thirteenth century and though they were subsequently governed by one and the same Mamlūk regime in the late thirteenth century, Egypt and Syria certainly did not form one monetary unit.

From the late twelfth century onwards the Egyptian gold dinar was no longer of a standard weight, yet large numbers of dinars of a high degree of fineness continued to be struck.[75] Curiously, though the dinars were not of a standard weight, they were almost invariably heavier than the old Fatimid dinar or the legal dinar of c. 4.25 g.

Egypt's silver dirhams, unlike those struck in Syria, were mostly of a poor alloy. The bulk of the dirhams were probably 'black' or 'waraq' with alloys of c. 27-32% silver. According to the fifteenth-century chronicler Maqrīzī, Saladin variously struck a Nāṣirī dirham of pure silver and/or a Nāṣirī dirham which was only half silver in content. Other Ayyubid princes after Saladin, notably al-Kāmil, seem to have attempted to produce dirhams with a high silver content, but the inferior dirhams, 'black', 'waraq' and Nāṣirī, continued to circulate into the early Mamlūk period. From c. 1250 onwards there was a fairly steady improvement in the alloy of the dirham (the crisis-beset reign of al-Muzaffar Quṭuz was an exception), this improvement culminating in the Ẓāhirī dirham of the Sultan Baybars which had a silver content of approximately 70%.

Supplies of the copper coin, the fals, seem to have been unstable. For long periods in the thirteenth century no copper coins were issued. On the other hand problems were caused by excesses in the supply of copper coins in 630/1232 and again in 695/1295-6.

In Syria everything was different.[76] It appears that scarcely any dinars at all were minted by the Muslims in thirteenth-century Syria. (Claude Cahen has argued from the near non-existence of Syrian gold coins that Christian gold coins cannot therefore have been minted for use in Syrian markets,[77] but the logic of that argument is not obvious, for it is surely possible either that Christian-minted bezants caused the disappearance of the Muslim Syrian dinar or, alternatively, that the disappearance of the Syrian dinar for other reasons encouraged an influx of other gold coins precisely to fill the gap.)

By contrast dirhams were normally plentiful in Syria and of a fine alloy too, usually ranging from 80 to 90%. But there does appear to have been a silver famine in Syria c. 1230-40. There was also a temporary reduction in the fineness of the dirham to 72-74% in the reign of al-Nāṣir Yūsuf and again it would appear that no dirhams were minted in Damascus from 1260 to 1266. Incidentally dirhams were struck with remarkable rapidity by short-term regimes and usurpers in Damascus. Tūrānshāh had dirhams minted in his name there as he passed on down to Egypt. Hulagu issued dirhams in Damascus and so did the rebel emirs Sanjar al-Ḥalabī and Sunqor al-'Ashqār. It seems likely that some of these issues were struck to declare a change of regime rather than to meet a genuine economic need.

Copper coinage was in fairly constant demand and, as we shall see, there was a shortage of it c. 1259-60.

Egypt's abandonment of the standard-weight dinar and the discrepancy between the Syrian and Egyptian dirhams, at least until Baybars' issue of the Ẓāhirī dirham, might lead one to conclude that until then Syria had been growing richer and Egypt poorer, as Egypt lost its stock of precious metals.[78] However the validity of that conclusion is dependant upon a number of assumptions, among them firstly the assumption that there is some necessary correlation between the issue of debased moneys and the impoverishment of the economy. No such necessary correlation exists. The issue of coins of low or variable alloys by the Egyptian mints might be taken as an indication of the impoverishment of the state but not the economy or of the greed of the state issuing authority but not of its impoverishment or simply of the increased demand for money by the thriving Egyptian economy. Nor can we take it for granted that the Syrian Muslim dirham, with its high silver content, was the common or standard currency in Syria at that time. There is evidence that in the late thirteenth century large quantities of dinars and dirhams may have been brought into Syria from Egypt. One has the impression that this phenomenon owed less to commerce than it did to the requirements and expenditure of sultans, officials and soldiers coming from Egypt. Thus, for example, when the Sultan Baybars, encamped in Palestine in 663/1264-5, wished to reward a garrison and a relief army on the Euphrates, he had to send to Egypt for 200,000 dirhams to be brought north to supplement those available in Damascus.[79] Yet it would be perverse to argue from such instances as this that Syria in the thirteenth century was becoming richer and Egypt poorer. A variety of other evidence suggests the reverse and, as we have seen above, it was Syria, not Egypt, which bore the brunt of Khwarizmian, Kurdish, Turkoman and Mongol depredations in the thirteenth century. The contrast between high-grade Syrian dirhams and low-grade Egyptian dirhams would remain but would become less important if one were to speculate that most of the population of Syria used Egyptian-minted Nāṣirī or 'waraq' dirhams most of the time.

Though a great deal of Egyptian money did come into Syria from the time of Saladin onwards, and some Syrian gold and silver presumably percolated into Egypt, the rate of exchange between dinar and dirham in the two areas was not necessarily the same.[80] Even within Egypt, (for which the evidence is more plentiful), the rate could vary from year to year, or perhaps according to the transaction. Thus the rate for a low grade 'waraq' dirham could vary between 1:35 and 1:40, while the rate for Baybars' Ẓāhirī dirham with its much higher silver content, could vary between 1:20 and $1:28\frac{1}{2}$. A rate of 20 Ẓāhirī dirhams to the dinar suggests a gold:silver ratio of 1:9 or 10, a rate of $28\frac{1}{2}$ Ẓāhirī dirhams to the dinar a gold:silver ratio of 1:13.4 (so long that is as one assumes a direct dependence of the dinar:dirham rate upon the gold:silver rate).

In Damascus on the other hand, when Abū Shāma came to cite the rate for the Egyptian (Miṣrī) dinar against the (presumably) Syrian dirham in 636/1238-9 he gave it as 1:9.[81] Since the actual Egyptian dinar of the early thirteenth century had no fixed weight, Abū Shāma must have been intending to refer to the 'standard' or legal dinar of 24 carats fineness and 4.2 g (and perhaps we should take his estimate of wheat prices in 634/1245-6 expressed in Nāṣirī dinars, i.e. Saladin's dinars of irregular weight, in the same sense). Whatever sort of dinar Abū Shāma was referring to, the discrepancy between his figure and the Egyptian ones quoted above is startling.

It may be explained in two not incompatible ways. Firstly the rate given for dinars and dirhams in 636 reflects the temporary scarcity of silver in Syria in the 1230s—a phenomenon which has been suggested by another scholar of this period.[82] Secondly the rate between dinar and dirham is not only the product of the local scarcity of gold and silver moneys relative to one another, but is also determined by political and social considerations. In this particular case the high value placed upon silver may for example reflect fiscal demands by the authorities in Damascus to be paid in dirhams. Jawād, the governor of Damascus in that year, is said to have secured the sum of 600,000 dirhams through extortion from the city's notables.[83] Alternatively the rate quoted may be an official rate fixed by al-Ṣāliḥ Ayyūb or his predecessors which deliberately aimed at under-valuing the Egyptian-minted dinar.

Whatever the explanation for Abū Shāma's figure, the rate was clearly local and temporary. Why else should Abū Shāma explain to his readers what it was? Such a rate never applied in Egypt and in Syria Ṣāliḥ ibn Yaḥya gives the rate of 20 or 21 dirhams to the dinar by the early fourteenth century.[84]

Much has been written about the export of moneys to the Levant by Italian merchants, most notably by Lopez and Watson.[85] It has been argued (simplifying considerably) that the export of silver coins and bullion from the West and their exchange against Egyptian and Syrian gold (at a profit to the western merchants) and the shipment of that gold back to Europe may explain the West's return to a gold standard from the latter half of the thirteenth century. But it remains to be shown whether such movements of gold and silver took place on a sufficiently large scale to be significant.

In any event some of the gold and silver taken out East by the Europeans seems to have been taken to Muslim mints where it was recoined as dinars and dirhams. The Italian gold and silver was sold to the mint at a privileged rate and sometimes it would appear that the work in the mint was done by the the Italians themselves. Of particular note in this respect are the commercial agreements concluded between the Italian merchant communities and the Muslim rulers of Egypt and Syria. In Venice's treaty with al-Ẓāhir Ghāzī of Aleppo in 1207-8 the sale of silver by the Venetians to the mint was covered. In 1238, during the reign of the Egyptian ruler al-'Adil II, the Venetians negotiated an agreement which seems to have covered payments for gold sold by the Venetians to the mint and further to have allowed the Venetians themselves to use the mint in Alexandria. A similar agreement with Mu'izz Aybak in 1254 covered the sale and minting of gold and silver by the Venetians in Egypt.[86] In 1290 the agreement concluded between the Genoese and the Sultan Qalāwūn fixed a tariff payable by the Genoese on the import of gold and silver and also allowed them to mint dirhams which they could use to trade with in Cairo without paying any further charges.[87]

It is noteworthy that similar clauses covering the import of gold and silver and minting privileges are to be found in a series of agreements negotiated between Venice and Cilician Armenia in 1202, 1245, 1271, 1307 and 1321. It seems possible also that Venice had had at some time minting privileges in the Crusader cities of Acre and Tyre.[88]

Since many of the surviving agreements cover Egypt where the price of gold in relation to silver does not seem to have been more favourable than in Europe and since the import of gold as well as silver is covered in most of these agreements, it appears unlikely that the Italians were engaged in anything so simple as the sale of silver from Europe in exchange for gold in the

Near East. Rather, the clauses dealing with money and bullion in these agreements indicate that the Italians were concerned to secure options which would allow them to take advantage of regional differences and fluctuations over short periods of time in the relative value of dinars and dirhams. Beyond that, they were of course keen to provide themselves with locally-acceptable currency while at the same time avoiding exchange premiums in the market or seignorage at the mint. The concession of such privileges may have had vast implications for the monetary history of the Near East. On the other hand of course they may never or only rarely have been taken advantage of.

Besides the dinars and dirhams struck by Muslim mints in Syria, a range of moneys were struck in gold, silver and copper by the Christians in the Crusader States. Coins were struck not only by the kings of Jerusalem, the princes of Antioch and the counts of Tripoli but also on a smaller scale by the Frankish seigneuries in what remained of the kingdom of Jerusalem—among them Sidon, Tyre, Beirut and perhaps Jaffa. These issues were perhaps supplemented by moneys from Cyprus and Cilician Armenia. Gold and silver coins were taken to the Near East by western, mainly Italian merchants, and we know from the evidence of both coin hoards and documents that large quantities of gold and silver—particularly silver—were brought out to the East by crusaders in the thirteenth century.[89]

It would be superfluous for me now to elaborate on the above. For my present purposes only one particular range of moneys is of interest—the bezants and dirhams minted by the Franks in the Levant in imitation of Muslim coins. Even here the numismatic evidence has been carefully presented by others so that it is not necessary to do more than summarise the points of particular interest that arise from a numismatic examination of these coins, before proceeding to look at the textual evidence for their circulation.[90]

At some time in the twelfth century, perhaps as early as the 1130s or 40s, but probably not on any very large scale until the second half of the century, the Christians in the Crusader principalities began to mint gold coins with Arabic Muslim legends and dates in imitation of the Fatimid gold dinars. Though similar in appearance to the Fatimid dinars, the Crusader coins were not of the same high standard of fineness. These coins are referred to frequently in western documents as 'bisancii saracenati'.

The issue of such coins continued on into the thirteenth century, but in 1250 as a result of an intervention by the papal legate to the Holy Land, Odo of Châteauroux, the minting of coins with Muslim legends seems to have ceased. From 1251 issues of imitation dinars appeared bearing Christian legends and Christian dates in Arabic, and some of these were marked with crosses on one or both sides. On the strength of the numismatic evidence, however, we should be justified in concluding that the striking of these latter coins was abandoned by 1258 at the latest. Lopez, writing in 1957, was of the opinion that the Crusader bezant was gradually phased out and replaced by the new Italian gold coins.[91] Yet the appearance of these new Italian moneys (the genovino and others) is not noticed by the Arabic sources dealing with Syria in this period, nor, so far as I am aware, have any Italian gold coins been found in coin hoards in Syria until the very end of the thirteenth century and the beginning of the fourteenth.[92]

Imitations of Muslim dirhams and half-dirhams were also minted though no examples have been found for the twelfth century. In the early thirteenth century the dirhams of Aleppo were copiously imitated. From c. 1240 onwards it was the turn of the Damascus dirhams of al-Ṣāliḥ Ismā'īl (ruler of Damascus in 1237 and again from 1239 to 1245). These imitations have al-Ṣāliḥ Ismā'īl's name on the obverse and the name of the caliph of Bagdad, al-Mustanṣir, on the reverse. They are somewhat difficult to identify, for, as Balog has remarked, they are skilful copies and, as Bates has remarked, the surviving copies outnumber their original models. They are identified by the failure of the dates shown on the coins to correspond with the years in which al-Ṣāliḥ Ismā'īl ruled over Damascus and in which al-Mustanṣir was caliph of Bagdad. Also some of these dirhams show crosses on their margins, and examples of imitation dirhams analysed by Balog were found to have a silver content of 76-79% while their Muslim models had a silver content of 80-89%.[93] (But Muslim issues from Damascus later in the 1240s had an alloy closer to that of the Crusader imitations). These Crusader imitations, types I-IV in Bates' classification, were struck from 641/1243-4 to perhaps as late as 647/1249-50.

In 1251 and 1253 dirhams with Christian legends in Arabic were struck by the Crusaders (and some of these overtly Christian coins even had crosses in the centre). In 1253 imitation dirhams bearing the names of al-Ṣāliḥ Ismā'īl and al-Mustanṣir, but also a religiously neutral inscription were struck (type V in Bates' classification). A further type of coin (type VI), very similar to the above but bearing the (almost certainly fictitious) date 641, has been identified and Bates has argued that it was struck at around the same time as the type V dirham. It would seem from the numismatic evidence that minting by the Crusaders of imitation dirhams ceased in 1253 or soon after.

However if the date on the type VI '641' dirham is fictitious, then it is possible, though not likely, that other Muslim dates shown on imitation dirhams of the types I-IV are equally fictitious and arbitrary. Most of the imitation dirhams minted by the Crusaders which have been published in recent years have come from two hoards of Egyptian, Syrian and Crusader silver. One, discovered at Fayyum, has been dated to the year 655/1256-7, on the basis of the latest date borne by any of the Muslim coins in the hoard. The other, a Syrian hoard, has been dated to 653/1255. No dirhams from al-Nāṣir's Damascus are known after 654/1256-7. As far as Egypt is concerned, though dirhams minted for Nūr al-Dīn 'Alī in 655 are known to exist none are for 656, and al-Muẓaffar Quṭuz (657-8) minted no dirhams until 658. Therefore both hoards might date from as late as 657 or 658 (the years of the Mongol invasion, plausible years for a Syrian refugee to bury a hoard). Since imitations form such a large portion of these two hoards, much depends upon the dating of the imitations, and, as we shall see later, there are some grounds, though not decisive ones, for thinking that a lot of Crusader dirhams may have been minted in the late 1250s.

Of course it was not unknown for Muslims in this period to counterfeit dirhams. In the early 1260s for instance the overseer of the mint in Damascus was disgraced and imprisoned by the governor of the city after dies for the striking of counterfeit coins had been discovered stored in a box in the mint.[94]

In principle it is possible that Muslim forgers could have produced some of the imitation dirhams mentioned above, following the conventionalized epigraphic errors of the widely current crusader dirhams. However while crude counterfeits of al-Ṣāliḥ Ismā'īl's dirhams have been discovered, it would seem that the imitation dirhams classified by Bates are too fine and too consistent in the distribution of their weights around a modal value to be confused with such counterfeits.

In discussing the evidence in Arabic sources for the circulation of imitation moneys, the first coin to be considered is the Ṣūrī dinar. The equation of the term 'dinar Ṣūrī' with the gold coin minted by the crusaders in imitation of the Muslim dinar has been taken for granted by some and firmly denied by others.[95]

Qazwīnī, the traveller and geographer who died in 682/1283, explained the term thus: 'From Tyre (Ṣūr) the Ṣūrī dinars are derived, which the people of Syria and Iraq use in their transactions.'[96] Unfortunately what Qazwīnī has to say about the Ṣūrī dinar does not necessarily apply to his own time. Arab geographers were even more prone to plagiarize from their predecessors than were Arab chroniclers.[97] Indeed, in the light of what has been said earlier about the closing of the frontier between Syria and Iraq to commerce, it is very unlikely that Ṣūrī dinars circulated to any significant extent in Iraq in Qazwīnī's lifetime, and Ibn al-Fuwāṭī, the thirteenth-century Iraqi chronicler makes no reference to any such coin. When Qazwīnī refers to the Ṣūrī dinar he may be referring to a twelfth-century coin minted by the crusaders in imitation of the Fatimid dinar, or even to the Fatimid dinar itself, which was minted in Tyre up to 1124. According to Ibn Khallikān, when the Crusaders captured Tyre from the Fatimids they took over the mint there and continued to mint coins for a further three years until 1127 when they stopped.[98]

At all events it is absolutely clear that by the early thirteenth century the term 'Ṣūrī' was no longer being applied by Arab writers to the Fatimid dinar minted in Tyre, for the Fatimid dinar was 90% fine or even finer, but al-Nābulsī's report on administrative and financial malpractices in Egypt (presented to al-Ṣāliḥ Ayyūb in 1242) described Ṣūrī gold brought to the mint as being only 60% fine.[99] Actual Crusader bezants which have been analysed have been found to range between 60 and 80% in fineness; this is broadly compatible with al-Nābulsī's 60% when we allow for the inaccurate assaying techniques of the time and the tendency of the Egyptian mint to undervalue foreign dinars.

While it is plausible that the adjective 'Ṣūrī' did indeed originally refer to coins struck in Tyre by the Fatimids or the crusaders immediately after them, it is virtually certain that the revived use of the term from the late twelfth century onwards was a calque based on the French 'besant de Syrie'. The coin referred to by the Arabs as Ṣūrī then may have been minted in Acre, Tyre, Tripoli or anywhere.

In al-Shayzārī's late twelfth-century manual of ḥisba (market inspection) the sale of Egyptian dinars against Ṣūrī dinars was forbidden, so it would seem that the Ṣūrī dinar was by then regarded as a foreign coin or a coin of lower alloy or both.[100] In Ibn al-Athīr's chronicle al-Kāmil fī al-Tārīkh the price of wheat in Damascus in 574/1178-9 is given in 'old Ṣūrī dinars', surely implying that a new Ṣūrī dinar was by then circulating.[101]

Generally, the period in which the term 'Ṣūrī dinar' is used corresponds too closely to the crusader period and appears too frequently in the context of transactions with or by the crusaders for the term not to have referred to a crusader coin.

Among early appearances of the Ṣūrī dinar in the works of Ibn al-Athīr and Bahā al-Dīn ibn Shaddād, we find a Frankish lord ransoming prisoners from the Muslims for 150,000 Ṣūrī dinars in 575/1179-80 and we find grain prices in Acre and Antioch in 586/1190-1 expressed in Ṣūrī dinars.[102] The last reference to the Ṣūrī dinar known to me occurs in Ṣāliḥ ibn Yaḥyā's Tārīkh Bayrūt. In 702/1302-3 a Buhtorid emir, taken captive by the Franks during a raid on the Lebanese coast, was ransomed for 3,000 Ṣūrī dinars.[103]

References to the Ṣūrī dinar are especially frequent in Arabic chronicles and documents of the late thirteenth century dealing with matters connected with the Crusader principalities. In particular, the tributes, taxes, and blood prices mentioned in Mamlūk-Crusader truce negotiations are commonly fixed in Ṣūrī dinars. However it is also clear that the Ṣūrī dinar was not the only gold currency in the area but was competing with (or co-existing with) the Egyptian dinar. Thus in 665/1267 Baybars allowed the Hospitallers 50 Ṣūrī dinars annually as compensation for the loss of certain rights over straw west of the Orontes and the Hospitallers renounced the tribute they had been levying on Aynab of 500 Ṣūrī dinars annually. On the other hand they also renounced a tribute they had formerly been levying on nearby Abū Qubays of 600 Egyptian dinars annually.[104]

Again, when Baybars sent a deputation of Muslims into Tripoli in 669/1271 to ransom prisoners, they took with them 3,000 Egyptian dinars, but in 673/1275 the sultan's sabre-rattling induced the count to pay him 20,000 Ṣūrī dinars.[105]

Though Ṣūrī dinars were used for payments between Muslim and Christian, or at least for computing such payments, I have found no references to the Ṣūrī dinar being used for payments between Muslim and Muslim in Damascus or elsewhere in Syria or Egypt. When the type of dinar is specified in such circumstances it is either the Egyptian dinar or a pure gold ('aynan) dinar. The Ṣūrī dinar was not an international currency in any sense save that its gold content and Arabic form made it an occasionally acceptable means of payment in Muslim Syria.

There are a few mentions in western commercial and notarial documents of a coin known as the Tripolitan bezant (bizantius Tripolatus).[106] I know of only one reference in Arabic to the coin. In 1267, at the same time as the Hospitallers formally renounced their tribute upon Aynab levied in Ṣūrī dinars and that upon Abū Qubays levied in Egyptian dinars, they also renounced the tribute they had formerly been taking from the Ismā'īlī castles of Masyāf and Rusāfa of 1,200 dinars Qumsiyya (i.e. of the comes or count of Tripoli), and a few years later the Ismā'īlīs began to bring the gold (dhahab) which they had formerly payed to the Hospitallers to Baybars instead.[107] Instances such as the above make it unlikely that the Ṣūrī dinar was a money of account, used to make notional estimates which would then be paid in silver or copper, for there is no point in having a money of account if it does not actually simplify one's accounts and provide a fixed yardstick of value.

The above figures have been taken from a copy of the treaty document in a chancery manual. Unfortunately when chroniclers mention sums of money in Ṣūrī dinars, their employment of the term is slapdash and so casual as to suggest that they took little care to distinguish between dinar and dirham. Thus, according to Ibn 'Abdal-Ẓāhir, in 665/1267 Baybars demanded that Tyre should pay 15,000 Ṣūri dinars as blood money for a murdered Mamlūk and that half this sum should be payed instantly, but when Ibn 'Abd al-Ẓāhir's nephew came to abridge and gloss his uncle's chronicle, he gave the figure as 25,000 Ṣūri dinars, which he added was equivalent to 1,000 Egyptian dinars and of this sum 7,000 dinars were paid straight away![108] Similarly when Ibn 'Abd al-Ẓāhir came to give the blood prices which had been fixed in the agreement with Tyre in 684/1285, he gave that for a knight as being 1,100 Ṣūrī dirhams (sic), that for a turcopole as being 200 dinars and that for a peasant as 100 dinars.[109]

It would seem from the above that the Ṣūrī dinar continued to circulate widely after the 1250s, until at least the 1280s (and the continued circulation of such a coin is also suggested by numerous references in the Genoese notarial acts witnessed at Ayas to the sarracenate bezant of Acre in the late 1270s—and also to the sarracenate bezant of Armenia).[110] It is disturbing that the numismatic evidence for these coins has not yet been found and therefore the possibility that, at some time around the mid-thirteenth century, the Ṣūrī dinar became a ghost money should be borne in mind.

Turning now to the minting of imitation dirhams and half-dirhams by the crusaders, it has been noted above that no examples of crusader dirhams or half-dirhams have been found which date from the twelfth century. Nevertheless there is evidence in al-Shayzārī's twelfth-century hisba manual that such coins may have circulated. The author has this to say about the purchase of bad coins:

> 'There are those who purchase dinars with dirhams of silver or Frankish qarātīs and then such a one says to the seller "One of your debtors has brought these to me so that you can be dispensed from counting them or weighing them; or he has contracted debts to me for small sums". He profits in this from the ignorance of others and it is forbidden'.[111]

The overall sense of this passage is unclear to me, but evidently Frankish coins, probably of poor silver alloy, were known to the Muslim money changers of the twelfth century. It is quite possible that the term qirtās (pl. qarātīs) was used to designate the Frankish denier, but this must remain uncertain as long as the composition, alloy and weight of the Muslim coin of that name remain in doubt. The Muslim qirtās, as we have already seen, was circulating in Syria during the reign of Nūr al-Dīn. The Muslim qirtās seems to have been a half-dirham. Its rate against the dinar fluctuated from 50:1 to 60:1

or even higher. It continued to circulate widely in Syria and Egypt in the late thirteenth century and was sometimes called the 'black qirtās'.[112]

This brings us finally to what the Arabic sources have to tell us about the imitation dirhams produced by the Franks. The problems that these coins caused in the markets of Damascus in 658/1259-60 are discussed by two Arabic sources.[113] After recording the soaring price of food in the city, Abū Shāma, the first of these sources adds:

> 'This was due to the Franks who were striking dirhams known as 'bāqiyya' dirhams (al-darāhim al-ma'rūfati bi'l-bāqiyya) which were of a bad alloy. I heard that in every hundred parts, there were only fifteen of silver, the rest being of copper. These dirhams became very abundant. Several times there was talk of suppressing them. As everyone who held them tried to get rid of them, fearing that they would be suppressed, so there was a lot of spending on different things, which made prices rise. When it was suppressed at the end of the year, four dirhams of this money were exchanged against one Nāṣirī dirham, and the Nāṣirī dirham itself was only half (silver).'

The British Museum manuscript of the continuation of Abū Shāma's history, the Dhayl, gives 'bāqiyya'; the Paris manuscript, used by the editors of the Recueil des Historiens des Croisades, apparently gives 'bāfiyya'. The sense of 'bāqiyya' (if that is the correct reading) is unclear. Does the adjective refer to a place or does it mean 'left over', or 'still owing as a debt', or 'calamitous'? The obscurity of the term and the context in which it appears has prompted the editor of the Arabic printed text to emend the word to 'yāfiyya' i.e. Jaffan.[114] This emendation, while speculative, is plausible enough, and has been followed by Lyons and Riley-Smith in their edition and translation of parts of Ibn al-Furāt's chronicle. The Vienna manuscript of Ibn al-Furāt gives 'bāqiyya' and has been emended by the editors to 'yāfiyya' so that their translation of the relevant passage in Ibn al-Furāt reads:

> 'Prices rose very high indeed because of the shortages (of food) and because of the poor quality of Jaffan dirhams. The people asked for help because of these (dirhams) and al-Malik al-Mujāhid, the Sultan of Damascus, suppressed this coinage and minted a new one. The new dirhams appeared in his name, with an inscription on them: "Al-Malik al-Mujāhid 'Alam al-Dīn Sanjar, the ruler of Damascus".'[115]

Maqrīzī, a fifteenth-century compiler seems to be relying on a third source. In covering the causes of the rise in prices in Damascus in 658 (which seems to have begun even before Sanjar's usurpation), he makes no mention of the Frankish dirham, but says:

> 'The people returned to Damascus (i.e. after the Mongol withdrawal), the prices became very high through lack of provisions and there was a lack of fulūs (copper money) there and the people suffered harm in the market through having to use dirhams, and what had been easy became difficult.'

Coming from Maqrīzī this explanation is notable, for he normally displays a ferocious prejudice against copper money. It is also noteworthy that

Maqrīzī does not give any credit to al-Malik al-Mujāhid Sanjar for solving Damascus' monetary crisis during his brief period of authority over that city. According to Maqrīzī prices were still high in the following year, and Baybars took steps to bring grain into Damascus and Syria.[116]

Ibn al-Suqā'ī's biographical dictionary confirms the impression that, whatever monetary measures Sanjar may have taken, they were not really successful in bringing down prices, for he says that two years after Baybars' victory over Sanjar, prices were still very high in the city. He gives examples of inflated prices in darāhim judad ('new dirhams'—but whose?) and adds that Baybars took steps to have seed-corn imported into Syria from Egypt.[117]

It is in fact very unlikely that Sanjar could have succeeded in suppressing the Frankish dirham, or in replacing it with dirhams in his own name, or that this would have solved Damascus' price problem. For one thing, if one accepts Abū Shāma's statement as to the rate at which the Frankish dirham could be exchanged against the Nāṣirī dirham (note that the latter would seem to be the Egyptian dirham issued by Saladin which was only 50% silver), then it is evident that on the basis of silver content alone, those who sold to the Damascus mint would be making a substantial and unnecessary loss. Sanjar's writ scarcely ran outside the walls of Damascus, and coins similar to the 'Jaffan' or bāqiyya dirham were circulating elsewhere, for the emir Fakhr al-Dīn al-Ḥimṣī was alleged to have extorted 1,600,000 Beiruti dirhams from the population of Aleppo in 659/1261.[118]

Then again Sanjar's own issue of dirhams does not seem to have been a large one. Only two surviving examples have so far been discovered.[119] Even in the most favourable circumstances it was difficult to suppress 'bad' coins, and the declared reluctance of rulers like Nūr al-Dīn and Baybars to do so may have concealed their impotence. The attempts of the Circassian sultans in the fifteenth century to remove Italian coins from circulation in Egypt furnish an instructive example of the difficulties involved.[120]

Besides, the crisis in Damascus was not entirely or even mainly monetary in origin, but a product of other special circumstances. In the wake of the Mongol invasion the harvest will have been a poor one. The refugees who had taken shelter in the Crusader towns on the coast would then have returned to Damascus, and it is conceivable that it was they who brought in the large quantities of Frankish dirhams. Certainly the vengeful fine of 150,000 dirhams which the Muslims imposed on the Christians of Damascus after 'Ayn Jalūt is likely to have brought large numbers of such coins into circulation in the city.[121]

Sanjar and Baybars both struck dirhams in Damascus upon assuming control there, but between 660 and 666 there does not seem to have been any issue of silver by the Damascus mint, though copper money may well have been issued.[122] In the light of the testimony of the Arabic chroniclers quoted above, it would appear that the suspension of the minting of silver there was due to the excessive numbers of dirhams already circulating—Frankish, Egyptian and others. The resumption of minting in 666/1268 in Syria was the product perhaps of the conversion of silver acquired in the sack of Crusader towns into Muslim coinage—Jaffa and Antioch both fell in that year.

Though Frankish dirhams were alleged to have been the cause of a monetary crisis in Damascus in 658/1259-60, it is in a sense more remarkable that in other years these coins did not produce a similar stir. Superficially Abū Shāma seems to be describing the operation of Gresham's law—bad money driving out good—but it is precisely a consideration of the context of Abū Shāma's information that suggests the opposite conclusion: though locally within Damascus 'bad' Frankish money circulated from person to person with increasing rapidity like the Bottle Imp, this was only because it was expected that an attempt would be made by the authorities to suppress it that year. This would not apply in other towns and in other years. Presumably Frankish dirhams had circulated in Damascus before 658 and perhaps they continued to do so afterwards as well. As Udovitch has observed, 'In the absence of special circumstances, such as the enforcement of a state-imposed exchange rate, all coins in circulation found their own level of values and were equally good or equally bad'.[123]

Very large numbers of bāqiyya or 'Jaffan' dirhams must have been minted, yet no actual dirham has been published by numismatists which can either be assigned to Jaffa, or to the late 1250s, or, most importantly, possessing a silver content of only 15%.

To conclude, the speculative nature of most of the above must be apparent. It is disconcerting to find that the textual evidence about the issue of coins in this period matches the numismatic evidence so badly. It is not only the bāqiyya (or 'Jaffan') dirham which awaits identification, but also the Beiruti dirham, the twelfth century qirtās, the Ẓāhirī dirham issued in Anatolia, the sarracenate bezant of Armenia and the Ṣūrī dinars of the late twelfth and late thirteenth centuries. A satisfactory matching of coins and texts may not always be possible, for in some cases doubtless we are the victims of the Arab chroniclers' misunderstandings concerning their own monetary system and, in some cases, it may be that they are referring not to real moneys but to moneys of account, yet it is clear that the Arabic texts raise important questions about the circulation of imitation dinars and dirhams and the dates when these coins ceased to circulate.

NOTES

I am grateful to M. L. Bates and D. M. Metcalf for reading and criticising this paper. The errors that remain are, obstinately, my own.

1. Some excellent studies of the commerce and economy of the Crusader principalities exist and have been consulted here, notably: J. Riley-Smith, The Feudal Nobility and the Kingdom of Jerusalem, 1174-1277, 1973, pp. 62-98; idem, 'Government in Latin Syria and the commercial privileges of foreign merchants', in Relations between East and West in the Middle Ages (ed. D. Baker), Edinburgh, 1973, pp. 109-32; J. Prawer, The Latin Kingdom of Jerusalem, 1972, pp. 352-415; J. Richard, Le royaume latin de Jérusalem, 1953, pp. 275-83; C. Cahen, La Syrie du Nord à l'époque des croisades et la principauté franque d'Antioche, 1940, pp. 472-500.

2. J. Sauvaget, Alep, 1941, p. 143. On the Khwarizmians in Syria and Palestine generally see R. S. Humphreys, From Saladin to the Mongols, New York, 1977, pp. 269-71, 274-5.

3. Though of course it is true that from the 11th century onwards there had been some Turkoman settlement in Syria. See F. Sumer, Oguzlar, Ankara, 1967, pp. 132f.; C. Cahen, op. cit. pp. 473f.

4. 'L'Estoire d'Eracles', RHC Occ. II, p. 435.; 'Continuation de Guillaume de Tyr, de 1229 à 1261, dite du manuscrit de Rothelin', RHC Occ. II, p. 623f.; Cartulaire général de l'ordre des Hospitalliers de S. Jean de Jérusalem (ed. J. Delaville Le Roulx), 1894-1906, II, no. 2605, pp. 726f.; 'Annales monasterii Burtonensis' (ed. H. R. Luard), in Annales monastici, I, p. 371.

5. 'L'Estoire d'Eracles' pp. 437, 445; Les Gestes de Chiprois (ed. G. Raynaud), Geneva, 1887, p. 445; 'Annales de Terre Sainte' (ed. R. Röhricht and G. Raynaud), in Archives de l'Orient Latin II, 1884, 443, 449-51.

6. Abū al-Fidā, al-Mukhtaṣar fī akhbār al-bashar, Cairo, n.d. III, p. 212.

7. Humphreys, op. cit., pp. 341, 343, 347, 362.

8. Maqrīzī, Kitāb al-Sulūk (ed. M. M. Ziada), Cairo, 1934-58, I, ii, pp. 689f.

9. I. M. Lapidus, Muslim Cities in the Later Middle Ages, Cambridge, Massachussets, 1967, pp. 13-4, 50.

10. E. Ashtor, A Social and Economic History of the Near East in the Middle Ages, 1976, p. 285.

11. G. L. Tafel and G. M. Thomas, Urkunden zur alteren Handels- und Staatsgeschichte Venedig etc (3 vols, Fontes Rerum Austriacarum, XII–XIV), Vienna, 1856-7, XIII, pp. 62-6, 256-60, 274-6, XIV, pp. 60-2.

12. Lapidus, op. cit., pp. 14f.

13. Ibn Shaddād, Muḥammad ibn Ibrāhīm, 'Alāq al-Khatīra (BM. MS Add. 23,334), passim.

14. On the importance of refugees in this period, see Ashtor, op. cit., pp. 289f; and Lapidus, op. cit., p. 84 and n. 13.

15. Ashtor, op. cit., pp. 262f.

16. Marco Polo, The Description of the World (ed. A. C. Moule and P. Pelliot), 1938, p. 100.

17. Ashtor, op. cit., pp. 244, 289; Lapidus, op. cit., p. 13 and n. 9; D. Haldane, Mamluk Painting, Warminster, 1978, p. 6.

18. J. Richard, 'La Confrèrie des Mosserins d'Acre et les marchands de Mossoul au XIIIe siècle', L'Orient Syrien XI (1966), 451-8. J. Riley-Smith, 'A Note on confraternities in the Latin Kingdom of Jerusalem', Bulletin of the Institute of Historical Research XLIV (1971), 303-8.

19. C. Cahen 'La "Chronique des Ayyoubides" d'al-Makīn b. al-'Amīd,' Bulletin des Études Orientales XV (1955), 172.

20. Ibn 'Abd al-Ẓāhir, al-Rawd al-Ẓāhir (ed. A. Khowaiter), Riyad, 1976, p.308.

21. M. Rogers, 'Evidence for Mamluk-Mongol Relations 1260-1360', in Colloque internationale sur l'histoire du Caire, Cairo, 1969, pp. 385-404.

22. Sauvaget, op. cit., p. 143.

23. D. Ayalon, 'On one of the works of Jean Sauvaget', Israel Oriental Studies I (1971), 299-302.

24. Ibn 'Abd al-Ẓāhir, al-Rawd, p. 221.; D. S. Margoliouth, Cairo, Jerusalem and Damascus, 1907, pp. 208-11.

25. R. S. Lopez, 'L'attività economica di Genova nel Marzo 1253 secondo gli atti notarili del tempo', Atti della Societa Ligure di Storia di Patria LXIV (1935), 163-270; M. Balard, 'Les Génois en Romanie entre 1204 et 1261', Mélanges d'archéologie et d'histoire LXXVIII (1966) 467-502; H. L. Misbach, 'Genoese commerce and the alleged flow of gold to the East, 1154-1253', Revue Internationale de l'Histoire de la Banque III (1970), 67-87.

26. J. Riley-Smith, What Were the Crusades? 1977, p. 45. On the continuing expenses of the French crown in Outremer, ibid., pp. 67f., and J. R. Strayer, 'The Crusades of Louis IX' in A History of the Crusades, II (ed. R. L. Wolff and H. W. Hazard), University of Wisconsin, 2nd edn., 1969, p. 508.

27. See below, p. 82 and n. 54.

28. Ibn 'Abd al-Ẓāhir, al-Rawd al-Ẓāhir, p. 171; idem, Tashrīf al-Ayyām, (ed. M. Kamil), Cairo, 1961, pp. 165-7; Maqrīzī, Sulūk, I, ii, 621; W. Heyd, Histoire du commerce du Levant au moyen âge, Leipzig, 1923, II, p. 417.

29. See below, p. 83 and n. 65.

30. L. T. Belgrano, 'Trattato del Sultano d'Egitto col Commune di Genova nel MCCLXXXX', Atti della Societa di Storia Patria di Ligure XIX (1887), 161-75; cf. Ibn 'Abd al-Ẓāhir, Tashrīf, pp. 165-8.

31. Tafel and Thomas, Urkunden, XIII, pp. 336-41, 416-8, 483-92; M. Amari, I diplomi arabi del R. Archivio Fiorentino, Florence, 1863, pp. 283, 285-7.

32. Clauses in the two Pisan agreements, the Venetian agreement of 1238 and the Genoese agreement are explicit on this.

33. Maqrīzī, Sulūk, I, ii, p. 304.

34. L. de Mas-Latrie, Traités de paix et de commerce, supplement, 1872, pp. 81f. ('Seme' must be read as 'Sham' i.e. Syria).

35. Amari, I diplomi, pp. 70f.

36. J. Riley-Smith, The Knights of St. John in Jerusalem and Cyprus c. 1050-1310, 1967, pp. 439f.

37. 'A crusader's letter from the Holy Land' in Palestine Pilgrims' Text Society V, 1890, p. 13.

38. U. and M. C. Lyons and J. Riley-Smith, Ayyubids, Mamlukes and Crusaders, Cambridge, 1971, I, p. 81, II, p. 82; Ibn 'Abd al-Ẓāhir, al-Rawd, pp. 96, 118, 187. (It is possible that some of the grain harvested in Palestine in 662/1264 was sold in Egypt, as there was a famine there in that year and a consequent monetary crisis. Ibn 'Abd al-Ẓāhir, al-Rawd, pp. 188-90 and see above, p. 85). On the grain trade between Egypt and Syria generally, see Lapidus, Muslim Cities, pp. 51f. and idem, 'The grain ecomony of Mamluk Egypt', Journal of the Economic and Social History of the Orient XII (1969), 1-15.

39. Richard, Le royaume latin, pp. 276, 278; Riley-Smith, The Feudal Nobility, p. 79.

40. Qalqashandī, Ṣubḥ al-A'shā, Cairo, 1919-20, XIV, pp. 31-9. On this treaty and those from Qalqashandī listed below, see W. Bjorkmann, Beitrage zur Geschichte der Staatskanzlei, Hamburg, 1928, pp. 172f.

41. Qalqashandī, op. cit., XIV, pp. 39-42.

42. Op. cit., XIV, 42-51.

43. Ibn al-Furāt, Tārīkh al-duwwal wa al-mulūk (ed. Q. Zurayk), Beirut, 1942, VII, pp. 205f.

44. Qalqashandī, op. cit., XIV, pp. 51-63; P. M. Holt, 'Qalāwūn's treaty with Acre in 1283', English Historical Review XCI (1976), 808-12.

45. Ibn 'Abd al-Ẓāhir, Tashrīf, pp. 103-10.

46. Ibn 'Abd al-Ẓāhir, al-Rawd, pp. 282, 378, 383.

47. Ibn al-Furāt, Tārīkh al-duwwal wa al-mulūk, VIII (ed. Q. Zurayk and N. Izz al-Din), Beirut, 1939, p. 2. On the location of al-Rūhā see G. Beyer, 'Die Kreuzfahrergebiete Akko und Galilea', Zeitschrift für deutschen Palästinavereins LXVII (1945), 239.

48. See above and Ibn 'Abd al-Ẓāhir, al-Rawd, p. 225f.

49. Ibn al-Furāt, Tārīkh, VIII, pp. 63f. ; Maqrīzī, Sulūk, I, iii, pp. 739, 741f.

50. Ibn 'Abd al-Ẓāhir, al-Rawd, pp. 122, 158; Ibn al-Furāt, Tārīkh, VII, p. 266; Ayyubids, Mamlukes and Crusaders, I, p. 216, II, pp. 99f.; Riley-Smith, Feudal Nobility, pp. 62f.

51. Lapidus, Muslim Cities, pp. 120-9; idem, 'The grain economy', passim.

52. M. Canard, 'Un traité entre Byzance et l'Egypte au XIIIe siècle', in Mélanges Gaudefroy-Demombynes, Cairo, 1935-45, pp. 210f.

53. Ibn 'Abd al-Ẓāhir, al-Rawd, pp. 256, 283-4, 299.

54. H. Rabie, The Financial System of Egypt A. H. 564-741/A.D. 1169-1341, 1972, pp. 42-4. On the variety of forms of iqṭā', see R. Irwin, 'Iqṭā' and the end of the Crusader states', in The Eastern Mediterranean Lands in the Period of the Crusades (ed. P. M. Holt), Warminster, 1977, pp. 62-73.

55. Encyclopaedia of Islam (2nd edition) s.v. 'Khalīl' (U. Haarman). The view, found elsewhere, that the merchants of Alexandria urged the Sultan Qalāwūn to remove a commercial rival by attacking the Crusader port of Lattakia in 1287 rests upon Reinaud's unsupported opinion (in Bibliothèque des Croisades, IV, pp. 560f.), as it is not to be found in Ibn 'Abd al-Ẓāhir's Tashrīf or Maqrīzī's Kitāb al-Sulūk, the two sources Reinaud seems to have been using on the capture of Lattakia.

56. Ibn 'Abd al-Ẓāhir, al-Rawd, p. 400; Heyd, Histoire du commerce, I, p. 420.

57. Heyd, op. cit., I, pp. 415f.

58. Qalqashandī, op. cit., XIV, pp. 72-8; Canard 'Un traité', pp. 210f.

59. Ibn 'Abd al-Ẓāhir, Tashrīf, pp. 92-103.

60. Op. cit., 156-164.

61. C. Desimoni, 'Actes passés en 1271, 1274 et 1279 à Aïas (Petite Arménie) et à Beyrouth par devant des notaires génois', Archives de l'Orient latin, I (1881), 434, 441f.

62. On Lattakia's status in the Ayyubid period and on the Venetian colony in Muslim Lattakia, see Tafel and Thomas, Urkunden, XIII, pp. 65, 258; Cahen, La Syrie du Nord, pp. 343f.

63. Ibn 'Abd al-Ẓāhir, al-Rawd, pp. 445f.; Ibn al-Furāt, Tārīkh, VII, p. 34.

64. Cahen, La Syrie du Nord, p. 479; J. Heers, Gênes au XVe siècle, 1961, p. 349; F. Braudel, The Mediterranean and the Mediterranean World in the Age of Philip II, I, 1972, pp. 103-8.

65. Desimoni, op. cit.; Riley-Smith, Feudal Nobility, p. 79.

66. A. Lombardo and R. Morozzo della Rocca (ed.) Nuovi documenti del commercio Veneto dei secoli XI-XIII (Monumenti Storici, (new series) VII) 1953, pp. 74f.

67. On the commercial importance of Cilician Armenia in this period see Heyd, op. cit., I, pp. 365-72, II, pp. 73-92; Desimoni, op. cit.; P. Z. Bedoukian, The Coinage of Cilician Armenia, New York, 1962, pp. 25-87.

68. C. A. Owen, 'Scandal in the Egyptian Treasury', International Journal of Middle Eastern Studies XIV (1955), 17. On the profits of the Egyptian mint generally see Rabie, The Financial System of Egypt, pp. 115-7.

69. Ibn al-Shihna, "Les Perles choisies" d'Ibn ach-Chihna (ed. J. Sauvaget), Beirut, 1933, p. 165.

70. Ibn 'Abd al-Ẓāhir, al-Rawd, p. 190.

71. Ibn al-Suqāʿī, Tālī Kitāb Wafayāt al-Aʿyān, (ed. and tr. by J. Sublet), Damascus, 1974, pp. 30f.

72. Ibn 'Abd al-Ẓāhir, al-Rawd, p. 208.

73. Op. cit., p. 467.

74. Abū Shāma, Kitāb al-Rawdatayn fi Akhbār al-Dawlatayn, Cairo, 1870, I, p. 14. Cf. N. Elisséef, Nur al-Din, un grand prince musulman au temps des croisades, Damascus, 1967, III, p. 817.

75. The literature on Egyptian coinage in this period is vast, but there is little consensus on even its most basic features. The following have been found particularly useful here: E. Ashtor, Les métaux précieux et la balance des payements du Proche-Orient à la basse époque, 1971; J. L. Bacharach, 'The dinar versus the ducat', International Journal of Middle Eastern Studies IV (1973) 77-96; J. L. Bacharach and A. A. Gordus, 'Studies in the fineness of silver coins', Journal of the Economic and Social History of the Orient, XI (1968), 298-317; P. Balog, The Coinage of the Mamluk Sultans of Egypt and Syria, New York, 1964; idem, 'The history of the dirham, from the Fatimid conquest until the collapse of the Mamluk Empire', RN^6 III (1961), 109-46; M. L. Bates, 'The coinage of the Mamluk Sultan Baybars I, additions and corrections', ANSMN XXII (1977), 161-81; A. S. Ehrenkreutz, 'Contributions to the knowledge of the fiscal administration of Egypt', Bulletin of the School of Oriental and African Studies XVI (1954), 502-14; G. Henneqin, 'Points de vue sur l'histoire monetaire de l'Egypte musulmane', Annales Islamologiques XII (1974), 1-36; idem, 'Nouveaux aperçus sur l'histoire monétaire de l'Egypte à la fin du moyen âge', ibidem, XIII (1977), 179-215.

S. Labib, Handelsgeschichte Ägyptens Spatmittelalter (1171-1517), Wiesbaden, 1965, ch. viii, 'Geld und Kredit', pp. 261-85; Rabie, op. cit.

76. On Syrian money in this period, see the works listed above; also: P. Balog, 'The Coinage of the Mamluk Sultans: additions and corrections', ANSMN XVI (1970), pp. 113-71; idem, 'Un fals d'al-Kamil Shams al-Din Sunqor, Sultan Mamelouk rebelle de Damas', RN^6 XI (1969), 296-9; A. Berman, 'The turbulent events in Syria in 658-9/1260, reflected by three hitherto unpublished dirhems', Numismatic Circular LXXXIV (1976), 314-16; Cahen, La Syrie du Nord, pp. 469-71.

77. C. Cahen, 'Notes sur l'histoire des croisades et de l'Orient latin. III. Orient latin et commerce du Levant', Bulletin de la Faculté des Lettres de l'Université de Strasbourg XXIX (1951), 337.

78. Balog, 'A history of the dirham', p. 144.

79. Ibn 'Abd al-Ẓāhir, al-Rawd, p. 227.

80. On the dinar-dirham exchange rate, see: Ashtor, Les metaux precieux, p. 37; A.S. Ehrenkreutz, 'The standard of fineness of gold coins circulating in Egypt at the time of the Crusades', Journal of the American Oriental Society LXXIV (1954), 163; idem, 'Contributions to the knowledge', pp. 504f; S. D. Goitein, 'The exchange rate of gold and silver moneys in Fatimid and Ayyubid times: a preliminary study of the relevant Geniza material', Journal of the Social and Economic History of the Orient VIII (1965), 1-46.

81. Abū Shāma, Tarājim Rijāl al-Qarnein (ed. Kauthari), Cairo, 1947, p. 168. Cf. Cahen, La Syrie du Nord, p. 470n.; A. M. Watson, 'Back to gold—and silver', Economic History Review^2 XX (1967), 27.

82. M. L. Bates, 'Thirteenth century crusader imitations of Ayyubid silver coinage: a preliminary survey' in Near Eastern Numismatics, Iconography, Epigraphy and History. Studies in Honor of George C. Miles (ed. D. Koumijyan), Beirut, 1974, pp. 393-409, at p. 406.

83. Humphreys, From Saladin to the Mongols, p. 249.

84. Ṣālih ibn Yahyā, Tārīh Bayrūt, Beirut, 1969, pp. 108f.

85. R. S. Lopez, 'Back to gold, 1252', Economic History Review^2 XX (1956-7), 219-40; A. M. Watson, 'Back to gold—and silver', Economic History Review^2, XX (1967), 1-34. See also H. L. Misbach,'Genoese commerce and the alleged flow of gold to the East, 1154-1253', Revue Internationale de l'Histoire de la Banque III (1970), 67-87.

86. Tafel and Thomas, Urkunden, XIII, 62-6, 336-41, XIV, 483-92.

87. Belgrano, op. cit. (note 30); see also L. Blancard, Essaie sur les monnaies de Charles Ier, 1868, pp. 489f., 541f.

88. Bedoukian, op. cit., pp. 27f, 45; H. Lavoix, Monnaies à legendes Arabes frappées en Syrie par les croisés, 1887, pp. 59f.

89. On transfers of bullion and coins from the West, see in particular Watson, op. cit., pp. 7-9.

90. The literature on these imitations is extensive. The following have been used here: P. Balog and J. Yvon, 'Monnaies à legendes Arabes de l'Orient Latin', RN^6 I (1958), 133-68; Bates, 'Thirteenth century crusader imitations of Ayyubid silver coinage', pp. 393-409; P. Grierson, 'A rare crusader bezant with the Christus Vincit legend', ANSMN VI (1954), 169-78; Lavoix, op. cit.; Prawer, op. cit., pp. 385-7; G. Schlumberger, Numismatique de l'Orient Latin, 1887, pp. 130-43.

91. Lopez, 'Back to gold'. pp. 227f.

92. L. Y. A. Rahmani, 'A fourteenth century hoard from Tiberias' Israel Numismatic Journal II (1964), 47-55; J. Yvon, 'Monnaies et sceaux de l'Orient Latin', RN^6 VIII (1966), at p. 91.

93. Balog, 'A history of the dirham', p. 149.

94. Ibn al-Suqā'ī, loc. cit.

95. For views on the Ṣūrī dinar, see Ehrenkreutz, 'The standard of fineness', p. 163n.; Cahen, La Syrie du Nord, pp. 469f.; Balog and Yvon, 'Monnaies à legendes Arabes', p. 136n; Misbach, 'Genoese commerce', pp. 75f.

96. Qazwīnī, Athār al-Bilād, Baghdad, 1960, p. 217.

97. G. Le Strange, Palestine under the Moslems, Beirut, 1965, pp. 1f.

98. Ibn Khallikān, Biographical Dictionary (tr. and ed. M. de Slane), Paris, 1843-71, III, p. 456.

99. Owen, 'Scandal in the Egyptian Treasury', p. 76. Ehrenkreutz's opinion ('The Standard of fineness', p. 163 and n.) that the early thirteenth-century treatise on the mint by Ibn Ba'ra described Ṣūrī dinars sold to the Egyptian mint as being over 90% fine appears to be based on a mis-reading of 'Ṣūrī' for 'Yaqūbī'. I am grateful to Mr. M. L. Bates for drawing my attention to this. I have not found it possible to consult A. Fahmi's edition of Ibn Ba'ra's Kitāb Kashf al-Asrār, Cairo, 1966, on this point.

100. Al-Shayzārī, 'Abd al-Raḥmān ibn Naṣr, Kitāb Nihayāt al-Rutba fī Ṭalab al-Hisba (ed. al-Arīnī), Cairo, 1946, pp. 74f. On al-Shayzārī see Encyclopaedia of Islam (2nd ed.) s.v. 'Ḥisba' (C. Cahen and M. Talbi).

101. Ibn al-Athīr, al-Kāmil fī al-Tārīkh Leiden, 1851-76, XI, p. 184.

102. Ibn al-Athīr, op. cit., XI, p. 186, XII, p. 23; Bahā al-Dīn ibn Shaddād, 'Ancedotes et Beaux traits de la Vie du Sultan Youssof' RHC Or. III, 195f.

103. Ṣāliḥ ibn Yahya, Tārīh Bayrūt, p. 156.

104. Qalqashandī, op. cit., XIV, pp. 31-9.

105. Ibn 'Abd al-Ẓāhir, al-Rawd, pp. 383, 447.

106. C. Desimoni, 'Actes passés', pp. 457, 491; RRH nos. 1355, 1396, 1398.

107. Qalqashandī, op. cit, XIV, p. 36; Ibn 'Abd al-Ẓāhir, al-Rawd, p. 274.

108. Ibn 'Abd al-Ẓāhir, al-Rawd, p. 282; Shafī b. 'Alī, Ḥusn al-Manāqib (ed. A. Khowaiter), Riyad, 1976, p. 121.

109. Ibn 'Abd al-Ẓāhir, Tashrīf, p. 108.

110. Desimoni, op. cit. See also RRH, index s.v. 'bisantius sarrazenatus'.

111. Al-Shayzarī, Kitāb Nihayāt al-Rutba, pp. 75f.

112. For (conflicting) views on the qirṭās, see Elisséeff, Nur al-Din, III, pp. 817, 874.; E. Ashtor, 'Le cout de la vie dans la Syrie mediévale', Arabica VIII (1961), 63f., 69.

113. On this episode see also Cahen, La Syrie du Nord, p. 471 and n.; Ashtor, Les métaux précieux, p. 36.

114. Abū Shāma, Mudhayl 'alā al-Rawdatayn, MS. B. M., Or. 1539, f. 123b; idem in RHC Or., V, p. 203; idem, Tarājim, p. 211.

115. Ayyubids, Mamlukes and Crusaders, I, p. 51 and n., p. 223, II, p. 42 and n., p. 192.

116. Maqrīzī, Sulūk, I, ii, pp. 434, 442, 446.

117. Ibn al-Suqā'ī, Tālī, p. 66.

118. al-Yunīnī, Dhayl al-Mir'āt al-Zamān, Hyderabad, 1955, I, p. 440, II, p. 93.

119. Berman, op. cit.

120. Bacharach, 'The dinar versus the ducat', passim; W. Popper, Egypt and Syria under the Circassian Sultans, Berkeley and Los Angeles, 1957, II, p. 47.

121. See above page 75 and 'Chronique des Ayyoubides', p. 176; Maqrīzī, Sulūk, I, ii, p. 443.

122. Bates, 'The coinage of the Mamluk Sultan Baybars', pp. 167, 171.

123. A. L. Udovitch reviewing Balog's Coinage of the Mamluk Sultans, in Journal of the American Oriental Society XC (1970), 290.

THE AMALRICUS COINS OF THE KINGDOM OF JERUSALEM

Roberto Pesant

The Amalricus coins of Jerusalem, that Schlumberger[1] illustrated as pl. III, 19 and 20 (see Fig. 1), may be briefly described as follows:

 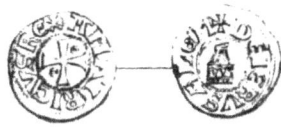

On the obverse, the legend AMALRICVS REX around a cross pattée; generally with a bead or annulet or a combination of both in the first and fourth quarters of the cross. At times there are either one, two, or even three annulets or beads at the start of the legend, but often there are none. The cross is within a circle, either beaded or plain. On the reverse there is a small crosslet that starts the legend DE IERVSALEM around the portrayal of the church of the Holy Sepulchre within a circle; again either beaded or plain.

These coins are of two denominations, namely the denier and its half, the obole. The deniers, which are fairly numerous, can be divided into groups on the basis of their quality. There are, first, those larger coins, about 17 to 18 mm, heavier (average 0.8 to 0.95 g), perhaps of better alloy, and from dies in good condition which indicate, because of these characteristics, that they are of the earliest minting. Then one finds others which, though lighter (0.6 to 0.78 g) and of smaller size, about 16 to 17 mm, are in just as good a condition as the larger and heavier ones. They could also be considered to be early issues; probably either concurrent with or shortly after the larger ones. Lastly the majority of the coins, which have about the same diameter as the smaller ones just mentioned, 16 to 17 mm, are not only lighter (0.45 to 0.5 g) but are in such a woeful condition as to have led many to think that they belonged to an entirely different series. These are possibly the later products of the mint.

It is therefore not impossible to think that a sequence could perhaps be established based upon the gradual decline and impoverishment of the Latin Kingdom as shown by the deteriorating dies and shoddy workmanship of the planchets.

The oboles, which are far more scarce than either kind of denier, are nearly always found in better condition and appearance, but even when slightly worn their weights are closely similar, at about 0.4 g.

The most interesting thing about these coins, and one which has not excited comment among the various scholars who have written about them, is the remarkably successful design in portraying the Holy Sepulchre. This imposing and difficult building has been rendered within a circled area of about 8 mm (5 mm for the oboles), by a few simple lines. Quite apart from the artistic achievement, this may be another contributing factor for the attribution of the coins.

Their attribution has, as is often the case with other series, been a subject of controversy among numismatists. The Amalricus coins have been given either to king Amaury (1163-74), or to another king with a slightly different name, Aimery (1197-1205), to whom earlier students mistakenly referred as Amaury II—or to both of them, notwithstanding the difference in names and a twenty-year gap during which four other rulers and a usurper reigned.

Dr. Metcalf, who knows of my intense interest as an architect on the subject of the Holy Sepulchre, provided me, à propos of this paper, with the following historical account. I include it here not only for its own merits but also because it adds interest to the artistic portrait of this edifice on the coins of Amaury.

'The architectural features represented on the Amalricus coinage are usually described simply as the Holy Sepulchre, or the church of the Holy Sepulchre. The conical roof with its open 'eye' presents no problems, and the colonnade has apparently been assumed to be the circle of columns within the rotunda. Thus we are offered a schematic representation, combining an inside and an outside view. This interpretation is not without its problems, and an explanation of them provides an excuse to say something about the architectural history of this endlessly fascinating building.

'The rotunda of the church of the Resurrection, the Anastasis, was roofed (until its great beams were destroyed in the fire of 1808) by an incomplete dome, open to the heavens. Fulcher of Chartres describes it in these words: 'There is, further, a handsome basilica above the tomb of our Lord, with a dome. The summit of this dome is skilfully made in such a way that it lacks a covering. The aperture being open to the splendour of the sun, the basilica always enjoys the light' ('Inest insuper basilica decens supra dominicum Sepulchrum rotunditate facta; cuius rotunditatis summitas ita artificiose tegmine caret, ut foramine illo solis splendori patulo, clara semper habeatur').[2] Through the opening, several metres in diameter, sunlight was admitted to the church; and the rain, too, could fall on the edicule of the tomb directly beneath, and on the worshippers. Through the same opening, the Holy Fire could descend from heaven to light the lamps during the Easter vigil. This open roof was a unique and highly distinctive architectural feature. It dated, apparently, from at least as early as the ninth century, following earthquake damage, when no-one, perhaps, was too sure of their ability to repair or rebuild the very large dome of the original late Roman design (which may well also have had an oculus). The diameter of the rotunda was some 36 metres, and the diameter of the circle of columns was about 24 metres. If the roof sprang from the inner circle, the trunks of pines and cypresses which the patriarch Thomas I (807-20) fetched from Cyprus to use as beams must have been 13 to 16 metres (42 to 52 feet) long. The roof had to be renewed after the fire of 966, and again, of course, after al-Hakim's destruction of the church in 1009. William of Tyre tells us that the rebuilding of the church of the Resurrection as it was in his day had been completed under Constantine Monomachus in 1048. Indeed, Constantine's roof apparently survived until 1719, by which time the great beams were thoroughly rotten, and it was a marvel that the lead-covered roof held up. The roof and tambour were replaced strictly and exactly as they had been before, and 132 beams of Belgian pine were used for the purpose.[3]

'The Latin kings from a very early date placed the conical roof on their seals, as part of an imaginary skyline symbolizing the Holy City. The upper part of the church is seen rising above the wall to one side, and similarly the dome of the Temple of the Lord to the other side, with the citadel, the Tower of David, between.

'The Typicon of the Church of Jerusalem records the orthodox rites of Holy Week, which were taken over by the Latins. On Easter Eve, the lamps were cleaned and placed in the tomb. All the other lamps in the church were then put out, and the patriarch closed and locked the edicule. During the vigil that night, after prolonged chanting of Kyrie Eleison in the darkness, the lamps hanging in the tomb were seen to be miraculously lit (by an angel, or by celestial fire), and the patriarch or some other bishop, after prostrating himself, crept along the low passage into the tomb to take a light from the lamps, and brought it out to the archdeacon, who gave it to spread from one to another, until all the lamps in the church were relit. The Muslims viewed this ancient ceremony with some scepticism. Mas'udi, writing in A.D. 943, says that for the Christians, the fire descends from Heaven and they light the lamps from it; in reality the fire is produced by a cunning trick of which they jealously guard the secret.

'Below the conical roof, on Amaury's coins (but not on any of the royal seals) there seems to be depicted an arched colonnade <u>blocked by a low wall</u>. The same low wall, if that is what it is, can be seen again on the larger and carefully executed drachmas. What is it intended to represent? It has been assumed to be the interior of the rotunda, but if it were, the designer would surely have included the most important element of the architectural whole, namely the tomb edicule itself—as was done on various seals of religious communities. It is true that a circle of columns separated the deambulatory of the rotunda from the central space, and there was a second range of columns above. But these could not be seen from the outside of the building, for the outer wall was solid (the fourth-century work survives to the present day to a height of 11 metres).[4] We have no reason to suppose that there was ever a clerestory of any kind. It is doubtful whether such an open-work structure could have supported the roof; and in any case the tambour of 1719 followed very exactly the work that was demolished at that time.

'Moreover, William of Tyre speaks about the church being dark, which would seem unlikely if the arcading shown on the coins were a clerestory. 'The Church of the Resurrection', he says, 'is in the form of a rotunda. Because it is situated on the slope of a hill, so that the slope of the ground is almost equal to the height of the walls, the interior is dark. The roof is made of long beams raised into the air, skilfully assembled in the form of a crown, of which the central part, open to the sky, lets into the church the necessary light.' (S. Resurrectionis ecclesia, forma quidem rotunda: quae, quoniam in declivo praedicti montis sita est, ita ut clivus eidem eminens et contiguus Ecclesiae pene superet altitudinem, et eam reddit obscuram, tectum habet, erectis in sublime trabibus, et miro artificio in modum coronae contextis, apertum et perpetuo patens, unde lumen ecclesiae infunditur necessarium...').[5]

'One of the seals which depicts the edicule of the tomb[6] shows a cross-section cut through the rotunda, and the tambour on which the roof rests is there shown as a row of shallow arched columns, which might seem to be windows. But they correspond with the 14 niches of the 1719 reconstruction, which were not carried through to the outside of the wall. This can be seen in the well-known drawing published by Le Bruyn.

'The royal seals are of little value as evidence, as the buildings below the two distinctive roofs are almost always shown alike, to make a symmetrical design.

'A manuscript in the Vatican Library[7] contains a drawing of the basilica which offers the essential clue. All the main elements of the building complex are shown: the rotunda—with the dove (representing the Holy Spirit) descending through the open roof; the much-admired belfry; the Crusaders' new church; the beautiful double doorway with its carved lintels; the windows above the doorway, quite accurately drawn; and the steps leading up to the Golgotha chapel (Fig. 2). The colonnade seems to be detached from the roof of the rotunda, and to stand outside it. It would seem, therefore, to have been some kind of parapet, on the circle of the principal columns beneath. The outer roof then spanned the deambulatory.

Fig. 2

'De Vogüé has pointed to a change in the formulas used in charters dealing with the church, between 1167 and 1169, and he suggests that the church of the Resurrection and the crusaders' new choir church were until then legally separate although physically connected, but were at that date made into a single legal entity (the basilica of the Holy Sepulchre). He supports this suggestion further by arguing that the high altar was moved in 1167.[8] These changes may help to explain why the Holy Sepulchre was chosen as a coin type by Amaury. They also suggest that the reform of the coinage may have occurred after the new arrangements were made for the church, i.e. not earlier than 1167. Changes in coin types in the twelfth century rarely coincided with the accession of a new ruler, and it need not surprise us if Amaury continued to strike Baldvinus deniers for the first four years or more of his reign'.

The object of this paper is to reinforce the attribution of the coins to King Amaury while acknowledging that perhaps they continued to be struck for a few of his successors, thus becoming an 'immobilized type' after Amaury's death. For this purpose some new evidence will be introduced as well as original thoughts and a re-examination of information already available.

But first, a short review to serve as background to some of the ideas expressed here. It is curious that up to the present no coinage is known to have been struck by and for the Latin Kingdom during its first forty years of existence and the reigns of its first three kings. It supposedly had to make do with all the various sorts of contemporary monies brought in by barons, soldiers, merchants, pilgrims, and sundry others, as well as those from former rulers and from the warring states that surrounded it.

I am, of course, ignoring those coins of gold and silver imitative of the Islamic states issued by the kingdom because the dates when they were produced are still controversial, and even if struck during the first forty years, they may have been destined as a 'coin of exchange'; that is, for interchange and trade with the neighbouring countries and not for internal use.

One is not surprised that no coins have been attributed to the first ruler of Jerusalem, Godfrey of Bouillon (1099-1100), but with the next two kings, Baldwin I (1100-18) and Baldwin II (1118-31), the absence of coinage in their names becomes somewhat problematical. Both kings had previously struck large coppers in their own names, in the manner of contemporary Byzantine folles, for their remote barony of Edessa. It used to be assumed that the series of deniers and oboles with the legend BALDVINVS REX and the portrayal of the Tower of David could be attributed to either or both of them. But at the present, and mainly due to M. Yvon's scholarly work,[9] it has become generally accepted that this series should be attributed solely to a later king of the same name, Baldwin III (1143-63).

Between Baldwin II and Baldwin III, there is another king, Fulk (1131-43), who breaks the continuity of the same-named monarchs, and the fact that no coinage can be attributed to him helps maintain the idea of the attribution of the Baldvinus coinage solely to Baldwin III. For among other things, it is hard to imagine this able and forceful king, who ruled over a kingdom appreciably stronger and more stable than it had been under his two predecessors, would have forgone the privilege of striking coins in his own name throughout the twelve years of his reign.

The opinions regarding the attribution of the Amalricus coinage may be summarized as follows. De Saulcy,[10] de Mas Latrie,[11] and de Vogüé [12] argue for both Amaury and Aimery; Miss Cox[13] for Aimery, but with the distinction of assigning one kind of denier to the kingdom of Cyprus and the other kind to the kingdom of Jerusalem; finally, Duplessy and Metcalf[14] attribute the coins to Amaury and subsequent kings as an immobilized type.

There have been two basic reasons for attributing the Amalricus coinage to King Aimery: firstly, the supposed evidence of the various hoards in which these coins have been found; and secondly, as already mentioned, their division into two broad groups based on their differing appearance. This distinction is so pronounced that Schlumberger[15] wondered whether the coins of inferior workmanship were no more than forgeries. His suggestion has not met with approval.

Regarding the evidence of the hoards, this can be questioned quite forcefully. The following table will serve to illustrate my point.

Kings and their reigns		Hoards, with suggested burial dates	
Amaury	1163-74	Samos	1170 x 1185
Baldwin IV	1174-85	Châtellerault	1221 x 1225
Baldwin V	1185-6	Tripoli	ca. 1222
Guy of Lusignan	1186-92	Kessab	ca. 1225
Conrad of Montferrat (in competition)	1190-2	Ras Shamra	in the 1220s
Henry of Champagne	1192-7	Djebal	1230 x 1235
Aimery	1197-1205		

It reveals two things:

1. That only in the case of the Samos hoard, where two Amalricus coins were found, is there a definite attribution to Amaury.

2. That the dates of burial for all the other hoards are late enough for an attribution to Aimery; but still allow us to think of Amaury as well. A seventy-year circulation 'life' was not extraordinary during the medieval period. This would also concur with the coinage of Amaury becoming an immobilized type.

The coins with the legend Baldvinus have been, as already mentioned, pretty well accepted as belonging exclusively to Baldwin III, whose reign (1143-63) immediately preceded that of his brother Amaury. To the evidence presented by Yvon[16] there can now be added the important work by Brady[17] on gold Jerusalemite fragments. Dr. Brady, although discussing entirely different coinages from those of this paper, does show the close affinity in the space of time between the coins of the two kings.

There is one more argument that, to me, is almost conclusive for the attribution of at least some of the coins to Amaury, and which can be mentioned before we proceed to discuss the condition of the coins. Longuet,[18] in his study of the Kessab hoard, although respecting Schlumberger's attribution to both Amaury and Aimery (to whom he mistakenly refers as Amaury II), had this to say:

'Une raison péremptoire pour que les deniers lourds, le prototype, n'appartiennent pas à Amaury II, vient de m'être donnée par le comte Chandon de Briailles: Amaury II ne s'est jamais appelé Amaury, mais bien plutôt Aimery ...l'erreur vient d'historiens postérieurs et, si le type des deniers en question avait été conçu du temps d'Aimery, que nous appelons à tort Amaury II, la légende n'eût pas été AMALRICVS mais, comme sur les textes contemporains, AIMERICVS.'

At the end of his analysis, Longuet makes this odd comment:

'Et: nous arrivons à constater ce fait étrange qu'Amaury II ou plus exactement Aimery, prince qui joua une rôle de premier plan dans l'histoire du royaume de Jérusalem et dans celle du royaume de Chypre, ne nous a laissé, ni à Jérusalem ni à Chypre, de monnaies à son nom, puisqu'elles sont toutes au nom d'Amaury Ier.'

Now, with reference to that group of coins which are the most numerous and so wretched in appearance, I believe that these coins were made on shoddy planchets with overworked dies which were used and reused to a condition of almost total dilapidation. This situation could most likely be the result of various factors. The kingdom of Jerusalem was, in comparison with other states, a poor country beset by almost continuous warfare with its neighbours and internal quarrels among it ruling class. Even though it is recognized that during Amaury's reign it reached its height of prosperity, the resources available to the mint must have been meagre at best and the production of coins on a relatively modest scale.

Dr. Metcalf[19] has estimated for the Baldvinus coinage a total amount of from 5 to 8 million deniers of the so-called 'rough' style and from $5\frac{1}{2}$ to $8\frac{1}{2}$ million deniers and about half a million oboles of the 'neat' type. These figures are arrived at by a formula that estimates the total number of dies based on die duplication in a supposedly random sample, and then conjectures the average output per die as between 10,000 and 15,000 coins.

As it has not been possible to arrive at a meaningful number of die links in the slightly over two hundred Amalricus coins that I have examined, due to their poor condition, no reasonably acceptable figure could be given at this time of the total production of the series.

One must consider, however, the insatiable demands on the mint by the king himself. Grousset[20] described a characteristic of Amaury which might have some bearing on the forced production of the mint thus: 'The Archbishop of Tyre, who nevertheless thought kindly of him, depicts him as greedy for money and not very scrupulous as to how he got it, even at the cost of church property. But, as he told the prelate himself, this harsh taxation had no purpose other than the defence of the realm. The proof of this is that no-one spent more lavishly when the country's interest was at stake.'

With Amaury's death at the age of 39, the kingdom lost a competent and untiring leader and it soon fell into discord and quarrelling among the barons, with only a sick child of 13, his heir, Baldwin IV (1174-85), around whom the struggle for power began. This tragic figure, a victim of leprosy, had to devote practically his entire reign to warding off the powerful thrusts of so determined a foe as Saladin. It is not hard to imagine the mint continuing to

strike the Amalricus coins, instead of issuing a new series, amid all the
turmoil and dissentions. The same, if not a worse, situation must have ensued
when Baldwin IV was succeeded by his nephew, Baldwin V (1185-6), whose
short reign under a regency was a time of even greater intrigue and turmoil.

Even more important was the shattering blow to the kingdom of the loss
of its capital, Jerusalem, in 1187. There are no records to ascertain where
the mint had been located, but with the loss of the city one must assume that
the Amalricus coins were struck elsewhere if their production continued—
perhaps, for example, in Acre. The dies may have been salvaged, and taken
to a new location, where their production was renewed with ever more dilapidated dies and shoddy planchets.

The condition of the coins has, I think, been misunderstood. It has been
considered by some that the reduced size of the dilapidated deniers was mainly
due to their having been pared and clipped by other parties for the purpose
of thievery. Longuet[21] has remarked that this reduced size was due to the
reduction of the planchet by the mint, prior to striking, if only because most
of the coins are found in this condition. Clipping could not have been so consistently prevalent. Furthermore the metallic alloy appears to be so poor
that one would not have imagined that it would have been profitable for anyone
to steal it.

The coins themselves offer proof that the irregular and seemingly clipped
planchets were reduced in size prior to striking. The forces created by the
hammer blows caused radial splits in many instances. Most of these splits
show a wedge-shaped opening which grows wider as it approaches the rim of
the coin. On the rim, the shoulders of the wedge are generally curved and
this would not be so if the coins had been clipped or sheared after striking.

There is another oddity which, I think, helps to dispel the idea that the
vast majority of the coins were clipped. On many of the coins, the central
design (the cross, or the Holy Sepulchre), which is enclosed within a circle,
is consistently off-centre in the same manner—as if the planchets "nestled"
in the same way in the striking process.

There is yet another piece of evidence which I think is being presented
here for the first time, and which is important in that it not only closely
relates the two series (the Baldvinus and the Amalricus series), but also,
naturally, reinforces the attribution of the Amalricus series to Amaury. In
his recent paper on the Baldvinus coinage, Dr. Metcalf mentions the curious
effect on the design caused by a second concentric 'wire' border upon which
the letters of the legend rest. This produces a sort of trench between the
two concentric circles. This design is only found on some of the Baldvinus
deniers that have been denominated as 'neat' by Dr. Metcalf to differentiate
them from the rough variety. This same curious effect of two concentric
circles with the letters of the legend resting on the outer circle also occurs
on some of the deniers and oboles of the Amalricus series. In spite of
differences in legends and designs, there is a marked affinity between the
two types of coins, which indicates that either the dies for both types were
cut by the same hand or that one type was closely copied from the other. I
believe that it is more reasonable to assume that this affinity is more in the
nature of a personal 'nuance' of the die sinker who presumably cut the dies

for both coinages, rather than the result of strict copywork. This double 'wire' and trench effect serves still another purpose in trying to establish some sort of sequence within the Amalricus series, as follows: coins with this feature are found among both groups, manely the heavy, neat, large kind of deniers, and also the smaller, dilapidated, and lighter ones, and on the oboles too, and it indicates that the coins do not belong to two separate periods of two separate kings, but rather that they form only one series, at most, a long one continued for the kings after Amaury. It also to some extent demonstrates that the same dies were used over and over again almost to the point of disintegration, which, together with the parallel shoddiness in the production of the planchets, causes the one group to appear altogether different from the other.

I have already mentioned the extraordinary artistic achievement in the portrayal of the Holy Sepulchre. Considering the simple and limited tools and punches of that age, as explained by Fox,[22] it must have been the work of a highly gifted die-maker.

Admittedly there are slight variations in the building, such as slight differences in the proportions of the various components, additions of beads to the columns to express the capitals and the presence in some cases of beads inside the arching as well.

But these are insignificant details which do not detract from the thought that the design and its execution were the work of one person, and that the various dies were produced under the guidance of the same person. Furthermore, if one considers that the mint must have been on the modest side in accordance with the limited resources of the Latin Kingdom, then the idea that only a limited personnel made dies under one master becomes more plausible.

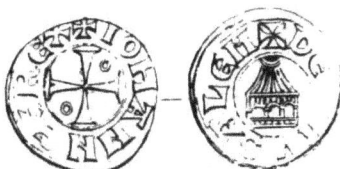 

Fig. 3

I am aware that the design of the Holy Sepulchre was repeated about 50 years later on the large silver coin of another king, John of Brienne (1210-25), as also on the equally rare anonymous drachm of Acre (see Fig. 3, taken from Schlumberger, pl. III, 30 and pl. XX, 3). On these extremely rare coins, the Holy Sepulchre seems to be but a close copy of the original design of the Amalricus coinage.

The fact that the obverse dies have various styles of crosses, such as short fat ones, others with large serifs, and still others with flared arms; or that the beads and annulets in the quarters of the cross vary in combinations, does not detract from the uniformly stylish rendering of the Holy Sepulchre because, except for the varying legends, the use of the cross for the obverse design was an extremely common practice in medieval times.

Prior to the portrayal of the Holy Sepulchre in the Amalricus series, one finds this same building, together with those other two which were such important landmarks for the kingdom, the Tower of David and the Temple of the Lord, displayed on the seals of the earlier kings, but the representation of the Holy Sepulchre on these seals is both clumsily executed and quite different from the one on the coins. Comparing the two conceptual representations of the same building, it is obvious that the one on the coins, which originated later, was neither inspired by nor copied from the earlier version on the seals. This, I believe, also serves to mark the beginning of the series.

Unlike some other series of coins where variations in style, features and workmanship may help to establish a sequence, the Amalricus series does not appear to have, or display, a progressive, perhaps gradual, change in the basic design.

There are, of course, variations in some of the letters of the legends as well as in the stops and in the quarters of the cross, but these are not, I feel, sufficient justification to attempt a classification for a sequence of issues. Miss Cox,[23] in her study of the Tripoli hoard, did separate them into classes, but I think that the main achievement was a mere pictorial separation of the differences into varieties.

A summary of the main points set forth here may be made as follows:

1. The Amalricus coins should be attributed to Amaury (1163-74), and considered as an immobilized type for some of his successors.

2. The series may have commenced shortly after Amaury's accession, ca. 1165 (although we have no way of knowing how promptly the new type was introduced), and may have continued during the reigns of Baldwin IV (1174-85) and Baldwin V (1185-6).

3. The fall of Jerusalem in 1187 may have caused the discontinuation of this series.

DISCUSSION

Mr. Pesant's paper was followed by a lively discussion. Some of the comments that were offered are taken up in the notes printed below.

Capt. Sabine. There is a clear distinction between the heavy fine-style Amalricus coins and the presumably later poor quality specimens. So far I have come across only four distinct varieties of the heavy coinage, and they can be distinguished only by the commencement of the obverse legend. One variety has no stop between the words REX and AMALRICVS, another has a single annulet stop, the third has two annulets, and the fourth has three annulets vertically disposed. The overall style and the lettering are very similar on all four types, although there is some variation in the barring of the letters. Again all four types seem to have the inner wire border although this feature is sometimes difficult to see. The second variety seems to be the most plentiful.

A further type has been noted which is of quite good fabric, although not so good as the finest style. On this type the lettering is not so broad and flat, and sometimes has a somewhat 'spidery' appearance. The Holy Sepulchre has a lower conical top with a narrow apex but often with rather broad crescents surmounting the building (compare Fig. 4b with 4a). This gives the edifice a rather more squat appearance than on the previous four varieties where the rotunda is shown fairly tall and narrow. It seems that this fifth type might be a step in the degeneration of the <u>Amalricus</u> deniers between the fine-style coins and the very poor specimens. The cross-bars on the lettering of the fifth type are much more variable, many letters being double-barred.

Fig. 4, a. Fine-style coinage, first four types.
b. Fifth type, heavy coinage. c. Degenerate type.

The poor-quality coins show many differences from those previously mentioned—a fact also noted by Miss Cox (<u>NNM</u> LIX 1933, pp. 51f.). The representation of the Holy Sepulchre is much degenerated, the facade often shown as a mere simple crossing of lines, like a grill (see Fig. 4c), rather than the carefully-cut arches of the fine-style coins. The conical top of the building is often very broad at the top on the poor coins, and sometimes is not even conical in shape at all having the outer lines cut vertically. The lettering is often very carelessly formed, and the whole aspect of these degenerate coins is very far removed from the fine-style series, not only in the careless striking but more significantly in the actual dies themselves. Many varieties occur in the degenerate series, with in some cases pellets instead of annulets, and different combinations of pellets/annulets in the quarters of the obverse cross; sometimes these quarters are left plain, and the actual form of the cross is often very different from that of the fine-style. These varieties simply do not seem to occur on the fine-style coins, and the dies for the degenerate coinage must surely belong exclusively to that series, and cannot be the earlier dies of neat workmanship used to destruction.

Mr. Pesant tells us that some of the deniers have wire borders instead of the beaded type—I am quite sure that this feature does not occur on the fine-style coinage. If the wire borders are deliberate, rather than the result of bad striking and/or worn dies or coins, then this to me suggests that such coins may be very much later than we are here led to believe, perhaps as late as <u>c</u>. 1215 (see my remarks concerning the use of wire borders, in my own paper, above, pp. 49-50). John of Brienne is known to have used the Holy Sepulchre design on his drachmas, and these must have been produced after 1210. I think great caution is needed before we rule out the attribution of some at least of the degenerate deniers to the early thirteenth century.

Dr. Metcalf: The Amalricus deniers and oboles were a reform coinage, replacing those in the name of Baldwin. They circulated in the Latin Kingdom for fifty years or more, and we have a certain amount of numismatic evidence from the beginning and from the end of that fifty-year period, but singularly little from a long stretch in the middle.

We do not know that the coinage reform took place promptly after the accession of Amaury in 1163, for changes of type in the twelfth century were often delayed or deferred. But it is certain that the introduction of the Amalricus issue antedates the Samos hoard, in which there were five specimens, along with one of Baldwin. Difficult as the Samos hoard is to date precisely, it seems to fall in the period 1170-85. If a particular explanation were sought for its concealment, it might be found in the events of the year 1182, when the Franks living in Constantinople rose in revolt and launched destructive raids widely throughout the Aegean area. But whatever its exact date, the hoard proves that the Amalricus coinage originated with Amaury, not Aimery, and it must, therefore, have begun before Amaury's death in 1174.

The Tripoli and Kessab hoards, concealed in the 1220s, show that Amalricus deniers remained in use even after John of Brienne had struck large quantities of deniers on an improved weight-standard at Damietta (from 1219 onwards). The Jerusalem hoard ostensibly shows the same, as it contained 3 coins of Baldwin, 74 of Amaury, and one of John, but its integrity is very questionable. In the Tripoli hoard, there were one Baldvinus denier, 652 of the Amalricus type, and 206 of John. At Kessab similarly, there were 263 Amalricus coins and 82 of John.

Thus the Amalricus coins were struck before 1174, and perhaps even as early as 1163, and similar coins, although smaller and lighter, were still in circulation in the 1220s. Were these the same coins, by now old and clipped?—or different coins struck on smaller and lighter flans?—and if different, were they essentially from dies cut before 1187, as Pesant has argued, or were they still being struck in the thirteenth century, as Sabine has suggested? Pesant's idea about the prolonged use of the dies is difficult to reconcile with what we know about dies in medieval England: their working life was normally measured in weeks rather than months.

What happened to the currency between the 1180s and the 1220s? We have a gap of no less than 40 years in the hoard evidence. Until some new hoards come to light to help us, our reconstruction of monetary history during those 40 years is bound to rest on extrapolation. Numismatists would, I think, be very surprised indeed if such future discoveries revealed that Baldwin IV and V struck coins in their own names, but one cannot categorically rule that possibility out from the evidence of the Samos hoard, in which the eastern element consisted of so few coins. Nevertheless it is reasonable to assume that the first introduction of the Amalricus deniers was accompanied by the recall and re-minting of the Baldvinus coinage. Thereafter, the new type remained current, although there were intervening issues on a small scale by Guy of Lusignan and Henry of Champagne (bearing their names). But these were of a different monetary denomination: they were copper oboles or pougeois.

Partly no doubt for reasons of commercial familiarity and confidence, the type of the deniers was unchanging; but the currency was not. It should not surprise us that by the 1220s the good, heavy coins had either disappeared from circulation or, if a few survived, had been heavily clipped. By the 1220s the bulk of the currency consisted of poorer, lighter coins, at least some of which (as Pesant has shown) were actually struck to a lower weight-standard.

It would be a legitimate ambition of numismatic research (given the hoard evidence, without which little progress can be made) to define and date the transition more precisely. The gradual disappearance of the early coins would be a perfectly normal phenomenon in any series that lasted for 40 or 50 years. In English experience, for example, late Short-cross hoards, or late Edwardian hoards, would in each case contain relatively few of the earliest classes or varieties of the series. The currency dwindled away in use, at a rate which may typically have been around 2% per annum—thus 20% in a single decade. And this was without the powerful incentive to cull provided by a falling intrinsic value.

With the _Amalricus_ deniers there is, of course, the further complication of the collapse of the Latin Kingdom in 1187. We do not know how many mints originally struck the coins: perhaps only one, but this is the merest subjective impression. In that case, it would surely have been at Acre, not Jerusalem. The heaviest demand for minting was undoubtedly at the ports, where travellers arrived carrying European silver or billon coins which, at least up until 1187, they were (so far as we can judge from the hoards and stray finds) strictly required to change into the official issues of the Latin Kingdom. Acre was not recovered until 1191; where had the stock of currency, amounting to perhaps ten or twenty million deniers, been scattered in the three or four intervening years?—was it still in existence? How soon was the minting of _Amalricus_ deniers resumed, how much did the new issues weigh, and which are the dies that struck them? These are questions to which we cannot give firm answers. On the one hand, there are difficulties in supposing that Henry struck coins in his own name and in that of Amaury concurrently. On the other hand, the issues represented in the Tripoli and Kessab hoards seem to have been minted, and to have circulated, over a considerable period of time. As the issue of an immobilized type was almost certainly resumed by Aimery, it could be said that there is no extra difficulty in supposing that it was resumed already by Henry.

Lacking the vital hoards which (provided they could be dated convincingly) would answer our questions, we have to fall back on evidence which is less conclusive—in particular, that of metrology. It is worth being clear about the evidence of the published hoards, for which the weights of the _Amalricus_ coins are at least partly available. Whereas the average weight of the earliest issues was the same as or close to that of the _Baldvinus_ coins, i.e. between 0.95 and 0.9 g, fifty 'undoubtedly complete' coins in the Tripoli hoard averaged only 0.55 g, varying from 0.29 to 0.72 g. A hundred "clipped" deniers in the same hoard averaged 0.48 g 'which though less than the weight of the complete coins is by no means in proportion to the extent of the clipping'. Although Miss Cox does not tell us the weights of _all_ the coins, what she says is, I think, very good evidence that _Amalricus_ coins were at some stage minted at a weight-standard of a little less than 0.55 g (the 'undoubtedly complete' group may have been better-than-average), say 0.5 g—and also that heavier, earlier coins were clipped in order to reduce them to the same half-gramme standard. What weight these were clipped from is uncertain. Miss Cox offers a hint that it was less than 0.9 g when she says that 'a number of badly clipped deniers weigh between 0.6 and 0.64 g'—i.e. these would originally have been 0.9 g, while coins that looked less heavily clipped, but averaged only 0.48 g, would originally have been less.

Miss Cox then goes on to relate the silver contents (note, not the alloy and not the weight) of the Jerusalem coins to those of Cyprus in the name of Guy. This was a more tricky procedure than she realized, because it is very difficult to establish accurately the original alloy of billon coins which have been buried for centuries. It is better to keep closer to the metrological evidence, and not to introduce too many hypotheses.

Miss Cox, then, does not say what the average weight of all the Amalricus coins in the Tripoli hoard was, but we may perhaps assume that the samples were representative.

Longuet, faced with 263 'mauvais deniers' (sc. Miss Cox's smaller, poor-quality variety), weighed 250 at 61.5 g, to arrive at an average weight of 0.47 g. (Something has gone very wrong with his arithmetic here, and it is not obvious what has happened. We should probably accept 0.47 g as correct.) Ten of the largest of these coins ranged from 0.60 to 0.42 g, and nine especially small specimens averaged 0.32 g. (In other words, Longuet judged that there was no reason to suspect that the 250 coins were on more than one weight-standard, related to their size.) He did not, unfortunately, follow up Miss Cox's observation about 'undoubtedly complete' and 'clipped' coins. Nor do either of them record the varieties of inscription, etc. in these two categories. Had they done so, it might have shown that the proportions of the different varieties among the coins apparently clipped down to half a gramme were inconsistent with their being drawn from the original 0.9 g currency. Formal proof of the theory of prolonged use of dies would come from die-linked specimens of different quality: none is to hand; and the statistical argument is perhaps almost as conclusive.

The Kessab hoard evidently matches that from Tripoli closely, and the Amalricus coins in it are essentially all on the half-gramme standard.

The Jerusalem hoard of 1927, otherwise known as the YMCA hoard, is represented by 96 Crusader and medieval French coins, including 74 of the Amalricus series, in the Rockefeller Museum. They are presumed to be a hoard; another parcel from what may have been the same hoard was acquired by the Jerusalem YMCA and subsequently disposed of in America. A few of the Rockefeller coins were pierced, and not all had the same thin purplish patina. One cannot, therefore, exclude the possibility of mixed provenances. The museum authorities kindly allowed me to study the coins in 1973, and I weighed them all on that occasion. The average weight of 67 unpierced deniers was 0.91 g. A histogram (using the same step interval of 0.1 g as those published for the Baldvinus coins in NC 1978) shows a very compact distribution, with 64% of the coins in the central step, centred at 0.91 g

(see Fig. 5). There is no evidence of any variation in weight according to
the dots or annulets in the angles of the cross, or according to the mark after
REX. There are a couple of coins with unbarred As on the obverse, which
each weigh only 0.82 g. (These might reflect the intermediate weight-standard
hinted at above.) Ten or more coins with chevron-barred As are possibly
a little heavier, but essentially there is no discernible variation.

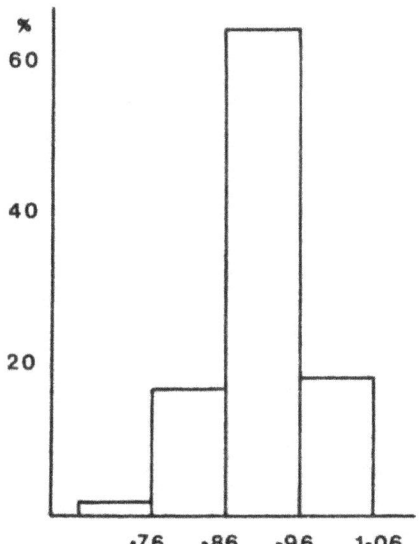

Fig. 5.

These coins are obviously quite different from those from Tripoli or
Kessab, and it is much to be doubted whether the worn coins of Hugh and
Henry I or Cyprus in the parcel can really belong with them. There is one
coin of Bohemund IV of the Tripoli mint which may have been associated,
but frankly the dating of the hoard by the non-Jerusalemite coins is a worthless exercise. Whenever the YMCA coins were concealed, they represent
a phase of the Amalricus coinage when its weight had not declined below ca.
0.9 g (or when it was just beginning to do so); and we see that this early
phase had lasted long enough, or been varied enough (if there was after all
more than one mint) to embrace a great range of varieties of stops and
lettering. These are summarized in Fig. 6.

REX	6		1		
REX o	20		1		
REX 8	10	2			
REX 8	1	1			
REX •	7	1	1	5	1
R•EX	1				

Fig. 6. Varieties in the Jerusalem hoard

Finally, the stray finds from Acre include four Amalricus coins (nos.
9-12, in ANSMN XX, 1975, 139ff.) which one would say were clipped deniers,
but which weigh 0.28, 0.27, 0.26, and 0.23 g. These weights are both very
low, and consistent. Making some allowance for the extra wear and corrosion
of stray finds (three other deniers of more normal size weigh 0.84, 0.80,

and 0.75 g), the small coins are just, but only just, within the range weights found in the Tripoli hoard, and one wonders whether they could conform to an even lower standard—or whether they could be oboles. Their interpretation must remain uncertain for the present. The chemical analysis of a similar very light piece is mentioned below.

There is no evidence of any change in the alloy of the Amalricus coinage during its period of issue. The problems which surface enrichment of very thin billon coins pose, however, are such that it is difficult if not impossible to assess the original alloy, and all the more so by non-destructive methods. Assays performed for Miss Cox on the two halves of two coins gave average results of 33.3% and 31.4% silver. These are no doubt very accurate and reliable measurements of the samples which the analyst used, but experience with other billon series suggests that when these particular coins were new, the proportion could have been distincly less—one would guess between 25 and 30%.

Professor A. A. Gordus and I analysed a dozen Amalricus coins from among those in the trays of the Ashmolean Museum. All but two fell between 29 and 32.5% silver (including traces of gold), and the exceptions were 28.7 and 27.6% 'silver'. Unfortunately our sample included only one coin on the half-gramme standard (28.7%). There was also one very light coin (0.28g), for which the result was 30.8%.

The deniers of John of Brienne are on a reduced standard. Miss Cox had one assayed, and found that it contained 22% silver. She points out that the average weight of John's coins is 0.74 g, and its pure silver contents accordingly 0.163 g, or almost exactly the same as the half-gramme coins in the name of Amaury. This entitles us to think that the quarter-gramme coins are oboles.

NOTES

1. Schlumberger, pp. 89f.

2. H. Hagenmeyer, Fulcheri Carnotensis Historia Hierosolymitana (1095-1127), Heidelberg, 1913, I, XXVI, 10.

3. H. Vincent and F.-M. Abel, Jérusalem. Recherches de topographie, d'archéologie et d'histoire, vol. II, Jérusalem nouvelle, 1914, pp. 89-300.

4. C. Coüasnon, The Church of the Holy Sepulchre in Jerusalem, 1974, pp. 30 and 56-7.

5. William of Tyre. 'Historia rerum in partibus transmarinis gestarum', RHC Occ., i, book VIII, cap. 3, p. 524.

6. C. J. Sabine, 'Numismatic iconography of the Tower of David and the Holy Sepulchre', NC CXXXIX (1979), 122-32 and pl. 17, 5.

7. J. Williams, Knights of the Crusades, 1963, p. 53 gives a photographic reproduction. I am indebted to Capt. Sabine, who drew my attention to this important piece of evidence at a late stage in the preparation of the paper.—D. M. M.

8. M. de Vogüé, *Eglises de la Terre Sainte,* 1860, pp. 217-21.

9. J. Yvon, 'Monnaies et sceaux de l'Orient latin', RN^6 VIII (1966), 89-107.

10. F. de Saulcy, *Numismatique des Croisades* (Paris, 1847).

11. L. de Mas Latrie, 'Notice sur les monnaies et les sceaux des rois de Chypre de la maison de Lusignan', *Bibliothèque de l'Ecole des Chartes* V (1843-4), 118 and 413.

12. M. de Vogüé, 'Monnaies inedités des croisades', RN NS IX (1864), 275-93.

13. D. H. Cox, *The Tripolis Hoard of French Seignorial and Crusader's Coins* (NNM LIX) (New York, 1933).

14. J. Duplessy and D. M. Metcalf, 'Le trésor de Samos et la circulation monétaire en Orient Latin aux XIIe et XIIIe siècles', RBN CVIII (1962), 173-207; D. M. Metcalf, "The Samos hoard: corrigendum", HBN XXII/XXIII (1968-69), 470.

15. *op. cit.*

16. *loc. cit.*

17. J. D. Brady, 'A firm attribution of Latin gold coinage to twelfth-century Jerusalem', ANSMN XXIII (1978), 133-47.

18. H. Longuet, 'La trouvaille de Kessab en Orient Latin', RN^4 XXXVIII (1935), 163-83, at p. 168, and p. 172.

19. D. M. Metcalf, 'Coinage of the Latin Kingdom of Jerusalem in the name of Baudouin' NC^7 XVIII (1978), 71-84.

20. R. Grousset, *Epic of the Crusades* (New York, 1970).

21. *loc. cit.*

22. S. Fox, 'Die making in the twelfth century', BNJ VI (1909), 191-6.

23. *op. cit.*

A NOTE ON THE REPAYMENT OF LOANS IN MID-THIRTEENTH-CENTURY ACRE

Peter W. Edbury

The Livre des Assises de la Cour des Bourgeois is a compilation of burgess and commercial law from Acre. Professor Prawer has dated it to the period 1240-44, though more recently Professor Riley-Smith has argued in favour of the 1260s as the period in which it reached the form in which it has survived.[1] Two aspects in particular of this treatise have excited attention: the presence within it of a tariff list which has much to tell of the variety of commodities which passed through Acre at this period as well as the duty payable, and the fact that it is modelled on a Provençal law code which derives ultimately from Roman Law.[2]

For the monetary historian the chapter on the repayment of loans is of especial interest. The central principle laid down is that the lender is under no obligation to accept repayment in anything other than the commodity loaned The full text reads as follows:

> Mutuum est quod de meo tuum fit, c'est à dire, prest est chose que dou mien est fait tien. Le donement de prest se fait par pois, si com est or et argent; par nombre, si come monoie; par mesure, si come huille, vin et forment, et aussi d'autres choses. Toutes ces choses sont aucunes foiz et presteez et renduez en quantité ou en qualité, ou en cele meisme semblance. Et por ce doivent savoir tuit li home que celui qui preste le sien à autre n'est mie tenuz par droit, se il ne veut, de recevoir autre chose que tel come il presta, et d'autel valor et d'autel bonté: si come est se il te presta forment, tu ne li doiz mie rendre orge; et s'il te presta oille, tu ne li doiz mie rendre vin; ne se il te presta besanz, tu ne lui dois mie rendre deniers. Mais comande la raison que tu es tenuz de rendre li tel chose come il te presta. Et si vos mostrerai la raison por quoi: por ce que maintes foiz avient que le besant vaut v. sols, et avient maintes foiz que le besant vaut x. sols; de dou forment, tel houre est vaut le mui un besant, et trois muis d'orge por un besanz. Et por ce comande la loy et l'assise qui il n'est mie droit que vos li doiez rendre deniers por besanz, ne orge por forment; mais tout itel chose com il te presta, tout autel li dois rendre par droit. Ne la court ne doit nullui destraindre de prendre autre chose que ce qu'il te presta, se il ne veut; et que la chose doit estre d'autretel valoir et d'autretel bonté com ele estoit quant il la te presta.[3]

It would be dangerous to build major theories upon an isolated piece of evidence without examining other documentary sources, not to mention the numismatic material, but the implications of this passage nevertheless deserve to be pointed out.

"The repayment of the loan is to be by weight in the case of gold and silver, by number in the case of money ...". Implied in this statement seems to be the idea that when loans (and presumably other payments) are expressed in terms of Latin Syrian currency at least in the period that this passage was composed, the sums were in actual coin and not money of account. The manner in which money is differentiated from gold and silver indicates that here by gold and silver the writer is thinking of bullion as distinct from coin. But it may well be that this provision applied specifically to the Frankish Saracen Bezants since there are numerous references elsewhere in this treatise to money owed expressed in this denomination.[4] The conclusion would thus seem to be that at least in the case of the gold coinage of the mid-thirteenth century there was a sufficient degree of uniformity of fineness and weight for the currency's value to be guaranteed by the authorities so that payments could be made simply by counting out the coins and not by resorting to weighing them and then calculating the inherent value of the bullion.

"... neither if he has loaned you bezants, should you pay him back in deniers ... often it happens that the bezant is worth five sous, and often it happens that the bezant is worth ten sous .... it is not right that you should pay back deniers for bezants ...." The relative value of gold and silver fluctuated, although the wide variation suggested in this passage should perhaps not be taken too literally. The gold bezant was divided notionally into twenty-four carats or 'karoubles'. The silver currency was expressed in units of denier, sou and the silver mark. Although on occasion the currencies are juxtaposed in the Livre des Assises de la Cour des Bourgeois,[5] they are never confused, and in this connection it may be relevant to remember that hoards containing a mixture of gold and silver coins are rarely found. It would appear that the simplest solution to the problem of bimetallism was to keep the two monetary systems—one based on gold, the other on silver—separate as far as possible. Thus to avoid complaints of profiteering by gambling of the relative price of gold and silver, loans in gold were to be repaid in gold; those in silver in silver.

NOTES

1. J. Prawer,'L'établissement des coutumes du marché à Saint-Jean d'Acre et la date de composition du Livre des Assises des Bourgeois' RHDFÉ[4], XXIX(1951), 329-51, esp. pp. 346-8; J. S. C. Riley-Smith, The Feudal Nobility and the Kingdom of Jerusalem (1174-1277) 1973, p. 85 and n. 186 (p. 268). Prawer's argumentation has also been criticized by C. Cahen, 'A propos des coutumes du marché d'Acre', RHDFÉ[4], XLI(1963), 287-90.

2. J. Richard, 'Colonies marchandes privilégiées et marché seigneurial. La fonde d'Acre et ses "droitures"', Le Moyen Age LIX (1953), 325-40; J. Prawer, 'Étude préliminaire sur les sources et la composition du "Livre des Assises des Bourgeois"', RHDFÉ[4], XXXII (1954), 198-227, 358-82.

3. 'Livre des Assies de la cour des bourgeois', RHC Lois, ii, 48-9. See also pp. 62, 73, 150 for allusions to the same theme.

4. Pp. 37, 40, 43, 49, 50-51, 52, 56, 59, 63, 65, 78, 99, 154, 155. I have noticed only one reference to a loan of deniers (p. 148).

5. Pp. 36, 117, 204, 221, 222.

CRUSADER COIN FINDS FROM CAESAREA MARITIMA, ISRAEL:
THE JOINT EXPEDITION'S EXCAVATIONS, 1971-1979

Robert L. Hohlfelder

Beginning in 1971, excavations have been conducted at Caesarea Maritima, Israel, the site of the ancient capital of Roman and Byzantine Palestine, by a consortium of American and Canadian universities, colleges and foundations known as the Joint Expedition to Caesarea Maritima under the direction of Professor Robert J. Bull, Drew University, Madison, New Jersey, U.S.A.[1] This consortium has completed eight seasons of field work (excepting 1977) under an archaeological permit awarded by the Israeli Department of Antiquities and through the sponsorship of the American Schools of Oriental Research. The archaeological explorations which have been conducted in various areas of the ancient city and its immediate environs have produced c. 10,000 coins or coin fragments to date. Most of these site-finds date from the Byzantine epoch of the city's history, that is from the fourth century to its capture by the Arabs in A.D. 639/640. Other historical periods are less well represented. In particular, the two centuries of Caesarea's history during the Crusader era, A.D. 1101-1291, have accounted for only ten coins in the numismatic record, nine from the excavations plus one chance find.[2] Although this number is very small, it may be useful to describe these specimens since the list of archaeological sites from which Crusader finds have been reported is itself limited. Moreover, three of these ten finds are scarce, interesting varieties.[3]

Latin Kings of Jerusalem
 1. Baldwin III, 1143-63, or later. Denier, (Schl., plate III, 21; Metcalf, Group 4 (with ✂ in REX)). 0.71g. (chipped).
    C76 6/21. A.5.83. 5035 C - 16
 2. Anonymous denier. Schl. pl. III, 27 (Siege of Acre, 1191?)
    MONETA REGIS / + REX IERL'M   0.79g.
    C72 5/22 C.2.3. 3201 C - 2.[4]
    Other specimens of this very scarce coin are illustrated in NC 1979, pl. 18, 12-13.

Kings of Cyprus
 3. Hugh I, 1205-18, denier, cf. Schl. pl. VI, 4. •+• hVGO·REX/CYPRI
    Cross with 2 crescents and ? two pellets in angles. Pierced twice. 0.75g.
    C72 7/12 C.5.56. 5045 C - 1.

Kings of Jerusalem and Sicily
 4. Frederick II, emperor, 1220-50. Spahr 112. Brindisi?
    +F. IPERATOR / REX IERL'M. SICIL.   0.60g.
    C74 6/26 H.5.O. 5004 C - 1
    Spahr lists this coin as RRR. It is one of the first Sicilian coins to bear the title of Jerusalem.

Kings of Sicily
5. William II, 1166-89. Trifollaro. Spahr 117. 10.63g.
C71 5/10 A.2.4 C.3

Bishops of Valence
6. Immobilized type. Caron pl. XIX, 9-12. Metcalf HBN 22/23, Group B (cf. pl. XVII, 7). Denier. 0.94g.
C75 6/26 P.C.6.0. 6006 C - 3.

7. Immobilized type cf. Metcalf Group D (note the triangular nose) but the legend is ✝ I I Ǝ I P∧VSII... / S∧P✿LL IN   0.98g. Chance find at Caesarea, 1978, by R. Hohlfelder. Perhaps an unofficial imitation. Hitherto unrecorded

Counts of Angoulême
8. Immobilized type in the name of Louis, third series. Dieudonné, Manuel, vol. IV, 70f. Obole. ✝ LODOICVS / ✝ EGOLISSIME   0.48g.
C78 6/15 C.22.10. 2208 C - 1.
Very similar coins occurred in a recent hoard; ANSMN XX (1975), pp. 149-52, nos. 79-87.

Counts of Provence
9. Alfonso I, 1185-1209. Obolo. Vidal-Quadras 5396; V. Ramon Benedito et. al., 10.16.2. **REX ARAGONE / POVINCIA**   0.42g.
C74 6/25 H.5.5. 5004. C - 4.

Zengids of Syria
10. Nur al-Din Mahmud, A.H. 541-69 (A.D. 1146-74). Copper fals. BMC Or III, p. 212, no. 601. (The mint is probably Damascus). 4.87g.
C72. 6/21. A.1.166. 1002 C - 1

NOTES

1. Notes on the various seasons of field work have appeared in the Israel Exploration Journal. The preliminary report of the first phase of the Joint Expedition's excavations from 1971-76 is in preparation (ed., Robert J. Bull). A report on the 1978 campaign by Robert J. Bull has been submitted to Bulletin of the American Schools of Oriental Research, as has a statement of the 1979 field work (by Kenneth Holum and Robert Wiemken). Some comments on the numismatic record of these excavations will appear in these publications. A complete catalogue with commentary and several specialized articles on different aspects of the coin finds are now in preparation.

2. The most recent study of Caesarea Maritima during the era of the Crusades is by Harry W. Hazard, 'Caesarea and the Crusades', The Joint Expedition to Caesarea Maritima, Vol. I: Studies in the History of Caesarea Maritima, ed. Charles T. Fritsch, Bulletin of the American Schools of Oriental Research: Supplemental Studies, 19 (Missoula, Montana, 1975) pp. 79-114.

3. I wish to thank Dr. Metcalf and Dr. Edbury for inviting me to present a brief note on the Caesarea Crusader coins and Dr. Metcalf and Mrs Helen W. Brown for their final assignments and confirmation of field attributions.

4. Inventory data are provided for each coin: season and date of the find (C76 6/21); archaeological field and area in which find was made (A.5.83); Locus and temporary catalogue number of the coin find (5035 C-16). Descriptions and maps of the fields of excavations can be found in publications cited supra n. 1.

SOME COIN EXPORTS FROM TWELFTH-CENTURY YORKSHIRE TO THE HOLY LAND

Paul R. Hyams

Movements of specie, coined or as bullion, are obviously fundamental to monetary history, as Michael Metcalf's paper reminds us.[1] A dozen years ago, Andrew Watson offered in his 'Back to gold—and silver'[2] a broad hypothesis about the direction and timing of large-scale bullion flows in the middle ages, which suggested a pivotal role for the Latin settlements in Syria, particularly during the twelfth century. Much of his argument hinged upon deduction from such matters as the gold-silver exchange rates at different times and places. The dearth of hard evidence on the movement of coin or bullion[3] must lead numismatists occasionally to look wistfully at historian colleagues and wonder why those apparently copious written sources cannot do more to help.

The present 'widow's mite' offers some minor assistance. This note required the study (initially for quite other purposes) of some four thousand Yorkshire charters and ancillary materials for the period up to the early thirteenth century.[4] That represents a high proportion of the early Yorkshire private charters still surviving; yet many times that number may have been lost or destroyed. Only a few of these documents record some of the arrangements made by Yorkshire barons and knights for crusades and pilgrimages to the East, and fewer still tell anything about the money raised for the purpose. They could certainly be matched from other parts of England and western Europe if the relevant materials could be collated. Perhaps readers who in the course of their own researches—for the proportion of product to effort invested does not justify a direct hunt—come across documents similar to those below might send the references to the editors of this volume. A comprehensive collection would at least enable us to make some intelligent guesses at the wealth exported eastwards by private individuals, to set alongside the guesses about the amount taken by kings or transmitted by the supranational corporations of the church.[5]

No Yorkshire document establishes the precise amount of coin or bullion with which any individual set out.[6] Four, however, record grants of money to assist pilgrims. In about 1174, Jocelin of Louvain granted one of his Percy wife's manors to Sixle Priory in perpetual fee-farm. He was to receive £12 per annum rent but in addition is said to have been given £100 'ad sumptus itineris mei' when he was about to set out for Jerusalem.[7] Two grants date from the Third Crusade. The nuns of Swine gave to Walter le Noir five marks 'ad peregrinationem meam faciendam in Ierosolimam' in return for two bovates of land in fee subject to services for the head lord,[8] and a royal _familiaris_, William f. Aldelin, gave various small pieces of land to his _serviens_, Durand f. Drew, for the ten marks which Durand supplied him 'ad iter meum de

Jerusalem'.[9] Then, at some date between 1231 and 1243, Thomas f. William de Malham surrendered two bovates of his land to his lords, the canons of Bolton Priory, for thirty marks 'ad peregrinacionem meam faciendam in terram Jerosolimitanam faciendam'.[10]

In three other cases, the timing of sales or mortgages to coincide with the start of a pilgrimage probably implies that the purpose was to raise the necessary cash. Roger de Mowbray, one of the area's major barons, participated in the Second Crusade and was to die in Palestine in 1188. How he financed these expeditions remains unknown. He also went to the Holy Land in the late 1170s, after he had backed the wrong side in the revolt of 1173-4. For this enterprise, he raised from the family's favourite monastery, Fountains Abbey, sums amounting to £420 for himself and sixty-five marks for his son Nigel.[11] These substantial sums raised by land grants and agreements probably represent only part of the money raised for the Mowbray voyage,[12] yet the other two examples are on a much more modest scale. During the 1150s, Henry of Octon, the younger son of a sheriff of York, 'Iherosolimam proficisciens', sold to Meaux Abbey his right in $2\frac{1}{2}$ carucates of the family's land at Octon for sixty marks.[13] Robert the Constable in his old age went on the Third Crusade as William de Mandeville's seneschal, to die at the siege of Acre. Before his departure he too made a grant to Meaux, some manorial demesne outright and gages of two vills in return for a loan of 160 marks.[14] Since one of the gages is dated to the year after the kings of France and England took the cross and vowed to go to Jerusalem, it seems likely that he too was raising money for his venture.[15]

In conclusion, I draw attention to two further grants, each made during the 1150s by men about to go on pilgrimage. They are phrased as grants for service (i.e. for value), but they provide that no service was due for the period when the grantors were expected to be absent in the East.[16] Very probably some pecuniary consideration was received but omitted from the charter for fear that it might appear to spoil the pious intentions.

I hope that the data presented here may at least stimulate thought. There is certainly no clear answer to the monetary historian's prayer. Charters like these only record transactions of some permanent importance, involving landed property. Disposals of other assets would normally pass unrecorded, unless perhaps by the occasional cautious Jew. Those with enough treasure in stock to finance their expedition would leave no trace at all. We are left with scraps about a small minority.

NOTES

1. Above, pp. 1-17.

2. Economic History Review[2] XX (1967), pp. 1-34, esp. pp. 7-9.

3. See, for example, the studies cited by Watson, p. 8, nn. 2-3.

4. Twelve volumes of Early Yorkshire Charters, ed. W. Farrer and C. T. Clay (hereafter referred to as E.Y.C.) have been published between 1914 and 1965, now under Yorkshire Archaeological Society, records series, extra series. D. E. Greenway (ed.), Charters of the Honour of Mowbray, 1107-1191 (London 1972) follows a similar format.

5. I await with high hopes the completion of Mr. S. Lloyd's Oxford D. Phil. thesis on 'English society and the Crusade, 1216-1307', although he is not directly concerned with the early period. J. P. Trabut-Cussac, "Le financement de la croisade anglaise de 1270", Bibliothèque de l'école des chartes CXIX (1961), pp. 113-40, shows what can sometimes be done for great crusaders at a later date.

6. See, however, Pleas before the King and his Justices, 1198-1202, ed. D. M. Stenton (Selden Society lxviii 1949), no. 248 for Robert de Marsh, whose father tithed his Cornish lands (as canon law authorised him to do for a crusader) and fitted him out with 20 marks, 20 bezants and a gold ring, as well as the necessary military equipment.

7. E.Y.C. xi.68.

8. E.Y.C. iii.1409 (1188X91).

9. E.Y.C. iii.1641 (1190)

10. E.Y.C. vii.89.

11. See Greenway, Charters of the Honour of Mowbray, 1107-1191, pp. xxxi-xxxii, lv and nos. 111-3, 120-2, 124, 126; Chartulary of the Cistercian Abbey of Fountains, ed. W. T. Lancaster (2 vols. Leeds 1915), i. 205 (7).

12. See Greenway, no. 388 = E.Y.C. i.547 by which Roger granted to William de Tickhill, a prominent York merchant, a manor he had only recently purchased for 220 m. (cf. Greenway, no. 389), 'quando iter arripui versus sanctam terram repromissionis'. Despite the address to 'amico meo', some substantial unstated consideration seems certain; see E. Miller, Victoria County History, City of York (1961), p. 45 and Greenway, pp. xxx, 349.

13. Chronica Monasterii De Melsa i, ed. E. A. Bond (Rolls series 1866), pp. 102-3.

14. Chron. Melsa, i.220; Roger de Howden, Chronicon iii, ed. W. Stubbs (Rolls series 1870), p. 89; E.Y.C. iii.1364.

15. Pipe Roll 3-4 Richard I, p. 76 (1191), cited Miller, loc. cit., refers to another crusader mortgage to York financiers, alas without detail.

16. E.Y.C. iii.1342 (1152): 2 bovates for 4 shillings per annum, waived for the first 7 years; E.Y.C. viii.102 (1154X9): 20 acres for 2 shillings per annum, waived until the crusader's death or return.

THREE RECENT PARCELS OF HELMET DENIERS
OF BOHEMUND III OF ANTIOCH
CONCEALED AT ABOUT THE TIME OF SALADIN'S CONQUESTS

D. M. Metcalf

I

A hoard which passed through the hands of Mr Carl Subak[1] in the summer of 1978 consisted of 202 'helmet' deniers of Antioch, together with five strays of other types. The 'helmet' series was classified by Derek Allen in 1937 into Types 1-5 and 1*-3* in the name of Bohemund, Raymond Roupen's coins, and Type 6 again in the name of Bohemund. The sequence of the early types 1-5 (to which this hoard is restricted) has been revised since Allen wrote, to the extent of moving Type 5 to the beginning of the series, and of placing the rare 'head to right' variant earlier still.[2] A fully-documented mise au point summarizing the evidence for these and other revisions is with the printer, and should appear in the Hamburger Beiträge zur Numismatik.[3] The sequence it suggests is Head right-5-1-2-3-4. But some very early and important new evidence to be published by Alistair Lilburn will suggest that even this is incorrect, and that the scarce Type 4 is in fact earlier than Types 2 or 3. As there is a stylistic progression through Types 2, 3, and 4, e.g. in the size of the crescent on the reverse, moving Type 4 might be expected to make it necessary to change the order of Types 2 and 3 as well.[4] It looks therefore as if Allen's much-reworked classification may now need to run Head right-5-1-4-3-2. Mr Subak's hoard published here adds a little evidence in support of that view, in that the irregularly shaped flans and the peculiar greyish colour, as well as the style of the dies, of the coins of Type 2 in it offer a contrast with Types 3 and 4: the history of the mint would be puzzling if the order were 1-4-2-3. The degree of wear is difficult to judge, because Type 2 is so poorly struck. Some specimens seem quite fresh. Certainly, most specimens of Type 4 in the three parcels discussed here look worn. Proof would be forthcoming if a hoard were discovered which terminated with Type 3 and lacked Type 2; but it would need to be a large hoard, since Type 2 is relatively uncommon, and its integrity would need to be assured. Lacking proof, it nevertheless seemed sensible to list the Subak coins on that working basis. One's estimate of the date of deposit of the hoard is not much affected by the uncertainty. It does not go beyond Types 1-5, and belongs in all probability to the last quarter of the twelfth century. It contained, in summary:

		Antioch %
Early variety, head r.	2	1
(?) Transitional variety	1	0.5
Type 5	4	2
Type 1	36	18

Type 4	3	1.5
Type 3	138	68.5
Type 2	18	9
Foreign coins	5	9

Ten specimens, illustrated on the accompanying plate, are marked with an asterisk in the notes.

Early coins

*1. (0.93 g) The A is ornamented with annulets on the obv., but with dots on the rev.
*2. (0.96 g) On the rev., a large crescent in the first quarter, with the points facing outwards. As with annulets.
*3. (0.97 g) Head r., but the style is that of Type 5. No star and crescent on obv. As with dots. This coin is presumably either a contemporary counterfeit, or a transitional issue standing at the head of Type 5.

Type 5

4-7. (0.92, 0.91, 0.88 g). One reading ... MVDNVS (1.03 g).

Type 1

8-32. Normal coins with a narrow bust. (1.08, 1.06, 1.02, 0.99, 0.98 (2), 0.97 (2), 0.96, 0.96 (2), 0.93 (2), 0.90 (3), 0.89, 0.88, 0.87 0.86 (2), 0.85 (2), 0.83, 0.70 g (clipped).)
33-5 Similar, but with . + . (0.94, 0.92, 0.86 g).
36-8. Similar, but with annulets on the letter C. These have a rather larger crescent, and a slightly more egg-shaped head (1.03, 0.96, 0.89 g).
39-40. With a bust which spreads out more at the base. These too have a rather larger crescent (0.95, 0.93 g).
41. In broader style, with a dotted letter O on the rev. (0.86 g).
*42. With rev. legend I ɪ O. This coin has a deep crescent, and a shorter letter C (0.85 g).
*43. With rev. legend I ❦ O. Spreading bust (0.81 g).

Type 4

44-6. (1.02, 0.91, 0.86 g).

Type 3

Among a total of 138 coins, 9 were somewhat in the style of Type 2, and a further 8 were noted with Ⳕ in the mint name (AⳐT...), coupled with the letter forms Ƀ and ⊙. Apart from this, all attempts to detect sub-groups on the basis of style were frustrated by the evidence.

47-167. (1.11, 1.09, 1.08 (2), 1.07, 1.06, 1.05 (2), 1.04, 1.03 (3), 1.02, 1.01 (2), 1.00 (5), 0.99 (10), 0.98 (14), 0.97 (6), 0.96 (7), 0.95 (5), 0.94 (5), 0.93 (6), 0.92 (3), 0.91 (5), 0.90 (3), 0.89 (9), 0.88 (6), 0.87 (3), 0.86 (3), 0.85 (2), 0.84 (6), 0.83, 0.81, 0.79, 0.78 (2), 0.77 (2), 0.71 g).

168-75. Reverse double barred N, dotted O. (0.99, 0.97, 0.96, 0.95 (2), 0.94, 0.90, 0.87 g).

176-84. Cf. Type 2. (1.08, 1.02, 1.01, 1.00, 0.98, 0.94 (2), 0.90, 0.82 g).

Type 2

It was noticeable that these 18 coins were on flans of a rough shape, i.e. not made as carefully circular as the rest. They seemed also to be greyer in colour than the rest of the hoard.

185-202. (1.19, 1.15, 1.08 (2), 1.04 (2), 0.99, 0.96, 0.94 (2), 0.91 (3), 0.88 (3), 0.84, 0.75 g).

Lucca

*203.   In the crude (imitative?) style of HBN XXII/XXIII (1968-9), pl. 18, 15-18. [2]. 1.01 g.

Valence

*204.   Group B? Cf. HBN pl. 18, 6. Worn. (1.12 g).

*205.   Group C. Cf. pl. 18, 9. Worn. (0.92 g).

*206.   Group E. Cf. pl. 18, 16. (1.01 g).

Lyon

*207.   Cf. pl. 19, 10. (1.49 g).

The weights of the Subak coins add some useful data for a study of the metrology of the series. The mean weights (which can vary from one hoard to another, not only because of different degrees of wear, but also depending on the physical conditions in which the coins lay buried) were

      Types 5 and 1   0.920
      Type 3   0.940 (mode, 0.98)
      Type 2   0.965

These figures are very similar to those for the ANS hoard (Types 5, 1-4, mean, 0.942, mode, 0.975 g), but higher than those for the Stewart hoard (mean, 0.903, mode, 0.935 g). The same skew distribution occurs again in Type 3, as may be seen from the histogram, Fig. 1. It has been constructed with a step interval of 0.05 g, and in such a way as to maximize the central step (33%).

The sample standard deviation for Type 2 (0.11) is noticeably higher than for Types 1 (0.07) or 3 (0.07).

If the relative chronology of the 'helmet' series has been more difficult to establish than might have been anticipated, because of the lack of early hoards, the same is even more true of the absolute chronology. It still rests on the very slender (but reliable) evidence of one coin in the Samos hoard. Its concealment was 1170 x 1185, perhaps 1182, and the 'helmet' coin is of Type 3. The very large output of the Antioch mint was cut short with Type 2, possibly in 1187. The 'irregular' varieties (not represented in our three parcels) may belong to the period of about ten years on either side of 1200,

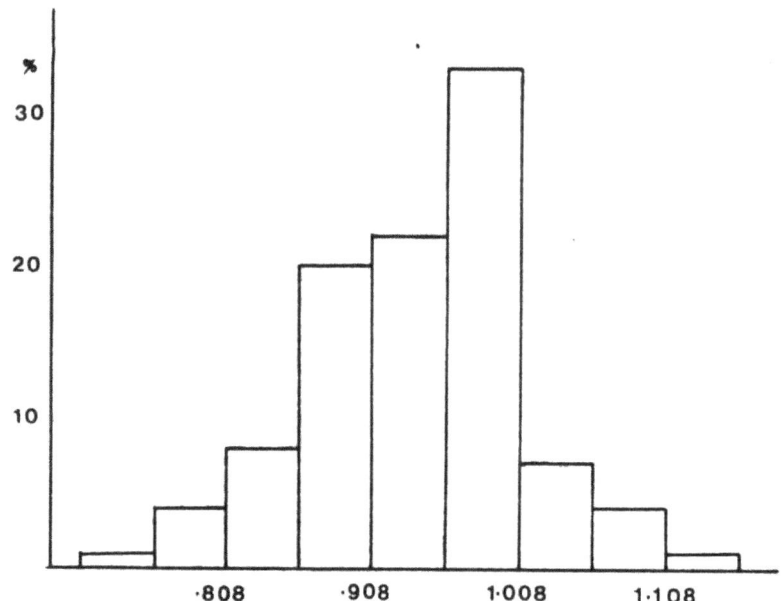

and the Rupinus varieties to the early thirteenth century. Ras Shamra lacked either of these but included a coin from the 1220s or 1230s; if it is not intrusive, it suggests a hoard concealed c. 1187 to which a small addition was made a generation later. But this interpretation, as has been said, is speculative.

II

A parcel of 'helmet' deniers belonging to Mr Havardjian was examined by Dr Bedoukian, who made foil impressions of all the specimens in the parcel. He then kindly made the impressions available for study. They may be listed as follows:

		Antioch %
Bare head	1	1
Type 5	2	1
Type 1	32	23
Type 4	3	2
Type 3	94	69
Type 2	6	4
Foreign coins	6	–

The proportions are so similar to Mr Subak's hoard that one immediately wonders whether the two groups of coins are not parcels originating from a single discovery.

Bare head coinage

*1. Variety 1b, with ANTI o OCHIA. Cf. Ras Shamra 4. Worn.

Early coin

*2. Head apparently to left, but in the style of the head to right var. Dotted As on rev. and also (?) on obv. Rev. ĀMTIOCNIĀ, with dotted C.

Type 5

3-4.   Dotted As.

5.   Similar, with . . . MVDNVS.

Type 1.

*6.   1/5 mule. Obv. annulets on A. Egg-shaped head. Rev. dots on A.

7-9.   Somewhat in the style of Type 5.

*10-11. Similar, with .+ and +. respectively.

12-30.   Typical specimens, with tall, narrow busts.

31-4.   With . + . , or possibly only one dot.

*35.   With ↑ , and bust in the style of Type 5.

*36.   With ❦ , and bust in the style of Type 5.

Type 4

*37-8.   (The group of 3 annulets on the rev., which distinguishes Type 3 from Type 4, is often indistinct, but on these two coins it is positively absent, and there is no room for it between the letters I and O.)

Type 3

*39.   Type 4/3 mule? (There is no formal distinction from a Type 3 coin.)

*40-122. Normal specimens.

123-5.   With dotted ☉ in BOAM...

*126-31. Type 3, but bust more in the style of Type 2.

Type 2.

*132-3. Type 3/2 mules. Double-barred N on obv., single-barred on rev. (The weak striking and shadowing on many of the coins listed as normal specimens of Type 3 do not allow one to be certain of the detail of the Ns. The style of the bust, and of the crescent on the rev., remains the best guide.)

*134.   Cf. Type 2, but with small neat lettering, V in the form ◢◣ , and bust in the style of Type 1.   ❦ pellets instead of annulets. Cf. Stewart 40.

*135-9. Normal specimens of Type 2.

Tripoli

*140.   Star denier, Raymond III (1152-87). (The obv. legend definitely begins with an R.) Sabine, type 1B (NC[7] XX, 1980, nos. 38ff.)

Valence

*141-3. Group E.

Melgueil

*144.   Obv. RAMVNOS. Rev. NAIBONA. Cf. Poey d'Avant 3843.

Guingamp

*145.   Obv. STEPHANOO. Rev. GVINGANP. PA pl. XXVII, 9.

III

Early in 1979 Mr Subak told me that he had acquired 'the other half' of the hoard he had shown me the previous summer. It proved to consist of 173 coins, of the following varieties:

		Antioch %
Early variety with head to r.	1	0.6
Type 5	2	1.2
Type 1	35	20
Type 4	4	2.3
Type 3	115	67
Type 2	15	9
Foreign coin	1	

The proportions are thus very similar to those in both the parcels described above; but these are not the self-same coins as the Havardjian specimens.

Early coin

1.   Var. with head to right. The A is ornamented with annulets on the obv., but with dots on the rev. (1.01g).

Type 5

2-3.   (1.03, 0.99g).

Type 1

4-22.   Normal coins with a narrow bust. (1.08, 1.04, 1.01, 0.99 (2), 0.98, 0.96 (2), 0.95, 0.94, 0.93, 0.92, 0.91 (3), 0.88 (3), 0.87g).

23-5.   Similar, with solid O in BOAMVNDVS (0.97, 0.92, 0.88g).

26.   Similar, with .+. (0.98g).

27-8.   Similar, with .+ (1.02, 0.95g).

29.   Similar, with +. (0.84g).

30-1.   Coins with bust similar in style to Type 5; one has ⊙ in BOAMVNDVS (0.95, 0.86g).

32-5.   Similar or spreading busts; all with NI•A (as Ras Shamra, nos. 25, 27) (1.05, 1.03, 0.97, 0.93g).

36-8.   Similar; with TI ⁞ O, and with deep crescent on rev. (0.93, 0.92, 0.80g).

Type 4

39-42. Four clear specimens, with characteristically small crescent on rev. (0.97, 0.96, 0.95, 0.91g).

Type 3

Many of these were somewhat in the style of Type 2, and fewer were in the normal Type 3/4 style. The letter B was occasionally in the form ℬ, but there were few if any coins with reversed Ns, as described above.

43-156. (1.20 (2), 1.12, 1.11 (2), 1.10, 1.09, 1.08 (5), 1.06 (2), 1.05 (4), 1.04 (7), 1.03, 1.02, 1.01 (6), 1.00 (8), 0.99 (4), 0.98 (2), 0.97 (5), 0.96 (8), 0.95 (8), 0.94 (4), 0.93 (2), 0.92 (8), 0.91 (4), 0.90 (5), 0.89 (5), 0.88, 0.87, 0.86 (2), 0.85 (3), 0.84 (2), 0.83, 0.82, 0.81, 0.80, 0.77, 0.76, 0.74, 0.73, 0.72g).

Type 2

These coins conformed very closely to those in the first parcel, e.g. the flans were irregularly shaped, the colour was different, and the 'heavy' style was distinctive.

157. Type 3/2 'mule' (in the style of Type 3, and it is very doubtful whether this is a true mule).

158. Type 2/3 'mule' (all in the style of Type 2, and it is rather doubtful whether this is a true mule) (0.99g).

159-72. (1.20, 1.12, 1.07, 1.05, 1.04, 1.03, 1.02, 0.99, 0.98, 0.97, 0.94, 0.91, 0.88g (2)).

Valence

173. Variety uncertain, possibly cf. HBN pl. 17, 6 (straight legs, feet not drawn). (0.86g). Worn.

The mean weights are a little higher (0.02 to 0.04g) than in the first parcel, and Type 2 is again heavier:

Type 1	0.942
Type 3	0.958
Type 2	1.005

The degree of skewness within Type 3 is very much less, as may be judged from the diagram, and this raises the technically interesting question whether the two parcels are statistically likely to be from the same hoard. If there

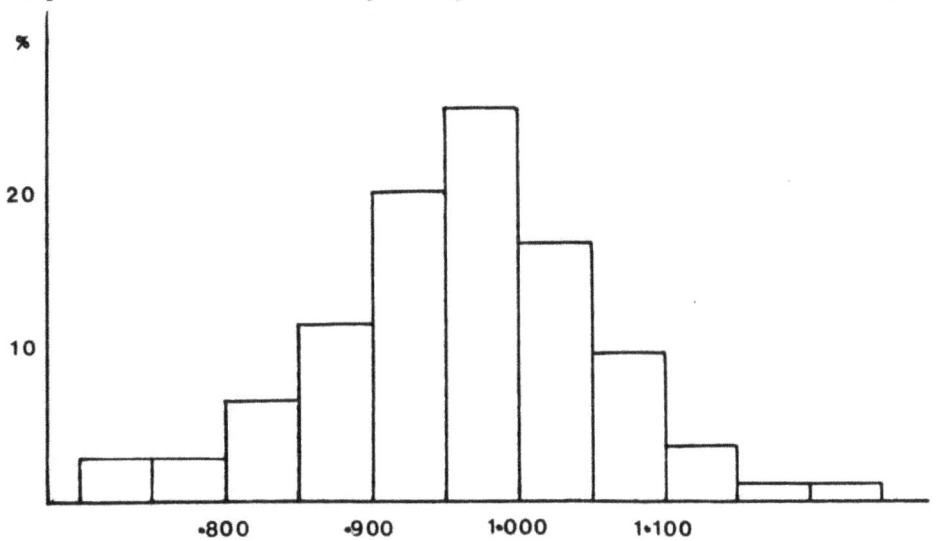

were two separate hoards, the date of concealment may have been ca. 1187 in each case. Because of the historical circumstances, the coincidence of date and composition would not be a strong argument against regarding the parcels as separate. There do seem to be minor differences of composition, e.g. the coins with NI.A which were found only in the second parcel.

The correct interpretation should become clearer when more hoards have been published in detail; after all we still have only half a dozen of any size. One can probably safely exclude selection by coin dealers and intermediaries in the Middle East, as there is little if any positive correlation between the appearance or attractiveness of a 'helmet' denier and its weight. It is more difficult to know whether coins were selected by weight in the twelfth century by the use of a tumbrel or trebuchet. If either of Mr Subak's parcels has been culled, it is presumably the first.

NOTES

1. I should like to express appreciation of Mr Subak's kindness in making the coins available for study.

2. D. F. Allen, 'Coins of Antioch, etc., from Al-Mina', NC^5 XVII (1937), 200-10; D. M. Metcalf, 'Billon coinage of the crusading principality of Antioch', NC^7 IX (1969), 247-67.

3. D. M. Metcalf, 'Notes on some hoards and stray finds from the time of the Crusades', HBN XXVII/XXIX (1973-5) (forthcoming). This includes a comparative analysis of the following hoards: Ras Shamra, Mağaracik, ANS hoard, Stewart hoard, Subak hoard, Al-Mina.

4. R. Pesant, 'The ANS hoard of Antioch deniers', ANSMN XVIII (1972), 73-85. At the Symposium, Mr Pesant graciously said to me that he believed he had been mistaken, and that he would now accept my views on the style of Type 2 (which were published in D. M. Metcalf, 'The Mağaracik hoard of "helmet" coins of Bohemond III of Antioch', ANSMN XVI (1970), 95-109. For Mr. Lilburn's hoard, see NC CXLI (1981), forthcoming.

THE SYMPOSIASTS

Dr. D. S. H. ABULAFIA, Fellow of Gonville and Caius College, Cambridge, CB2 1TA.

Mr. M. L. BATES, Curator of Islamic Coins, American Numismatic Society Broadway at 156th Street, New York 10032.

Dr. P. Z. BEDOUKIAN, 96 Warncke Road, Wilton, Conn., 06897.

Mr. S. BENDALL, 11 Adelphi Terrace, London WC2N 6BJ.

Dr. A. BORG, The Keeper, Sainsbury Centre for Visual Arts, University of East Anglia, Norwich NR4 7TJ.

Mr. J. D. BRADY, Associate Curator of Medieval Coins, American Numismatic Society, Broadway at 156th Street, New York 10032.

Mr. J. D. BRAND, 5 Ridley Road, Rochester, Kent MB1 1UL.

M. M. DHENIN, Conservateur, Cabinet des Médailles, Bibliothèque Nationale, 58 rue de Richelieu, 75084 Paris 02.

Dr. P. W. EDBURY, Lecturer in History, University College, Cardiff, P.O. Box 78, Cardiff, CF1 1XL.

Dr. B. F. HAMILTON, Senior Lecturer in History, University of Nottingham, NG7 2RD.

Dr. P. R. HYAMS, Lecturer in Modern History, Pembroke College, Oxford OX1 1DW.

Mr. R. IRWIN, 39 Harleyford Road, London S.E. 11.

Mr. J. JOHNS, Balliol College, Oxford.

Mr. N. J. MAYHEW, Assistant Keeper, Heberden Coin Room, Ashmolean Museum Oxford OX1 2PH.

Dr. D. M. METCALF, Assistant Keeper, Heberden Coin Room, Ashmolean Museum Oxford OX1 2PH.

Mr. P. MITCHELL, 11 Adelphi Terrace, London WC2N 6BJ.

Mr. R. PESANT, 325 Cypress Drive, Key Biscayne, Florida 33149.

Mr. J. PORTEOUS, 52 Elgin Crescent, London, W.11.

Mr. D. S. RICHARDS, University Lecturer in Arabic, St. Cross College, Oxford OX1 3TU.

Miss S. S. ROVIK, St. Anne's College, Oxford.

Capt. C. SABINE, 2 Delph Common Road, Aughton, Ormskirk, Lancs. L39 5DW.

Mw. Drs. A. B. SAPIR, Historisch Seminarium van de Universiteit van Amsterdam.

Mr. and Mrs. A. SPAER, P.O. Box 750, Jerusalem.

Mr. D. R. WALKER, General Editor, British Archaeological Reports, 122 Banbury Road, Oxford OX2 7BP.

Professor A. S. WATSON, The International Centre for Agricultural Research in Dry Areas, P.O. Box 5466, Aleppo, Syria; and Dept. of Political Economy, University of Toronto, 100 St. George Street, Toronto, M5S 1A1.

Mr. P. WOODHEAD, 65 Aldsworth Avenue, Goring-by-Sea, Worthing, Sussex BN12 4XG.

www.ingramcontent.com/pod-product-compliance
Lightning Source LLC
Chambersburg PA
CBHW061538010526
44111CB00025B/2964